DREAMSTREETS

Also by Jacqueline Yallop

Non-fiction
Magpies, Squirrels and Thieves: How Victorians Collected the World

Fiction
Kissing Alice
Obedience
Marlford

Dreamstreets

A Journey through Britain's Village Utopias

JACQUELINE YALLOP

JONATHAN CAPE
LONDON

1 3 5 7 9 10 8 6 4 2

Jonathan Cape, an imprint of Vintage Publishing,
20 Vauxhall Bridge Road,
London SW1V 2SA

Jonathan Cape is part of the Penguin Random House group of companies whose addresses can be found at
global.penguinrandomhouse.com.

Penguin
Random House
UK

First published by Jonathan Cape in 2015

www.vintage-books.co.uk

A CIP catalogue record for this book is available from the British Library

ISBN 9780224987274

Typeset by Palimpsest Book Production Ltd, Falkirk, Stirlingshire in Dante MT

Printed and bound in Great Britain by Clays Ltd, St Ives PLC

Penguin Random H⸍   ⸌rs and our planet. This

Contents

List of Illustrations

FIRST SECTION

The entrance to Arkwright's mill, Cromford.

The rear of the mill workers' cottages on North Street, Cromford, with the original 'weavers' windows' now blocked off.

The village square, Tremadog, with the Town Hall behind.

Nenthead village when the author lived there in 1992; the Methodist chapel is on the left with the reading room across the lane to the right and the current school on the hill above.

Italianate-style villa at Edensor.

A winter's evening at Edensor village with The Stand just visible on the hill beyond.

One of John Nash's nine Picturesque cottages at Blaise Hamlet.

Salt's mill at Saltaire.

Terraces designed by Lockwood and Mawson, Saltaire.

Miners' cottages skirting the green at Creswell.

'The Model', Creswell.

Cottages at 14–16 Church Drive, Port Sunlight, designed by Grayson and Ould with the initial L for Lever in the ornate decoration.

A seat in the bridge over 'The Dell' at Port Sunlight, designed by Cheshire architect John Douglas.

The bridge and cottages at Port Sunlight

The Town Hall at Portmeirion; in front, a bronze statue of Hercules by William Brodie (1863) and to the right, Angel Cottage, built in a traditional West Country style in 1926, the first cottage designed for the village by Clough Williams-Ellis.

The *trompe l'oeil* mock copper and sandstone turret hiding a chimney at Portmeirion.

A view of Portmeirion village with the pink Gothic porch from Nerquis Hall visible in the bottom left.

Foundations

During Advent, in the weeks approaching Christmas, one of the churches in my local town hosts a display made by hand by a local man: installed down one side of the nave, and across the altar, is a tiny village of houses, streets and workshops, intricate in detail. Most traditional trades are represented: there are masons cutting stone, blacksmiths in their forge, millers, shepherds and farmers. The women draw water from wells, launder clothes in the communal wash house or carry firewood. Paused in an imagined and undefined past, somewhere between the Middle Ages and the nineteenth century, the villagers go about their chores alone or in pairs against a painted backdrop of hills and fields.

There is no concession to seasonal good cheer. This is a place of hard labour and plain living, of oak and limestone rather than of tinsel and baubles. The palette is brownish, with hints of grey. There's no nativity scene, no angels suspended above or wise men lurking behind: the focus of the display is the people, working, and the structure of the village itself. I'm not quite sure what its theological purpose might be.

A surprising number of visitors each pay a small sum to wander the length of this model village and pick out the details which delight them most. Older people are tempted to reminisce. Children puzzle over habits of the past. Nearly everyone makes a connection in some way to this fictional place which seems, somehow, accurate and authentic, not just in architectural construction methods and details of costume and furniture, but in the more generalised picture of history it represents. This, we think, is how it once was. This is what a village was like. And perhaps this is the intention of the exhibition, in the end: to draw people together to consider what it means to live an ordinary life and reflect on how our experiences might be connected to those of the past.

When I told people that I was writing a book about 'model' villages, this is the type of miniature spectacle many of them thought I had in mind – but the model villages explored here are real places, life-size places, still changing and mostly still inhabited. The confusion over the idea of the 'model village' can be blamed on the Victorians, who first used the term to describe not a meticulous and tiny reconstruction but another sort of personal fantasy: new settlements created by the wealthy for their workers, often on landed estates, but also in the industrial heartlands, at mines, factories and mills. The term model was used in the sense of blueprint or exemplar, in the sense of the novel rather than the imitation, in the context of the ideal and the perfect. But there *are* moments of collision between the miniature model and the larger, working one; and this book explores those too.

Over 400 model towns and villages are recorded in Britain, built by philanthropic individuals and companies to house workers, to make concrete radical philosophies and to try out experimental solutions to social and economic problems. They are visible evidence of the effects of some of the most significant and controversial pieces of British legislation: the 1819 and 1833 Factory Acts, for example, the 1832 Reform Act, the 1834 Poor Law. Many are the work of the most progressive and innovative engineers and architects. Some, like Saltaire near Bradford – a World Heritage Site – are well known and celebrated; others remain little more than local curiosities or have slipped entirely into obscurity. From New Lanark in Scotland to Trowse in Norfolk and Tremadog in Wales; from picturesque Arcadian settlements to geometric rows of almshouses and industrial terraces, all are places that reveal the complexities of a society in flux, exposing the debates that preoccupied a developing nation: religion, class, education, reform, art, status, wealth, science, slavery, history, identity.

My own path has meandered through these model villages on a surprising number of occasions: as a child I lived close to Bournville in Birmingham, and later to Port Sunlight on the Wirral, which I visit again in Chapter 6; my first job after university was at Nenthead, a place designed for mine workers in the North Pennines, which I re-explore in Chapter 2; a cluster of Derbyshire workers' villages surrounded the place I settled for a while when I married. But the same might be true for many of us, if we just knew where to look: most people have the remains of these idealistic experiments close to their doorsteps. This seemed one good reason, after all, for writing about them.

Planned settlements have existed since Roman times, developing across Europe in response to political and military imperatives or as an expression of religious, ideological and social ideals such as those encapsulated by Thomas More in his *Utopia* of 1516: the *bastide* grid-towns of medieval France offered protection to strategic commercial centres; the *nuevas poblaciones* (new settlements) established by Charles III of Spain during the eighteenth century encouraged new settlers into de-populated mountain areas; the Polish nobility of the sixteenth and seventeenth centuries established a series of towns designed to stimulate trade and modelled on the Utopian vision of the perfect city; this was also the basis for Pienza, the Renaissance experiment constructed in Tuscany by Pope Pius II. The concept of the model village is not a distinctively British one: it was, however, in Britain from the end of the eighteenth century that the idea flourished, mapping the land with a variety of new settlements.

Inevitably, *Dreamstreets* is in part a biography of the manufacturers, philanthropists and far-sighted companies who created and sustained these places. Without their ambition and perseverance none of these villages would have existed; the complex interplay of private power and public authority features in the development of almost all of the settlements and the founders' idiosyncrasies make each place unique: the famously workaholic Isambard Kingdom Brunel sketched the parallel grids of cottages in Swindon himself; the Bolsover Colliery Company designed its settlement in Creswell, Derbyshire, around a miniature railway that delivered coal direct from the pits to each of the houses; George Cadbury's Bournville experiment was riddled with rules which included a requirement for each house to grow at least six fruit trees, and which banned alcohol within the village limits.

Dreamstreets is not confined to retelling individual life stories, however: this is a book about relationship with place, and about how people's histories shape the landscape. As a novelist, I'm curious about the ways in which individuals and communities interact with their environment; I'm fascinated by how we read the world around us. In the writing of this book, I've walked from grand avenues exuding power and prestige, to backyards, alleys and garden paths. This is a collection of some of the thoughts that occurred to me while I was walking; it's intended to give a sense of where these villages might have sprung from and why they exist at all; it touches as much on the contexts as the architectural decisions which shaped each place. The story stretches two hundred years, from the middle of the eighteenth to the middle of the twentieth centuries, attempting to trace the common impulses that lingered across time, and to point out the differences and changes. In particular, it highlights the factors that made these small, sometimes plain, settlements so influential: the radical thinking and politics that inspired them, the far-sighted philosophies of their founders, the fashions and contra-dictions and paradoxes.

If it's about anything more than a few interesting villages, this book is probably about ideals made real in a way that's rarely possible. It presents evidence of the *Dreamstreets* on the ground that link us, in time and place, to a history of visionary ideas, quirky desires and ambitious mistakes. It recognises, too, that most of us experience our lives through the communities in which we live – in the fabric of the houses and streets, in relationships with neighbours and the roaming of green spaces – and it broaches some of the connections between these intimate places and the social, political and cultural developments happening around them. Like the model village in the church, the book, I hope, offers the chance to reminisce and to question, to inspect the construct of workers' villages freely and precisely, and in so doing perhaps better understand the ways in which we live today.

DREAMSTREETS

I

Cromford, Derbyshire

We begin here: midwinter; mid-country; short, cold days. I come from the north, crossing open moorland before joining the main road through the Derwent Valley. Frost clings late to shaded hedges and pavements; the light remains metallic, dusky. The Derbyshire gritstone from which the houses are made lives up to its name and gives the villages a sombre, pragmatic air – a grittiness. Despite all the comfortable 4x4s, the seasonal lights and cosy fleeces, it's possible to imagine a tough life here, a not-so-long-ago past, bitter and thankless and industrial.

In the steep-sided gorge the river runs rapid and frothy, the rock pressing through with emphatic solidity. It's a landscape that encloses and intimidates; although mostly it's a mediated place, a trail of roads and signposts and drystone walls, it still offers brief moments of genuine, discomforting ruggedness, glimpses – nothing more – of something wild and brutal. It's like watching a piece of classic theatre with a dark villain stalking the back of the stage: there's the barely concealed promise of melodrama and menace.

A few miles from Cromford the natural landscape gives way to the distraction of a small town, Matlock Bath. Its original identity as a spa resort has become muddled, almost erased. Boxy 1980s cable cars dangle over Georgian and Victorian villas; the genteel row of buildings crouched beneath the lead mines on the Heights of Abraham is home to shops with a seaside feel, selling candyfloss, coloured windmills and car stickers. Beside the river there's a formal public gardens where eighteenth- and nineteenth-century visitors would stroll and chat, making brief acquaintances and indulging in small flirtations between taking the waters, but at this retreat – favoured by Josiah Wedgwood and Lord Byron and John Ruskin – a line of motorbikes now glints reflections along the length of the town; bikers in expensive leathers sprawl on the walls. This is still a meeting place, a place of convergence, but it thrums to the sound of powerful engines.

A little further along the road from Matlock Bath is the huge red-brick and gritstone edifice of Masson Mill, squeezed between the rock face and the river, simultaneously brutal and elegant. Built in 1783, it's a demonstrative expression of industrial progress. Driven at first by a single waterwheel, the mill drew its power from the Derwent along-side but its architecture suggests ambitions and influences far beyond the valley: the Italianate style – with a bell cote and a projecting exterior stairway – links it to a powerful cultural past. With its combination of stately European magnificence and practical efficiency, Masson Mill became the pattern for mills around Britain well into the nineteenth century. Now it is both a World Heritage Site and a shopping mall. Apparently it attracts almost half a million visitors a year, although the working textile museum – boasting the world's largest collection of bobbins – is probably less of a draw than the designer boutiques. Certainly on a Saturday afternoon only a few weeks before Christmas, the car park is full even though the museum is closed for the season.

At Cromford, just half a mile further on, the mill is more discreet. It could easily be missed. The main road cuts between the industrial site and the village square, separating one from the other; many travellers pause only at the traffic lights on the A6 before moving on again towards Derby. There is a fleeting sense, perhaps, of well-made old buildings on either side, enough to attract a quick glance, but Derbyshire is full of well-made old buildings; many of its villages are pretty and substantial, with wells and walls and churches, stone cottages nestling against green hills. Why pay particular attention to this one?

Turning at a set of traffic lights, I wind downhill. The lane narrows by a wide gate, a heavy wall stacked above it; either side two round towers thrust out like turrets. It could be the entrance to a castle or a prison. But it's the mill, its fortress-like presence suddenly imposing. The wall goes on, high and featureless, barricading the lane and creating closed, urban perspectives until quite suddenly, a few hundred yards further on, the prospect opens out: there's a wooded hill, the river widening between grassy banks and meandering under a stone bridge. The geometric certainty of the mill buildings dissipates into open waste ground by the canal, a scruffy collection of low walls and ruins, a wide gravel pathway. A wedding is just finishing at the church further down the lane: the bride and groom are standing by the gate, shivering, the photography not quite accomplished. The guests are picking their way over the scrubland, tripping in high heels around the puddles and clutching thin shirts across their chests. Mallards approach them hopefully. The bells ring.

In 1771, during the early days of the Industrial Revolution, Cromford was like many other Derbyshire hamlets, a scattering of poor cottages whose inhabitants were dependent on farming or small-scale mining. What set it apart was its water. This is a place where Bonsall Brook gushes between rocky banks, fast and furious. It is also a place where natural and man-made water courses run together: as well as the brook, there is Cromford Sough, which took over thirty years to dig, draining the seventeenth- and eighteenth-century lead mines deep in the hills, allowing the miners to work below the water table. It was said never to run dry and never to freeze.

To this place of constant streams came Richard Arkwright, a new breed of entrepreneur, an organiser, an inventor, a man of energy. He was thirty-nine years old and anxious to improve his small textile factory in Nottingham where the machinery was driven by horses. He was in search of something more reliable and efficient than exhausted animals, and at Cromford he found it. Water. In August 1771 he signed a lease to the land and to rights to the brook and the sough. In addition he bought Steeple Hall in the nearby village of Wirksworth and demolished it. The stone was transported to Cromford and by December the mill was built.

It's not easy to reimagine Arkwright's leap of faith. The connection between water and power has become an ordinary thing, an outmoded phenomenon. We've all learned about it at school, and we've all seen waterwheels. The idea of using water to drive machines has the sepia tint of heritage about it, a quaintness. But Arkwright's vision was truly extraordinary and experimental. He was attempting to change the way in which the world operated, to drive modernity in new directions. When the mill at Cromford was complete – the world's first water-powered cotton spinning mill – nothing of this kind had ever been seen before. It was hi-tech and high risk. As one stands now in the well-trodden yard, with its craft shops and interpretation panels, it requires an effort to appreciate this, an unremembering of the intervening years which have made this type of place familiar.

The mill building is five storeys high, each floor crammed with small, square windows. It has a certain brutal charm to it, but it might be considered ugly: the roof, flat and slight, seems out of proportion to the huge stone walls, an ill-fitting hat on a broad face. Arkwright, however, was unconcerned by architectural aesthetics. He was driven by a very practical, industrial vision and by 1775 his experiments with mechanisation had allowed him to take out a patent on ten types of machine for tackling many of the spinning processes, including carding and cleaning the cotton. The following year, he demolished an old corn mill on Bonsall Brook to make room for a second cotton mill, bigger than the first, seven storeys in height.

The industrialisation here took place with remarkable rapidity. Within a decade, Cromford was transformed from a nondescript hamlet into a world-leading centre of manufacturing and state-of-the-art mechanisation. Its landscape was altered beyond recognition, its water trussed and tamed, its old buildings demolished, improved and expanded. And all this activity, of course, required a change to the way people lived – and to the number of people who would call Cromford home. By the early 1770s, the first mill was employing 200 workers in twelve-hour shifts, carding and combing cotton during the day and spinning at night. When the second mill was opened in 1776, over 500 villagers celebrated with a parade, following a band to the new building where they were treated to cakes and ale. At all hours and on all days, Cromford was noisy and bustling, modern and anxious, a place of change and disruption where old habits were dislocated and new ones not yet formed: 'The rural cot has given way to the lofty red mill and the grand houses of overseers; the stream perverted from its courses by sluices and aqueducts will no longer ripple and cascade,' noted John Byng, 5th Viscount Torrington, when he visited. 'Every rural sound is sunk in the clamours of the cotton works, and the simplest peasant is changed into an impudent mechanic.'[1]

To accommodate the workers who were part of this ambitious vision for Cromford, Arkwright created a village. Up the slope from the river, on North Street and Cromford Hill, he built rows of grit-stone, three-storey cottages, each with a living room and bedroom and extra windows on the top floor to allow more light for frame-work knitters, who worked the yarn that was made at the mills. A chapel was constructed in 1777 and the following year the Black Dog Hotel (which has since been given the paler, less aggressive name of the Greyhound) was built in the market square, usefully accom-modating a bank in the same building and designed to cater for the constant stream of business visitors. Finally, in 1790, Arkwright – now with a knighthood and in the exalted role of High Sheriff of Derbyshire – managed to secure the right to hold a weekly market on Saturdays, so reinforcing the village's identity as a self-sufficient commercial centre. With the road running down one side, the marketplace linked Cromford to growing mercantile hubs: there were daily coaches to London, Birmingham, Sheffield and Nottingham. Occupying the flat land between the workers' houses and the mills, it also buttressed the domestic streets from the blatantly industrial activity near the river. Arkwright himself lived at Rock House, overlooking his original mill, although in 1788 he purchased a nearby estate from Florence Nightingale's father for £20,000 and began work on the creation of a grander residence which he named Willersley Castle.

The housing for the workers here at Cromford was the first planned industrial housing in Derbyshire, and some of the earliest in the country. Walking between the terraces, you quickly become aware how reminiscent the rows of cottages are of the mills: the high walls and small windows, the low, flat roofs, the blank stone frontages all recall the much larger buildings a few hundred yards down the hill. Today, the doors and windows are all painted to match each other, a tasteful shade of pale blue. Just at the end of the row, on the final door, someone has hung a small red Christmas wreath, a sharp moment of colour, but apart from this it becomes difficult to see where one cottage ends and the next begins: the lines of windows run into each other, and there is a single unbroken view, closed off at the end of the street by a pair of old yews and, beyond this, by the primary school. Built later than the cottages, in 1832, it's a low line of buildings around a square courtyard: with its large arched windows and tended gardens, it has a slightly ecclesiastical air, like a cathedral close or church almshouses.

The houses on North Street are featureless mill cottages constructed in a monolithic, undifferentiated block, successfully concealing their internal spaces behind the impersonal symmetry and simplicity of the facade. There is nothing very distinctive about them: there are similar rows in other Derbyshire and Yorkshire towns, with the same upper-storey windows, narrow doors and neat, undecorated stone. They are resolutely plain, sharing something in common with the modernist, even brutalist, architecture which shaped cities during the 1960s and '70s. I wonder what on earth I can say about them. Apart from its status as such an early planned village, there seems little to remark on here at Cromford. It doesn't seem a very good start for a book.

But something happens around the corner at the far end of the street, just beyond the yews, where the village school is fenced off with black metal railings and set behind small neat lawns. As you turn down between the school and the end of North Street, back in the direction of the mill, the view changes. A different Cromford is revealed, untidy and evocative. This is the back of the 1776–7 mill cottages. The top windows which are so evident on the front elevations have been blocked in here; low extensions have been added to provide space for toilets and kitchens, modern conveniences. But what is most striking is the view of the gardens, a jumble of tiny lawns and allotments, paths and pigsties, precarious satellite dishes, washing lines strung across small spaces, the ubiquitous trampoline enclosed in netting. And in this patchwork of land confined between houses and hidden from easy viewing, I begin to glimpse some of the contradictions of a place like Cromford, some of the tensions and complications, the things that make it interesting. Here, where Arkwright's cottages turn their blind backs on his mills, there is a way of connecting with the people who lived in these houses, growing food and keeping animals, bringing memories and habits from generations of country living to this new environment. Faced with a completely new way of life, forced into the factories and cut off from the collective conscious-ness of the past, the villagers at Cromford tended little squares of land as a way of improving practical conditions and rooting themselves in a different world. Today, despite years of transition and advance – despite the enormous impact of the Industrial Revolution – it's this evidence of hope and family, of idiosyncrasy and brief life, which remains.

The repercussions of the Industrial Revolution were merciless and abrupt. It seems obvious, but nonetheless it's worth remembering: the world was being quickly and irrevocably transformed, both physically and philosophically. And of course this was not just a process of technical invention, scientific discovery and capitalist enterprise – it was an evolution in the way ordinary people lived. On Friday 7 June 1776 a lead miner from Cromford called Anthony Coates hanged himself in one of the buildings hunkered over the mineshaft at Wirksworth, a market town around two miles distant, where the land rises away from the Derwent Valley. He was forty-two years old and married with three children. The local press attempted to explain the circumstances of his suicide: the *Nottingham Journal* suggested that he had been reckless with the family finances, having 'sold three Cows, by which his Wife maintained the Family, and 'tis suppos'd he went to Manchester Races, (and) lost all the money'; another newspaper also claimed gambling was at the root of the tragedy, but reported that the money had been lost at Newmarket. The detail of the affair seems unimportant. What *is* important is that physical changes at Cromford were impacting on individual lives. Five years after the building of the mill, the families who for generations had made their money from lead mining in the area were no longer flourishing – attention and prosperity had shifted to a new factory system of spinning cotton, to Arkwright's mill and the village surrounding it. Those who were left behind, bound to the old ways of life, were vulnerable and desperate. Taking a walk around Cromford, pausing within the symmetrical grasp of the terraces, I am brought face to face with evidence of what was happening 250 years ago, and its far-reaching effects.

These few cottages – Richard Arkwright's speculative village – established a pattern which was to recur throughout the country and the following century. Perhaps the best-known example of an early industrial village is at New Lanark Mills in Scotland, which sprang directly from the Cromford model. In 1784 Richard Arkwright was asked to travel north to view the Falls of Clyde with another entrepreneur called David Dale. It was a difficult journey, leaving Glasgow on poor roads and entering deep into the isolated and marshy Clyde Valley. But it was a spectacular place. By the early nineteenth century, as roads improved, it would become a major tourist attraction, a popular stopping point on the route from the Lake District to the Trossachs: William and Dorothy Wordsworth, Samuel Taylor Coleridge, Robert Southey and J. M. W. Turner were among those who came to admire the landscape.

Of a practical turn of mind, however, Arkwright was impressed less by the aesthetic impact of the scene than by its natural resources, particularly the rapid flow of water and its potential for providing reliable power. At Bonnington, about two miles upstream of Lanark, the River Clyde changes from a broad, placid river; it rushes through a reddish sandstone gorge, cascading in a series of waterfalls or 'linns'. Having seen the site, Arkwright immediately agreed to partner Dale in an effort to establish cotton mills there, providing technical expertise and training suitable men while Dale undertook the building work. The partnership proved short-lived: after just over a year the agreement was dissolved. But Arkwright had already left his mark, both in the systems employed in production and in the architectural character of the site which included both workers' housing and the projecting stair bays and Palladian windows which are a feature of Masson Mill.

Elsewhere, too, Arkwright was in demand as a kind of investor-consultant. At Stanley Mill on the River Tay near Perth, he entered into another brief partnership with George Dempster, building a typical first-generation Arkwright-style mill with a factory village attached. Greg's Mill at Styal in Cheshire – very close to the modern megalith of Manchester Airport – was constructed in 1784 to house Arkwright's water frames, and a nascent village was established close by. At first this was little more than an apprentice house to accommodate the pauper children who provided the bulk of the workforce, but by 1820 a more recognisable settlement had been developed, including a school and a chapel.

After Arkwright's departure from New Lanark, Dale continued to expand, quickly building four mills and attracting a population of over 1,500 workers, including almost 500 children brought in from Glasgow and Edinburgh workhouses – who were given food and lodging but no wages – and a large number of families from Skye and the Highlands who had been shipwrecked off the west coast of Scotland shortly after setting sail for a new life in America. Dale was, on the whole, a benevolent employer and the factory flourished, but living and working conditions were still difficult: shifts were long; most families lived in one room in large tenement blocks with little sanitation; theft and drunkenness were commonplace.

It was the arrival of Robert Owen, a Welshman working as a mill manager at Chorlton Twist Mills in Manchester, that was to transform New Lanark into a lauded model of industrial welfare and housing. Owen came from Newtown in the upper Severn Valley, a self-contained community that relied on the woollen industry. Then, as today, this was a pleasant but isolated country town with few opportunities for the budding entrepreneur; by his late teens Owen had completed a draper's apprenticeship at Stamford in Lincolnshire and moved on to London, trying his hand as a haberdasher's assistant. By 1788, at the age of seventeen, he had moved on again, working for Sattersfield & Co., a Manchester silk merchant, pandering to the fashions of the rapidly expanding middle classes. Owen seems to have had an eye for a trend and a profit. Despite his experience in wool and silk it was cotton which struck him as the fabric of the moment and perhaps the future. He decided to invest in the making of spinning machinery and to concentrate his efforts in the burgeoning cotton mills. By the age of twenty-one he had been appointed manager of Bank Top Mill in Manchester, where he was responsible for 500 workers, as well as another Arkwright-style factory at Northwich in Cheshire. His salary was an impressive £300 a year. Just three years later, having earned a reputation for efficiency and innovation, he went to work for the Chorlton Twist Company, a much larger operation with London partners and international trade connections.

Owen's rapid rise through the ranks is a clear indication of his taste for business and networking, his entrepreneurial talent and his sheer ambition. The site at New Lanark seemed to offer him everything he needed to nurture these qualities to the full – in September 1799, he married Dale's eldest daughter, Caroline, and invested £60,000 in his new father-in-law's business, becoming the managing partner a few months later, on 1 January 1800. He immediately turned his attention to improving the commercial efficiency of the mills – and to developing the workforce housing into a more recognisable village community. Over the next twenty years he provided schooling, recreation and a general store where workers could buy basic goods at close to cost price and where the sale of alcohol could be monitored, creating the kind of company village which would act as a prototype for many that came afterwards.

Owen's progress was apparently unstoppable and his confidence unshakeable: when his business partners voiced unease at the extra expense incurred by what they viewed as unnecessary welfare expenditure, he simply bought them out and relaunched the business with new investors. In 1813 he began to publish evangelical essays in which he expanded his philosophies to his fellow businessmen, to the political elite and *'to the dispassionate and patient investigation and decision of those individuals of every rank and class and denomination of society, who have become in some degree conscious of the errors in which they exist'*. These essays were ambitiously titled 'A New View of Society' and were couched in the language of Enlightenment conviction, expressing confidence that truth would ultimately make itself known, errors would be recognised and lasting change would result.

In particular, Owen's essays attempted to articulate the value of human life and suggest limits for the expansion of the factory system. On the subject of 'Man and Machine', for example, he wrote with fervour:

Many of you have long experienced in your manufacturing operations the advantages of substantial, well-contrived, and well-executed machinery.

Experience has also shown you the difference of the results between mechanism which is neat, clean, well arranged, and always in a high state of repair; and that which is allowed to be dirty, in disorder, and without the means of preventing unnecessary friction, and which therefore becomes, and works, much out of repair.

In the first case the whole economy and management are good, every operation proceeds with ease, order, and success. In the last, the reverse must follow, and dissatisfaction among all the agents and instrument interested or occupied in the general process, which cannot fail to create great loss.

If, then, due care as to the state of your inanimate machines can produce such beneficial results, what may not be expected if you devote equal attention to your vital machines, which are far more wonderfully constructed?[2]

In the space of just a couple of years, Owen poured out his vision into four essays, which became increasingly Utopian in tone, anticipating the coming of a better age that would see his ideas put into practice. He urged the government to intervene to counter rising levels of poverty and unemployment, and he set out proposals for new self-contained communities to be established by philanthropists, parishes or the state.

In many ways, these communities were an extension of the idea of the model village. Based on his experience at New Lanark, Owen proposed settlements of between 300 and 2,000 people on land of between 1,000 and 1,500 acres. These 'townships' would be largely agricultural in nature, combining a nostalgia for a pre-industrial lifestyle with a strict form of communism which made no concession to individual needs or desires: work, machinery and wages would be shared equally, with each person over the age of fifteen being given 'according to his needs'; the entire community would live in one large, square building, with public kitchens and mess rooms; children under three years of age were to be taken into communal care while older children would be placed in dormitories and allowed only occasional parental visits.

Owen's vision took the basic outline of the model village to its extreme, removing it from its new industrial context to a rural setting that rooted it in an idealised past and which isolated the inhabitants so thoroughly that every aspect of their lives could be planned and managed. His proposal suggests both a remarkable confidence in the pioneering social engineering he was trying out at New Lanark and a distrust of the industrial lifestyle which underpinned it. It had its roots in the traditional discourse around the idea of Utopia, the perfect place, a place of order and harmony where the beauty of the architecture reflected the collective happiness of the community.

Drawing on Plato, who described the perfect city state, the term 'Utopia' was first explored by Thomas More in 1516. His work attracted immediate attention and the Utopian ideal continued to intrigue and inspire philosophers and politicians over the following centuries: in the seventeenth century, Johann Valentin Andreae developed his version in *Christianopolis* (1619) and Francis Bacon re-examined the marvellous mythical city of Atlantis to create his vision for a better world in *New Atlantis* (1627). By the mid-eighteenth century, the concept was firmly embedded in social and literary culture: David Hume was discussing the 'Idea of a Perfect Commonwealth' in his *Political Discourses* (1752) and Samuel Johnson was setting his moral tale of happiness, *The History of Rasselas, Prince of Abissinia*, in a mythical Utopian valley.

Owen's ambitions sit neatly within this tradition but rather than develop one large perfect metropolis, his Utopian future was organised on a system of smaller settlements. He was confident that these communities would become so widespread and active that in time they would merge into larger 'federatively united' associations, creating 'circles of tens, hundreds and thousands' of townships across the country. In this way the villages would, he claimed, 'be found capable of combining within themselves all the advantages that city and country residence now afford, without any of the numerous inconveniences and evils which necessarily attach to both those modes of society'.[3]

Owen's revolutionary ideas for a scheme of linked villages were never tested: none of the planned settlements was ever built and the village at New Lanark was the closest he came to trying out his vision on the ground. But his writings did attract attention, giving him a platform on the national stage to address some of the major political concerns of the late eighteenth century: popular education, the impact of the factory system, the condition of the working class, Poor Law reform and economic regeneration. 'My four essays . . . and my practice at New Lanark had made me well known among the leading men,' he boasted.[4]

Not all the attention was welcome, however. Many of Owen's suggestions were quickly rejected, and even ridiculed. Critics pointed out that the ideas were not, in fact, as new as he liked to claim: 'It may be true but it is not new,' wrote William Hazlitt. '. . . it is as old as the royal borough of Lanark; or as the county of Lanark itself . . . as the Utopia of Thomas More, as the Republic of Plato.'[5] In addition, Owen's humble background and rapid rise to riches meant that many influential commentators simply regarded him as a charlatan and a chancer, speculative and scheming. They pointed to the enormous sums he was spending on what, they claimed, amounted to propaganda campaigns and self-promotion.

More controversial still was Owen's insistence that the townships should be free of religion. His conviction that in his Utopia there 'would be no public worship – no avowed recognition of God, no belief of responsibility to a higher tribunal than man's' drew the wrath of the Established Church and ensured violent opposition to his writing from the powerful Anglican hierarchy. Indeed, even many Nonconformists found Owen's anti-religious stance difficult to stomach: William Allen, a Quaker and one of the early partners at New Lanark, complained after the publication of 'A New View of Society' that Owen was promoting 'a manufactory of infidels'.[6]

Undaunted, Owen continued to spread the word, taking his message to Europe in 1818. A few years later, in 1822–3, he undertook a lengthy tour of Ireland, visiting Limerick and Clare and holding a series of public meetings in Dublin in an attempt to persuade the government to act as agent for his proposed reforms. But again, the message was not well received – disastrously, his ideas apparently 'caused a feeling of horror' among Irish landowners and manufacturers.[7] Typically, Owen brushed off such criticism and continued to articulate his vision with unabashed enthusiasm. If anything, the more people objected, the more determined he became – and the more extreme his blueprint for the ideal village.

Having failed to convert European minds to his most radical concept for a model settlement, Owen turned to America. In 1825, in an energetic middle age, he purchased the town of Harmony in Indiana, USA, a settlement along the Washbash River established by a Christian sect known as the Harmony Society. He broke up his family, leaving his wife and two daughters in Scotland and taking his four sons and another daughter across the Atlantic with the intention of establishing a community based on his principles of social reform, the ultimate expression of the ideal of the self-sustaining village which he had nurtured at New Lanark.

Owen's American dream was quickly over. The experiment proved chaotic and unworkable and just days after his arrival in March 1825 he was already confiding uncharacteristic uncertainties to his diary: 'I doubt whether those who have been comfortable and content in their old mode of life, will find an increase of enjoyment when they come here. How long it will require to accustom themselves to their new mode of living, I am unable to determine.' His son Robert was harsher still in his assessment of the scheme, which, he said, was an impossible muddle: 'a heterogeneous collection of radicals, enthusiastic devotees to principle, honest latitudinarians, and lazy theorists, with a sprinkling of unprincipled sharpers thrown in'.[8]

The town soon became overcrowded. It lacked sufficient housing, and there was a shortage of skilled craftsmen and labourers. The production of crops and materials was too poor to allow for self-sufficiency and there was little experienced supervision or management: Owen himself spent only a few months in residence. The community struggled on for a couple of years but finally disbanded into a series of smaller, squabbling groups in 1827, dissolving in constant quarrels over ownership in 1829. It was not possible, it appeared, to take the planned settlements of Cromford and New Lanark as archetypes for anything more ambitious and adventurous; it seemed as though the strong paternalistic direction of an Arkwright or Owen was the essential ingredient in holding together the disparate interests of a working community and shaping a village.

At New Lanark, Owen's character certainly loomed large. He considered the mills and village to be a very personal experiment: as his work attracted more and more attention he attempted to rewrite the early history of the project, taking complete credit for the development of the site, giving no mention to Arkwright's influence and reducing Dale's role to little more than an incidental footnote. In particular, Owen increasingly articulated the value of his experiment as a potential bulwark against a dangerous rising tide of working-class defiance and the uncertainties of international upheaval and manoeuvring, which alarmed his allies and threatened the growth of business. Moving to London to work on his essays in 1812–14, Owen arrived in a volatile city buzzing with news of Wellington's victories, Napoleon's progress, the war in the United States and a series of political and economic crises at home. He mixed with politicians and intellectuals, reformers and philanthropists, refining his ideas of the model village and what it might achieve. A mark of the mixture of influences – and the ambiguity of Owen's position – can be seen in the dedication of his first essay of 1816 which was addressed to both William Wilberforce – an Evangelical Christian MP, leading reformer and anti-slavery campaigner – and the Prince Regent – a hardline conservative, even reactionary, and a vociferous opponent of political reform.

In Europe the effects of the French Revolution and Napoleon's subsequent rise to power were being strongly felt: the dissemination of revolutionary ideas was inspiring widespread social and political protest while opposition to Napoleon's expansionist policies was creating unrest and financial hardship. By 1812, when Owen was beginning his series of essays, Britain was not only deeply involved in the European arena but had also been drawn into direct conflict with the United States, waging war at sea, fighting battles on the difficult American–Canadian border and attacking the south and Gulf coasts of the US in a number of invasions. Inevitably, the economy suffered, but at particular risk was the cotton trade which relied on raw materials from the US as well as the export market it provided. At the same time, to make matters worse, domestic protest was also targeting the cotton industry: the years 1812–13 saw the Luddite movement at its most active, breaking into mills and wrecking machinery in an attempt to protect jobs.

The government's response to these multiple challenges was to suppress discontent as quickly and effectively as it could. Legislation was pushed through to prevent organised protest: the Combination Acts of 1799 and 1800, for example, were put in place by Pitt's government to counter the threat of a workers' strike; following the Peterloo Massacre in 1819, the 'Six Acts' clamped down yet more repressively on the right to assemble and protest. Local militia were formed in many areas; articles in the press were censored. Anyone regarded as a radical or troublemaker was vigorously prosecuted. Owen's more personal response to such upheaval was to re-emphasise the role of the village. As industrial contexts became more uncertain and old habits more widely disrupted, he spoke up for the New Lanark-type settlement as a means of social engineering, asserting control and enforcing conformity.

Little of Owen's writing about politics, education, law and social order was new – but the simultaneous development of the village at New Lanark was the first time many of the ideas had been seen in practice. It was the settlement, rather than the rhetoric of *A New View of Society*, which demonstrated how economic progress and political change could be managed by applying practical solutions to the major problems of the period: poverty, poor housing, diet and health, and lack of educational opportunity. In the same year as Owen's essays were published in book form (1816), he opened at New Lanark an Institute for the Formation of Character, a direct practical expression of his belief in 'environmentalism' – that is, that character was not determined by divine creation nor inherent in race or class but was instead a product of the environment in which people grew up and worked. If he was able to prove this at New Lanark, then the experiment would have significant implications for eighteenth- and nineteenth-century planning and reform: if people were malleable and could be shaped by their surroundings, then changing those surroundings could ultimately produce an ordered and submissive workforce.

At the opening of the Institute on New Year's Day 1816, Owen gave a lengthy speech to 1,200 gathered villagers: 'It must be evident to those who have been in the practice of observing children with attention,' he said, 'that much of good or evil is taught to or acquired by a child at a very early period of its life; that much of temper or disposition is correctly or incorrectly formed before he attains his second year.' It was clear, then, that children were to be the focus of the new Institute – although technically separate from the school, it was to act as a school by another name. But the curriculum consisted of more than the usual three Rs. Alongside an elementary education in literacy and numeracy, geography and history, the children received dance and singing lessons, 'standing up 70 couples a time in the dancing room' and forming harmony choirs of over 200; they also took part in regular military-style drills 'with precision equal, as many officers stated, to some regiments of the line'; conformity was further enforced by a rather remarkable uniform, a 'beautiful dress of tartan cloth, fashioned in its make after the form of a Roman toga'.[9] Evening classes, balls, lectures and concerts were held in the Institute for adults.

In many ways, the Institute provided a progressive education, and the emphasis on teaching children rather than making them labour in the mills was a step forward in improving conditions. The example at New Lanark, along with Owen's campaigning, proved influential in forcing the government to act on child welfare although it was a further three years until the 1819 Cotton Mills and Factories Act put legal limits on the employment of those under sixteen years of age and it was 1833 before a modest burden of education provision was placed on factory owners. In addition, difficulties in enforcing the law meant that much was still left up to individual factory owners and managers: many mills continued to force workers, including children, into long hours in poor conditions in the search for profit.

For all the attention paid to working families, however, Owen's brand of rationality and progress was also clearly deployed to his own pragmatic, commercial ends. The mill was at the heart of a new type of far-reaching global capitalism which linked Britain to the New World and beyond, to an international marketplace that relied on both the worst inequalities of the slave-laboured cotton plantation and the excitement of a burgeoning consumerism. The village at New Lanark, despite its modest size, was an important part of this worldwide trade, a small but not insignificant cog in the growing mechanism of commercial success. The activities on offer to residents here were designed to make the business operate smoothly. The Institute was intended to produce well-trained, tractable and amenable workers, shaping them from infancy so that the mills could be harmoniously run. It provided a way of keeping an eye on future generations and weeding out troublemakers at an early age, with implications not only for productivity at New Lanark but for the success of the much larger global enterprise in which the village was invested.

Even the architecture of the site reinforced notions of civil obedience. If you take a walk around the mills and village, what becomes evident is how the design allows for supervision and control: Robert Owen's house stands centrally between the workers' housing and the mill buildings, well placed for the observation of movement to and fro; in the mill buildings themselves, large open-plan spaces act both to accommodate new forms of cotton-working machinery and to facilitate easy observation of the workforce; the Institute sits just the other side of the mill race, visible from both Owen's house and the mill; the yard in front of it, where military exercises took place, can be seen from all sides. This is a place built to discourage individualism, disobedience and secrecy; it's a village where privacy is not accounted for, or considered necessary. Its physical structure perfectly expresses the gap between those being watched and those doing the watching.

The New Lanark village would provide, Owen claimed, 'a model and example to the manufacturing community' with implications for the entire country: 'Without some essential change in the formation of their [the workers'] characters,' he warned in a *Statement Regarding New Lanark* in 1812, unruly elements would threaten 'to revolutionise and ruin the empire'. His village was clearly intended as something more than a physical home for the hundreds of workers at his mill. It was to be a blueprint for national security and prosperity. In Owen's vision for the settlement much was at stake. He was offering a means of permanently transforming the intrinsic nature of the British working man and woman so as to underwrite an orderly and successful empire. On his model of watchfulness and dance classes, he believed, the future of British interests depended.

Standing at the scramble of back gardens behind the cottages at Cromford, I become aware of how distant these domestic streets are from the mill. From here it's possible to see a rise of land, topped with bare trees, the roofs of other cottages, the edge of a terrace which forms one side of the market square – but the mill buildings are hidden. It could be a rural village; the industrial remains of the canal and mill race, the sweep of yard and the high walls might as well, for the moment, not be there. This is not a place of conscious scrutiny like New Lanark. At Cromford the topography of the land-scape forces the cottages and the mill apart. There's the marketplace between them and the sharp, bending hill that winds down to the river; today, you have to cross the busy main road, waiting at the lights for a break in the traffic – even at the end of the eighteenth century this road would have been a noisy, public, outward-looking thorough-fare interrupting the walk between work and home. When workers finished their shift and made their way to the cottages, they turned into streets which hid them from the gaze of the mill managers and, perhaps more significantly, hid the mill from their own view. They could not hear the rattle of the machinery or the gush of water which drove it. They could, perhaps, step out of their role as factory hands and become something more, or at least different – a mother or father, a gardener, a craftsman, a musician, a raconteur.

This distance between work and home, owner and worker, gives the village at Cromford an air of timelessness which is missing at New

Lanark. The Scottish site is unmistakably imposing; its World Heritage status lends it extra gravitas. But perhaps because of this perfect heritage preservation, it's a village without purpose in the twenty-first century. It has been left behind as a museum piece; the radical experiment has little life to it any more. In contrast, Cromford is a place which retains the air of a real village – it suggests that manufacturing is only a part of its identity, a moment in its history. For all their physical similarities, the thirty years between the birth of the mills at Cromford and the developments at New Lanark make a difference to the spirit of both places – Owen's village is the expression of an Industrial Revolution already moving on, gathering pace, becoming more confident and demanding; its scale and layout suggest that more is required, of both its leaders and its workers if they are going to keep pace. It is bigger and fiercer. Cromford seems less simple. It seems less sure of itself and its place in the world. Its buildings concede ground to human needs; its layers of history appear as much personal as institutional. I find New Lanark disconcerting, whereas there's something cheering about Cromford.

A detour: Tremadog, Gwynedd

A quarter of a century after Richard Arkwright began building his mill at Cromford an equally visionary, if less successful, entrepreneur called William Alexander Madocks bought the Tan-yr-Allt estate, an expanse of flat land which formed the estuary of the Afon Glaslyn in west Wales. It was low-lying, good-for-nothing sand and salt marsh, a tidal fenland of uneven sediment punctuated by islands and fragile trees. But Madocks had plans for it. With the help of an experienced civil engineer, John Williams, he began to drain the land, building a two-mile sand and turf embankment parallel to the river rising to a height of up to twenty feet. Behind the embankment, two catchwater drains and a large sluice were installed to further direct water away. The project cost £3,000, and took two hundred men six months to complete, but by 1802 Madocks was growing wheat and rape on the reclaimed fields. He also began to build a village, Tremadog, creating a settlement where before there had been nothing but shellfish and sedges, a mark of confidence in the safety of the increasingly dry land.

When I come up the coast towards Tremadog, I don't know what to expect. It's a small place, hardly known. It's not highlighted on the road maps for any special reason; no brown heritage signs direct tourists from the faceless modern bypass. I haven't seen any decent pictures of the village or read any histories. William Madocks is no Richard Arkwright with a settled place in school history books: although his basic biography is easy enough to find, the details of his enterprises are mostly obscure. The significance of Tremadog has slipped from sight; the many physical changes Madocks imposed on the landscape have now merged with the natural features, making the place seem deceptively untrammelled.

Along the estuary approach the hills are autumnal, yellows and oranges flickering on exposed banks, brownish patches of dying heather marking the open land. The mountains are close to the river here, bearing down; the sea is only briefly glimpsed through gaps, little more than a suggestion of distance. It is early morning, slightly misty, and the sky and land, the river and sea, come together in a contemplative palette of purples and blues. Arriving in the village more quickly than I expect, I'm thrust suddenly from the main road into a wide graceful square of handsome buildings, well aged in stone. It has the feel of a European piazza; it also feels like an inland place – a cliff rises directly behind the square, almost 100 feet high, sheer rock in places, buttressed with concrete. The houses have a Derbyshire feel to them. It's not unlike Cromford in its solidity and greyish tones; the elegance of the Georgian square recalls the dignified symmetry of the Cromford marketplace. But here a Welsh flag gusts out a big red dragon.

The general store is just opening for the morning and two men have arrived to collect newspapers, but generally the village is quiet; it feels sequestered. I begin in the centre of the square, scored with white lines which skirt a raised round plinth or dais in stone. There are four steps up to what is now a fairly ordinary black mock-Victorian lamp post; in the village's heyday there was a much more imposing flagpole here and pictures show it surrounded by old men. Up on the dais, with an excellent view of things, this was the place to come and gossip, the literal and metaphorical heart of the village. Today there are traffic bollards at either end and the island feels cut off and rather unnecessary. But I loiter here anyway, because there are no cars cutting past this morning and because it is a seductive piece of architectural punctuation, a giant exclamation mark.

From here the square peels out. It is crossed at the far end by the High Street and Dublin Street, a name which seems out of place in the middle of Wales. But Tremadog was from the first a village which looked westwards across the sea rather than inland, and this is where the first workers' cottages were built in 1805 in a row called Pentre Gwaelod, 'Bottom Village', and where the travellers' inns were later positioned. The harmonious frontage of the Royal Madoc Hotel still attracts my attention. But the most imposing building is certainly the Town Hall. It has three huge arched windows on the ground floor, with another two blocked on either side; above there are generous sash windows – its facade is mostly glass, plying reflections back and forth, drawing you in to the interior which originally bustled with the urgent business of an indoor market. Today, shamefully, the building is empty and slightly unkempt – two blue and yellow 'To Let' signs perch in the blind arches – but it remains an unmistakably ambitious landmark. The flattish roof is distinctive, sitting on top of the high walls like a severe haircut. Such roofs were a Madocks speciality – the same feature appears on the town Manufactory and on his own house, Tan-yr-Allt. Again, it recalls the mills at Cromford with their oddly out-of-proportion roofs.

I come down from my perch in the middle of the road and walk along the neat cottage frontages. This is a place which still manages to sustain three pubs and a restaurant, facing off across the square. On a Sunday morning, of course, they are mostly closed and deserted – breakfast is being served in one – but they all look lively and well used and I begin to wonder what it is about the nature of the village that encourages these businesses to thrive. Most other places of this size struggle to keep a single pub; here there is a gourmet's choice. I look again at the square. There's something very welcoming about its symmetry and its enclosure; it draws you in from the rugged land just visible beyond, offering shelter from cold winds. The homogeneity of stone and design is a further pleasure. But perhaps the strongest impression is one of purpose: this is unmistakably and unapologetically a market square. It seems to demand bustle and commerce – today, empty of people, it feels bereft. Tremadog's centre has been designed for business to flourish; it has been conceived with shops and inns in mind. This is town planning not with a social or moral purpose but with an unashamedly commercial one, and its success is still evident in the pub signs which animate it.

It doesn't take long to complete a circuit of the village. Even though I pause to take photographs and to view Madocks's old house at Tan-yr-Allt – where Percy Bysshe Shelley lived for a few months, running up enormous debt – my walk is quickly accomplished. This is not a large place. There are a few short terraces of modest stone cottages, and tucked away to one side there's a 1970s housing estate of greying pebbledash and boxy gardens, but it becomes clear that the sense of arrival and purpose signalled by the market square and the Town Hall is misleading: they seem as though they should sit at the junction of lengthy streets and stately thoroughfares; they suggest bustle and development, but in fact the village slinks away and dissipates into the hill. The outlying streets are overshadowed by the bulk of cliff; architecturally unremarkable, their proximity to the ambitious square suggests disappointment and embarrassment. Tremadog feels unfinished, unfulfilled.

Madocks's hopes for Tremadog are clear enough to trace. Most of the original houses open directly onto the square, in common with town houses of the period rather than rural cottages; ordinary housing was supplemented by villas a genteel stone's throw away. There was a general store supplied from London, a shoemaker and a tailor, even though shops were rare in Welsh villages at this period, and two inns. Madocks first transformed the place from a village – Pentre Gwaelod/Bottom Village – into a town: Tré Madoc or Madocks's Town. He drew up plans for aldermen and a town mayor. Not content, he decided he preferred the idea of a 'borough' and insisted on the use of this more imposing term to describe his new settlement. His intention was to attract investors, to create a thriving and fashionable commercial centre with architectural splendour signalling his ambitions.

But why would people come here, to this reclaimed marshland on the edge of Wales? That has to be the first question, of course. At Cromford and New Lanark it was the water, the promise of industry, that drew entrepreneurs and their workers. Tremadog is clearly not a place burdened with mills; it has the air of a country town, not a manufacturing one. But appearances can be deceptive and there are traces of early-nineteenth-century industry here. Madocks enlarged one of the drainage ditches to create a canal, carrying copper ore from a local mine for a while before eventually being converted to a tramline; in 1805, he built his Manufactory, one of the first woollen mills in Wales, where carding and spinning were powered by water drawn down from Llyn Cwm Bach through a series of catchponds and wheels; the Loomery alongside accommodated weaving and, from 1835, was used as a tannery. Just like most places, if you dig deeply enough, there is evidence of industry.

Madocks's vision for his village was not confined to processing wool and shipping copper, however. Such enterprises were a necessary part of any early-nineteenth-century business portfolio, but Madocks had bigger plans. His elegant, thriving 'borough' was to have another, more adventurous function – one which is less easy to discern from the physical remains and which is rooted in a political act apparently unrelated to this isolated cluster of Welsh housing: the 1800 Union with Ireland.

Passed in July and August 1800, the twin Acts of Union promised a fresh age of cooperation and trade within the expanded United Kingdom. Madocks was prepared. Having bought the Tan-yr-Allt Estate two years earlier, he quickly began to champion a major trading route between London and Dublin. With Tremadog at its hub, the route was intended to pass to the northern coast of the Llŷn Peninsula where a ferry port would link direct to the Irish capital. With this as his major aim, he also looked beyond Ireland: the market for Welsh wool was booming, with exports to South Carolina and the southern US states, the West Indies, South America and Russia. With his manu-factory in Tremadog he intended to be at the forefront of this increasing movement to transform an ancient cottage industry into a profitable multinational enterprise. The route to and through Ireland was the first step. Proposals by Madocks's competitors involved cross-ings at the River Conwy and the Menai Strait, neither of which had yet been built: he saw his chance to steal a march. By 1803 he had obtained the right to build a network of turnpike roads and in 1806 the Porthdinllaen Harbour Bill allowed for improvement to the local harbour. To avoid a long detour round the treacherous Traeth

Mawr sands, Madocks devised plans to build a huge embankment, the Cob, across the estuary.

Madocks's letters of the period to John Williams, his friend, agent and business partner, give a clear indication of his excitement and personal investment in the activity around Tremadog. He is concerned with all the detail and anxious to get things right. In July 1805, for example, he urges careful preparations for high tides, instructing Williams to ensure 'the ditch from the turnip field is cut as deep as possible'. During the winter of 1806 he writes at length about fences and ditches in general and about his new embankment in particular; five years later, in the summer of 1811, his interest in tidal flow is still strong and in fact seems to have become even more obsessive – perhaps an indication of the amount of money he is still being forced to spend. In August, he writes from London that he 'longs to hear the particulars of the high tide turning through the sluices'.[10]

Unfortunately, despite Madocks's obvious enthusiasm and commitment, plans for the Cob seemed doomed to failure from the outset. Having been elected MP for Boston in Lincolnshire in 1802, he found he was increasingly forced to divide his time, leaving Wales frequently for London and his constituency. Just as work began, his older brother died, so depriving Madocks of one of his key investors and weakening his financial position. Shortly afterwards his engineer, James Creassy, also died, leaving the plans for the Cob without an experienced supervisor. In addition, the practical arrangements proved more complicated than envisaged: the large workforce of around 300 men created a particular headache as Madocks struggled to find ways to feed them and places to accommodate them. In a major blow, an Act of Parliament designed to authorise the work on the Glaslyn Estuary was defeated.

Undeterred, Madocks pressed on. He finally won parliamentary approval in 1807, and he fully intended the work to be finished by 1809, by which time he could begin to recoup some of the £23,500 estimated cost of building the embankment. But progress still proved painfully slow. Battered on one side by the tide and on the other by the waters of the Glaslyn, stones tipped on to the site as the basis for the embankment were carried away or displaced; it was only when rush matting was laid down that they started to hold fast. The matting did not provide a complete solution, however. Because of the distance involved and the topography of the land, it could not be laid across the full length of the site. Large gaps in the embankment remained and the Glaslyn continued to flow down the middle of the estuary, scouring the back of the new construction. Despite the building of stone piers to buttress the bank and the extensive use of boats to take heavy stones into the heart of the estuary, the Cob could not be completed.

For four years the engineers and construction workers struggled against the natural obstacles and in July 1811 the gap was finally closed. Delighted, or perhaps simply relieved, to have achieved such a feat, the workmen celebrated. The *North Wales Gazette* reported that they seized Madocks 'with the native ardour of their ancestors'; they 'took his horses from his carriage and triumphantly drew him over that embankment, which was, comparatively speaking, the work of his own hands'. In September, when everyone had had time to catch their breath, the 'Embankment Jubilee' boasted an ox roast, new uniforms for all the workmen – 'by the munificence of W. A. Madocks' – horse races, a ball, an eisteddfod, performances in the new Tremadog theatre, and prayers and sermons in the new church.

The celebrations were short-lived. The construction of the Cob had cost at least £60,000, far more than Madocks had anticipated: by January 1812, he was effectively bankrupt and being pursued for his debts; only his position as an MP rescued him from immediate civil arrest. A month later, on St Valentine's Day, a storm whipped up high tides which breached the new embankment. Local landowners and farmers responded to a call for help but Madocks was in no financial position to launch any repairs and it seemed as though all the years of inventive work on the Cob had been pointless. One of Madocks's friends wrote poignantly to John Williams from Chester, asking, 'How could such a thing happen?' before encouraging him and Madocks to 'put their shoulders to the business' of repair: 'If the sea is allowed to trespass it forms a rent in the map that disfigures the whole. Fill it up. Fill it up.'

Despite such rallying cries, Madocks's hands were tied by his debts. The Tan-yr-Allt Estate was bought by one of his creditors, Samuel Girdlestone, and it was he who took on the task of mending the work on the Cob: in 1814 the breach to the embankment was finally and securely closed. But financial constraints did not altogether halt Madocks.

Tremadog remained an inspiration to him, and he continued to see the town as a centre of commercial activity – he simply had to identify what form such activity might take. Turning away from his unequal battle with the sea, he directed his attention inland, to the Blaenau Ffestiniog slate quarries. After 1831, when slate duty was abolished, these quarries boomed: by the middle of the nineteenth century, Blaenau Ffestiniog supported a population of over 11,000 and produced nearly 100,000 tons of slate a year. But when Madocks became interested, the business was still small in scale and hampered by the isolation of the mines. Elsewhere, however, horse-drawn tramways had been successfully trialled. In addition, because there was no tax on slates sent overseas, the export market to the United States was showing great potential. Madocks realised that a railway could transport slates from the mountain quarries directly to ships at the harbour, and from there to lucrative new markets. And his latest scheme positioned the village of Tremadog once again at the heart of a growing enterprise.

At the Caernarfonshire end of the Cob, anchored to a small outcrop of rock, Madocks envisaged a new port, constructed specifically to service the slate trade. In 1821 he obtained an Act of Parliament allowing him to build at Ynys y Tywyn, to be renamed Port Madoc, and by 1824 he had surveys in place to outline the best routes for tracks from Blaenau Ffestiniog. It was a typically ambitious scheme which again required work on difficult terrain. The harbour was completed with relative ease – by 1825 there were public wharfs capable of taking ships of up to sixty tons – but it was not until 1836 that the Ffestiniog railway opened. The effect on trade was immediate: more tramways soon followed, bringing slate to the harbour from local mines, and by the 1870s over 100,000 tons were exported annually through Port Madoc on more than a thousand ships. Madocks's vision had finally been fulfilled, his name remaining inextricably embedded in the port's identity.

But the Madocks story has an ambivalent, rather than a happy, ending. By the time the Ffestiniog railway opened and commercial success was guaranteed, Madocks had been dead for eight years: he died in Paris on 15 September 1828. Moreover, with the opening of the Britannia Bridge over the Menai Strait in 1826, the main route to Ireland shifted through Holyhead; Tremadog was sidestepped. The profits associated with the Union with Ireland were redirected elsewhere and the town was left behind. There had been little wrong with Madocks's plans – it was largely a matter of bad luck and unfortunate timing – but ultimately his grand schemes came to nothing more than than a square of improbably fine buildings.

Today it is the flourishes at Tremadog that make it so distinctive. It is a place of fashion and theatricality, the height of early-nineteenth-century chic. Walking away from the square, tempted by a view of a steeple to one side of the road, I am confronted by an extraordinary lychgate. It seems to have no connection at all with the rather conventional church. It is turreted and bold, a medley of styles and decorations with heavy geometric carving and conspicuous medieval-style crosses combined with flowers and rosettes and animal heads: a friend of Madocks complained that it was a 'foolish decoration' and it is certainly a bizarre concoction of owls and dragons, frogs, squirrels and boars. Each of the castellated turrets is surrounded by snub-trunked elephants which peer down like gargoyles – Madocks's family crest included elephants – and the overall effect is of a playful, irreligious celebration.

The stone is pale, cleanly carved, with a distinctive flat sheen. The lychgate is evidently not made of sandstone or gritstone or marble. I have a small guidebook, a pamphlet really, published by the local heritage society which salvaged and reconstructed both the church and its gate in 2005; it explains that the lychgate was shipped in kit form from London and is constructed from Coadestone, a type of ceramic stoneware which was perfected in the late eighteenth century by the London company Coade and Sealy. This explains the richness of the decoration – as though all the twirls and twiddles and sharp geometries have been pressed out of a fine plaster of Paris – and the unusual patina.

Later, I discover more about Coadestone. Easily moulded into complex shapes and resistant to weathering and pollution, it quickly became enormously fashionable – it was produced by appointment to George III and the Prince Regent and it graced high-profile buildings of the period including the Prince of Wales's Conservatory at Carlton House, St George's Chapel at Windsor and the Royal Naval College at Brighton where it provides the pediment for a statue of Admiral Nelson. With its modish, cosmopolitan associations – its modernity and practicality – it is fitting that this is the material which Madocks used to shape the finer details of his grand folly. What the Prince of Wales could have at Carlton House, home of voluptuous dances, bacchanalian feasts, sexual licentiousness and determined self-destruction, Madocks could have in Tremadog, if only to signal the boundless energy of his plans.

Coadestone crops up all over the village and is particularly evident in a series of medallions and keystones on the front of the Town Hall. There's a toothlessly smiling figure with a bushy beard and a jaunty hat; he could be a Scotsman in a tam-o'-shanter or Santa Claus. Alongside him there's a rather stern head with a lion on his cap, a flat nose and bushy sideburns, perhaps a military man of some sort. A giggling androgynous face, all curls and luscious fruit, looks down towards the criss-cross of white road markings which cuts through the centre of the square. Like the menagerie on the lychgate, these figures are roguish and joyful. They are also distinctly urban – they seem to belong to a city building, hinting at the excesses and sensuality of fashionable early-eighteenth-century society. Finding them here, in such a quiet corner of Wales, is like finding a neon sign in a field. They are deliciously out of place, and defiant.

It is the grandiose embellishments in the fabric of the town which reminds us of Tremadog's true nature. Unlike many of the philan-thropists who built villages across the country during the eighteenth and nineteenth centuries, William Madocks was not enormously interested in moral messages. As an MP he supported electoral reform and Catholic emancipation, but his plans for Tremadog had little to do with social engineering or better conditions for workers. The town was openly commercial and capitalist; it was an investment opportunity. It stands now as an interesting counterpoint to examples of authority and paternalism like New Lanark. The Coadestone faces not only nod quite openly towards the inherent theatricality of a model settlement, but they stand as an unashamed memorial to a man who liked dancing and play-acting; they capture the essentially frivolous nature of an experiment which aimed to create a commercial hub in undeveloped rural Wales, a scheme founded on an ambitious quest for wealth and a spirit of adventure. At Tremadog, the motives for the village are not concealed or mitigated. Here the way in which people lived and worked was changed for one reason: trade. Here it was the demands of business, and the fragile promise of great riches from bigger business, which constructed new houses and new lives, bringing people together where they had not been before. Madocks saw no need to hide his purpose for Tremadog nor to attach his enterprising ambitions to a social or moral crusade. I like the straightforwardness of this. I know that as we move to other places, and through other times, such clarity and openness will become rare.

Cromford again

I'm waiting, once more, to cross the road at the traffic lights on the A6. Dusk, which has lingered all day, is gathering in earnest now in the narrow streets behind the marketplace, crows settling noisily in the trees above. The lights in the shop windows tempt the last remaining visitors to step in out of the cold. Several heavy lorries pass, making the pavement rumble. Looking around while I wait for the green man, I notice – or rather I remind myself – what a dramatic fold in the valley the village inhabits: this is a place of natural beauty, of old trees and hills, of stone and water. It's a place which still feels pre-industrial, despite the bulk of evidence looming behind me.

1771: the year 'modern' Cromford began. For all the progress already made during the eighteenth century, this was a year on the cusp of greater change. The early 1770s saw an overlap between one way of doing things and another, between rural and industrial, between unknown and known. The Spinning Jenny had been patented by James Hargreaves in the summer of 1770 but was not yet the manufacturing revolution it was to become; Captain Cook was in the middle of his first expedition to the Pacific, a voyage which would change the way we understood the world; European governments were struggling to contain the growing social and political radicalism which would find far-reaching expression in the 1789 French Revolution.

All periods, especially when viewed from a distance, can be seen as times of waning and rising influence, of convergence and departure. This is how history works. But Cromford offers evidence of this process, of a particular moment caught between old and new ideas. This, the first industrial mill town, is both a beginning and an end. A few years later, Arkwright's Masson Mill, further down the valley, would offer a clearer statement of the power of mechanisation and commercialisation, a blueprint for later development during the nineteenth century. But here the presence of the mill is conciliatory; its buildings edge around the yard in a series of modest blocks – there are views between and around them; the landscape intrudes. The factory has more in common with the terraces of cottages on North Street than the monolithic constructions of the great Victorian cities. This is a place which seems to be trying out the structures and habits of a new kind of capitalist ambition, testing them for size.

One of the transitions this brings to mind is the shift in thought from the Enlightenment towards the Romantic. When Cromford was conceived and built many influential Enlightenment intellectuals were still working – Voltaire published his *Testament Politique* in 1771; Edmund Burke pressed for British constitutional change during 1770 and '71 – but the Romantic poets of the next generation were beginning to emerge. Wordsworth and Coleridge were both born within a couple of years of Arkwright's experiment beginning. And despite its position on the cusp of this change, in many ways Cromford strikes me as a romantic village – not only a village of weddings but a village of Romanticism.

This might seem an odd claim. This is an industrial site, of course, and although it's not easily defined, one of the characteristics of the Romantic view was resistance to the Industrial Revolution and its consequences: urban sprawl, population growth, the desecration of natural beauties, a growing distance between humans and their shared histories. Many of the evils which Romanticism attempted to escape can be seen here in the village and mill at Cromford. But Romanticism was also a reaction against the confident narratives of the rational ideal: in place of intellectual absolutes it emphasised the sometimes irrational human bond with nature, the value of the individual imagination and the importance of intense emotional experience. Accepted eighteenth-century ideas based on universal truths and moral certainties were debated and challenged – Romanticism recognised the process of change and the complexities and discomforts inherent within it. In 'The Excursion' of 1814, Wordsworth presents change as an 'urgent need'; he does not look backwards but forwards, towards a 'humanised society':

Change wide, and deep and silently performed,
This Land shall witness; and as the days roll on,
Earth's universal frame shall feel the effect.

From the end of the eighteenth and into the early decades of the
nineteenth century, the Romantic movement came to wield significant
power across Europe: its new ways of approaching the world were,
for a while, the dominant force in literature, music, art and intellectual
debate. There was evidence of increasing understanding of the
complexity of the human condition as well as a new interest in, and
awareness of, intricate psychology.

It is this spirit of Romanticism that seems manifest here at Cromford
– the spirit of enquiry and transition, a rejection of easy simplicities.
The moralising tone of New Lanark has no place here. Unlike Robert
Owen, Arkwright wrote nothing about the moral and social purpose
of his village. Rather than a planned project to prove a social theory,
Cromford feels like the rather serendipitous fruit of a powerful unfettered imagination. It is obviously commercial in tone; in many ways
it's the wellspring of the industrial evils that would overwhelm most
ordinary people during the nineteenth century – but Arkwright, of
course, could not know what would later emerge from his Cromford
experiment. And at this point, it feels like a place derived from a
uniquely personal and hopeful vision, a genuine belief in a better
world, fully consistent with the emerging Romantic ideal.

Indeed, it's interesting to note that for the middle and upper classes
– less touched by the brutalities of the Industrial Revolution – the
drama of the industrial village seemed to offer a perfect encapsulation
of the Romantic vision: they were delighted by the roar of the waterwheel and machines, the sublime vistas of the towering mills in the
rugged landscape, labourers perfecting ancient craft skills. Cromford's
adjacency to the great Derbyshire stately mansions of Chatsworth
and Hardwick Hall meant that many tours decided to include a trip
here after tourists had had their fill of ancestral houses – the village
was a place of new wonders. 'Everything wears the face of industry
and cheefulness,' noted one satisfied visitor, before going on to suggest
that even Richard Arkwright's humble beginnings could be overlooked
in the magnificence of his achievements: 'Mr Arkwright was born a
barber but true genius is superior to all difficulties.'[11]

Aside from the innate snobbery of this comment – the intransigent influence of class – what interests me is the focus on the idea of 'true genius' which was very much a Romantic preoccupation. In 1759, Edward Young's essay, 'Conjectures on Original Composition', began to detach the definition of genius from a focus on intricate skill and learned expertise and reposition it as a new Romantic concept which presented the genius as a visionary, driven by a force too great to control. New meanings of genius began to focus on the idea of it being some kind of gift, an inherent ability beyond the norm which allowed the human mind to reach new heights – by 1817, Coleridge was writing in *Biographia Literaria* of genius being 'impassioned' and 'lofty'. The use of the term 'true genius' in relation to the development at Cromford seems to capture what is potentially Romantic about Richard Arkwright's village by placing it in this new context of soaring achievement and unfettered imagination.

Most of the model villages we'll explore have their roots in Owen's influential approach at New Lanark: they are confident, if ultimately paradoxical, expressions of socialism and community, of utilitarian approaches and capitalist politics. In the next chapter, we'll venture to look at the role played by emphatic religious beliefs and a clear moral purpose. These are perhaps the characteristics we most commonly associate with such places. But at the beginning, here at Cromford, these certainties are yet to fully emerge. This is a village oddly divorced from the brutal demands that were to come; it is – like Tremadog a few years later – a personal vision, still bound to the land around it, still respecting the individual lives which are a part of it. This is a place in which the walk home from the mill still takes long enough to allow for a change of perspective.

2

Nenthead, Cumbria

The first time I came to Nenthead I was twenty-one years old and about to begin my first paid job. It was spring – or so I thought – almost Easter. I had spent the previous winter in the Lake District, in the comfortable fold of fells around Grasmere, and although I had often been to Scotland, I had never found my way to this forgotten stretch of upland that is the North Pennines; this high, open, unpeopled crest of moorland that lies out of reach of main roads or rail routes and which sweeps up to the long stony ridge of Cross Fell, the highest point on an escarpment of hard carboniferous limestone which dominates the skyline and which is known for its dense fogs, ferocious storms, unfriendly spirits and the banshee shriek of the Helm Wind.

I was unprepared for such a place. When I left the M6 motorway and began to cross Alston Moor on smaller roads, I was surprised that there was snow still lying in the shelter of the stone walls, in ditches and gullies and on the high tops. The narrow drifts were unexpectedly white and clean, and even now I remember the way they sliced through the otherwise black landscape, the moors stretching away darkly, apparently scraped free of foliage, the hills rising to a stony sky. It felt as though I had arrived in an alien place, and a hostile one.

There's no quick route to Nenthead. Leaving Penrith from the west there are twenty-five miles of picturesque but uneven road through the Eden Valley; from the east it's thirty miles twisting along Weardale from Barnard Castle. The nearest town of any size is Carlisle, an hour away by car. Even when you reach the market town of Alston, high in the North Pennines, you continue to climb, winding up the steep cobbled main street and out again on to the moors, winding and climbing until you reach a small summit from where you can see the village of Nenthead ahead of you. This is a good spot to pause and examine the view. Guidebooks might tell you that the village 'nestles' in the valley but that would suggest something comfortable, some kind of harmony between the houses and the landscape. It seems to me that if you stand on top of the hill and look towards Nenthead what you actually see is a village clinging on, like a fairground bareback rider, houses cleaving to the difficult topography, buildings out of place in the wilderness of the land. What you also see, all around you, is the enduring evidence of why such a village might exist at all: mining activity. Some features are obvious – ruined chimneys, heaps of worked stone, decaying mine buildings. Some are little more than a suggestion of the past: arched entrances into the hillside almost concealed by the dip of the land, bare ground where nothing will grow, a line of trees out of place, an odd contraction in the landscape. You begin to see why this bleak stretch of high moorland, 1,450 feet above sea level, might have become inhabited; you might begin to wonder what it would be like to carve out an existence in a landscape that neither seems meant for human communities nor seems to welcome them.

I originally came to Nenthead to work at the old lead-mining site, interpreting the mines and the village for visitors. The project was in its infancy. There were a handful of boards explaining some of the more obvious architectural features and there was a caravan – my office – parked on scrubland by the River Nent, offering passers-by a brief history of the place and displaying old photographs. I went to the mines every day in case visitors cared to take a guided tour. But very few people came. Days would go by without anyone calling in; over the course of an entire summer I must have given no more than a dozen tours, usually to middle-aged couples who fancied stretching their legs after a long morning in the car on the testing road from Weardale. I remember only one tourist who made the trip with the express intention of visiting the historic village. He seemed embarrassed by the one-to-one attention he merited simply by coming. We trundled around the mines together for several hours while I told him what I knew and then he bought me lunch at the pub, perhaps as some kind of recompense.

The past here was not entirely forgotten: most of the residents knew a good deal about the history of the mines and the village. Several of the older men had worked as miners during the last years of the dwindling operations. But these were mostly private stories; there was little sense that they should be shared or recorded. On Sunday mornings, when the large congregation spilled out of the Methodist chapel, a crowd would gather sociably around the caravan, smoking and chatting, ignoring me entirely. I seemed to be noticed only by the children, who would hang about at the doorway in their best clothes, making quick excursions inside when their courage was at the sticking point; but I was only worth attention as a novelty and after several weeks of giggling and snide comments even the children lost interest. Most weekends, cavers converged from around Alston to explore the riddle of workings but they, too, gave me a wide berth. The mines were already well known to them; they'd trodden most of the adits and levels many times; they'd felt along them in the dark until the shape of them was familiar to the touch.

So I spent the summer sliding down the banks of wild thyme to the hum of lazy bees and tending the sorry bedding plants installed in two disused tyres. Nenthead seemed like a place no one wanted to know about. Yet it tells one of the most remarkable stories of any of the planned villages. Its terraces of sturdy cottages, the Reading Room and school, the Miners Arms, the workers' lodgings and manager's office buildings are all testament to a courageous, perhaps reckless, experiment. Here at Nenthead, people were brought to a place where there had been little habitation before; miners were set to work in a brutal landscape and encouraged to tame it as best they could. Driven by the demands of industrialisation, a village was conceived and constructed more or less from nothing, creating a tiny mark on a huge and hostile moor.

Nenthead is not a village of architectural experimentation or flourish. It's a place of well-made but conventional stone buildings and functional housing; it looks very much like any other Pennine village, shaped by the climate and the land. It is sturdy and practical. Indeed, its plainness is rather insistent, its architectural understatement clearly considered. This is partly a result of the expense of hauling unnecessary materials to such an isolated spot simply to embellish a chimney or porch, but it is also an expression of intention and belief: this is not a village conceived as the extravagant plaything of a wealthy aristocrat but a place of work built by Quakers.

The village was constructed by the London Lead Company, which had extensive interests in copper, lead and sea coal – all, rather confusingly, outside London. Officially called the Company for Smelting Down Lead with Pitcoal, it was founded in 1692 by a group of entrepreneurs, most of whom were members of the Society of Friends. This was a period when the Quakers' form of speech and dress, as well as their beliefs, marked them out as a minority, one which was regarded as potentially dangerous by the established authorities. A Toleration Act, allowing for freedom of conscience and worship, was not passed until 1689; at the beginning of the eighteenth century, Quakers were still barred from taking university degrees or from occupying official positions or many of the professions. With traditional routes closed to them, a career in business was the obvious choice. Often these businesses flourished rapidly and although Quakers made up only 0.2 per cent of the population in 1800 (or one in five hundred) their influence far outweighed such a numerical disadvantage. Names which we now associate with mainstream nineteenth-century commerce – and with many of the innovations which drove the Industrial Revolution – are family names from the Quaker community: Abraham Darby I (and his sons), who developed the blast-furnace method of coke-firing pig iron at Coalbrookdale; Benjamin Huntsman who developed the crucible steel process in Sheffield; Edward Pease, a railway pioneer who ran the first train from Stockton to Darlington in 1825; the Bryant and May match manufacturers; Cyrus Clark, the shoemaker; the bankers Lloyd and Barclay; the Cadbury and Rowntree families, chocolatiers who founded the planned villages at Bournville and Earswick. There are plenty more. The Quaker network of businessmen and -women was lively, ambitious, astute and successful. Many of the companies which shaped the British way of life in the nineteenth century – and beyond – were, in turn, shaped by the ideas and beliefs of the Society of Friends.

The London Lead Company was another thriving example of Quaker entrepreneurship. It expanded quickly during the final years of the seventeenth century; through the course of the eighteenth century it continued to grow until it had mines scattered across the UK from Bristol and Derbyshire to Wales and Tynedale. From the middle of the century, it began to consolidate particularly in the north of England, acquiring several blocks of land leases around the Nent Valley in 1750.

A certain mythology seems to have grown up around the company's decision to move north. One story tells that:

> A north-country Quakeress, when attending a meeting of that religious body in London, called the attention of the gentlemen present to the great need of employment in the mining dales of the North of England, and expressed her belief that those mines abounded in lead ore, which, on being discovered, would not only give employment to the people, but be a source of wealth to their employers. She appealed alike to their philanthropy and to the spirit of commercial enterprise which she believed animated them.[1]

The unnamed Quakeress cannot be accurately traced, but her heartfelt plea to both the humanitarian and business concerns of her colleagues sets up a recurring pattern of dual interests. It is unlikely that concern for 'the great need of employment in the mining dales' was the deciding factor in the decision to consolidate in the area, but the undoubted 'source of wealth' promised by the ore seams was clearly an attraction and when the London Lead Company added more parcels of land in 1757 and 1765, it became the owner of almost all of the profitable but isolated Alston Moor mining field: its northern district now occupied an area of around 1,200 square miles of mountainous country between Hexham, Penrith and Darlington, much of it rough moorland over 2,000 feet above sea level, punctuated by occasional farms that worked the steep slopes and rocky crags.

Lead ore – galena – is not easy to find. The mineral veins in which it is found tend to occur irregularly, varying enormously in scale and content: sometimes there's a succession of deposits over a wide area with large quantities of ore while other veins of equal size might yield almost nothing. The North Pennines geology is complex, with the ore field made up of two blocks – the Alston Block in Durham, Cumbria and Northumberland, and the Askrigg Block to the south in North Yorkshire. These blocks largely consist of layers of limestones, sandstones and shales deposited during the lower and middle

Carboniferous Period (over 300 million years ago) and riddled with faults. These sedimentary layers rest in turn on a layer of granite, known as Weardale Granite, which influenced the mineralisation process by changing the flow of heat through the rock. The Alston Block has a particularly widespread system of fractures which allowed the minerals to be deposited, creating two types of ore field: vertical veins, created by hydrothermic action, and horizontal deposits known as 'flats' which are rich in mineralised cavities. As well as galena, deposits of flourite and quartz are common; the list of other minerals which can be found reads poetically, a geological incantation – sphalerite, ankerite, siderite, calcite, pyrite, marcasite, chalcopyrite, pyrrhotite.

The basic geology of the area had gradually been pieced together from the experience of miners since the twelfth century, when mining was first documented here. But it was not a simple case of mapping. There's no easy way of knowing what minerals might be deposited in the rocks, and to what extent. There are few clues in the shape of the landscape, and underground it can be a hit-and-miss affair trying to locate suitable areas for the commercial extraction of galena. The London Lead Company largely relied on miners to act as 'practical geologists' and spot profitable veins, but in turn the miners were quick to point out the difficulties inherent in their trade:

> The most intelligent miner amongst us cannot tell whether or not any particular vein of average strength and moderate throw will prove remunerative. His knowledge of it amounts to probability, not to a certainty. It may or may not contain ore in the great limestone. Hence it is that so many fortunes have been made and so many lost in lead-mining, that poor men have been suddenly enriched, and rich men impoverished.[2]

In addition to the fundamental uncertainty of the enterprise there was the inescapable severity of the site. This was – and still is – an area of high rainfall and severe winter snowstorms, of blizzards and flooding, stunted vegetation and poor soil. There were no roads, little housing, no markets or recognised supply routes. The mines required almost 4,000 people to operate successfully, but this meant bringing hundreds of families up on to the fells and away from more usual patterns of living. Establishing a skilled working community in this isolated and undeveloped location was clearly no simple matter of recruitment – it required energy, investment and a single-minded determination to make profit from such hostile land.

Undaunted, the London Lead Company took up the challenge. In 1753, in an attempt to provide all the services the new community might need, it began to build the village of Nenthead. The first community was clustered around the smelt mill and consisted of little more than a few solid cottages for the smelters alongside Gillgill Burn, a tributary of the Nent; the miners themselves were put out to lodge in the small farms that were scattered across the fells or into a system of 'Mine Shops'. These mine shops – which became a common feature of the landscape – were substantial stone buildings built near the mouth of each mine and fitted with lines of bunk beds and a cooking range, enabling miners to board for the working week and walk home to their families after a Saturday shift. In addition to providing for the miners, the Company began to establish a fitting 'headquarters': alongside the smelt mill, on Cherry Tree Hill, a new building was constructed to house the mines' agent and manager and to provide offices. With a country-house feel, this comfortable residence was set in a neat estate of gardens and plantations – improvements that amounted to a not inconsiderable investment of £2,200.

Although these early constructions began to create a visible network in the area, identifiable with the London Lead Company and reinforcing its ownership of the mines, it soon became clear that more was needed if the venture was to succeed. Conditions in the miners' lodgings remained harsh and with no settled community yet established, the house on Cherry Tree Hill threatened to become a one-off gesture of permanence. If productivity – and profit – were to be improved, then attention had to switch from expenditure on genteel management housing to investment in comfortable conditions for more ordinary families. With this in mind, the London Lead Company commissioned an improved, coordinated plan for Nenthead in 1825. This featured thirty-five cottages, a market hall, a school and a chapel, land for gardens and grazing and a suitably civic clock tower. It promised to address the problems of isolation and create a self-sufficient community.

The new village was constructed remarkably quickly, at a cost of £3,000 – perhaps not a great deal in comparison to the £2,200 spent on the gentleman's residence at Cherry Tree Hill. By the end of 1825

cottages were available to rent at between £4 and £6 per annum,
depending on their size and the amount of garden attached. These
houses were clean, spacious and weatherproof, which basic qualities
lifted them far above the usual conditions in which lead miners were
living: a government report in 1846, for example, over twenty years
after the new village was established at Nenthead, found that although
some lead miners' cottages in Halkyn, North Wales, were 'neat though
scantily furnished' with 'at least a rag rug to soften the hearth', many
were little more than huts, blighted by poor ventilation and drainage,
'a single room from 9 to 12 feet square . . . they are in general devoid
of furniture, the roofs are wattled, others are of straw, and full of
large holes open to the day'.[3]

Nenthead was now more than a series of mine workings, loosely
linked by temporary lodging arrangements, but if it was to become
a place that people might think of as home then the London Lead
Company's commitment had to go beyond the relatively simple
provision of adequate housing. One of the main challenges facing
the miners and their families was the most basic one – finding food.
The remoteness of the mineral fields from large markets meant not
only that food was scarce but also that prices were artificially high,
and supply tended to fall into the hands of profiteers. During the
late seventeenth and early eighteenth centuries, the Company's
agents had occasionally sent warnings to the London managers
suggesting that famine was creating not only hardship but also
worrying episodes of unrest; this prompted the delivery of vast
cargoes of grain, corn and rice to the northern mines to be sold on
at London prices – which were considerably cheaper than those
charged by the Newcastle merchants. As the number of miners and
their families grew towards the end of the eighteenth century,
however, such stop-gap measures became increasingly unsustainable
and the Company began to look for different ways of maintaining
the goodwill of its workforce.

There were no easy solutions. Miners negotiated quarterly
'bargains' which set a rate of pay according to the veins to be worked,
the skilled knowledge of the miners and the price of lead. These
bargains usually amounted to around 10 shillings per week per man.
As the price of lead remained stable, so too did most of these

bargains, but a sharp nationwide rise in food prices meant that most families experienced a steady decline in living standards. By 1800 famine was widespread among the populations of Alston Moor and Teesdale: an inquiry instigated by the London Lead Company found that a scarcity of corn was compounded by exorbitant charges on the part of millers and flour dealers, making bread unaffordable for many families.

Rather than make further shipments of grain, the Company decided to buy an old lead mill at Garrigill, in a parallel valley three miles from Nenthead, converting it into a corn mill to supply the whole area. In addition, the Nenthead agent was given authority to buy £500 worth of grain at Newcastle market, to store it in his offices and sell it on at cost price. The scheme proved enormously popular. Families were able to rely on affordable regular supplies and, in addition, no longer had to worry about dishonest merchants adulterating good grain with 'daft', which could be anything from plaster of Paris to powdered limestone. The only disadvantage of the arrangement was that it threw into sharp relief the plight of those excluded from the Company benefits: locals who were not employed at the mines felt they were being left to starve. In the face of such inequality, unrest began to simmer again, but the mine managers responded quickly, extending the benefits to all the residents in the district, whether or not they were employed by the London Lead Company.

In addition to constructing the corn mill, the Company also agreed to change the system of bargains so that the weekly wage was adjusted according to a monthly estimate of the cost of food, negotiated independently of the price of lead. By August 1800, this had raised the usual bargain to 12 shillings a week, and substantially reduced serious distress among the miners. But by 1815, conditions had worsened again. The occasional purchase of grain by the Company began to fail, and a winter of unusually harsh storms in 1816 meant that outdoor work had to be halted for months because of extensive flooding; unremittingly severe frosts froze the waterwheels and threatened to damage the dams. As the cold weather continued and more and more workers were laid off, the mines faced a crisis of unemployment. In turn, with the miners desperate for food and worried about their livelihoods, the managers noted a rise in aggressive behaviour and began to voice fears of growing radicalism amongst the workforce. In March 1817, mine notes recorded that 'on account of Snow, our outside men are all idle which causes us a troublesome time, a part of them being extremely uneasy'. A few weeks later, on 3 April, a delivery of oatmeal caused a near riot. The mines agent reported being 'almost smothered with the crowd', noting for the benefit of his London-based superiors that 'at the end of each month, a considerable part of the population is almost on the brink of starvation'.[4]

By the time the Nenthead village was built in 1825 two innovations had been introduced by the Company in an attempt to halt for good the cycle of need and intervention. The first experiment was a cooperative Corn Association: at the end of 1820 each worker was given an advance on a month's wages with the proviso that it was used to club together with other miners to buy corn in bulk, using the Company's system of carriers to transport it to Nenthead or the Garrigill Mill. Secondly, the new village included a Ready Money Store, conveniently situated between the warehouse and the market house and leased to a shopkeeper on the condition that only cash purchases could be made. The move was aimed at the credit traders who would advance goods at ruinous rates of interest, condemning many mining families to a state of constant debt. As before, access to the Ready Money Shop and the Corn Association – as well as the right to use the corn mill – was extended to include all the residents of Alston Moor, not just those directly in the Company employment.

Abutting two painted stone pillars and a metal gateway in front of one of the oldest Nenthead cottages – a substantial eighteenth-century whitewashed building with broad sash windows – there are two steps leading down to a cobbled lane. They are broad and rounded, like solid half-moons, and each is about four inches high; the bottom step has flaps poking out on either side, like stone ears. The lane rises quite steeply here, but the steps are perfectly horizontal, levelling out the gradient; the drop to the road is much less at the top than the bottom. A black boot-scraper sits on another large stone at the lower edge of the steps, as though to prevent them sliding back down the hill.

It's a natural platform, a place to pause on the climb or to stand and chat. It's almost a small thrust stage, the pillars at either side framing the space between. Taking advantage of its elevation, it was apparently from these steps that John Wesley preached in April 1748, long before the arrival of the London Lead Company or the construction of the planned settlement when Nenthead was a tiny hamlet of ad-hoc mining and subsistence farming. There is no memorial here to mark his visit, but the Methodist chapel has a plaque which records his influence in the area: he preached in the village again, over thirty years later, on 5 May 1780, before riding over the fells to Penrith.

By the time the Quakers arrived at Nenthead, Methodism was already well established. From the middle of the eighteenth century, Methodists had been able to boast substantial influence in the district, as well as west into Cumberland and east along the dales towards Newcastle. The Established Church had found the area difficult to reach – the huge distances between centres of population and the isolated nature of many of the settlements meant that few people had a local vicar to attend to their needs or easy access to a church for Sunday services. By 1851 only 70 people were regularly attending Church of England services in Weardale while 1,441 people attended the local Methodist chapels. Methodism seemed to speak more directly to poor families scraping a living in the harsh landscape, and in the early years of the nineteenth century, Primitive Methodism – a part of the movement which advocated day-long open-air meetings called Camp Meetings as well as communal meals or 'Love Feasts' – became particularly well established in Nenthead and the hamlets around. One commentator noted that after a Primitive Methodist preacher called Anthony Race turned his attentions to Nenthead and Garrigill in 1823 there was a popular revival: 'The work grew so mightily, and the excitement became so intense, that more frequent ministrations were imperative.'[5]

Many of the Methodist preachers were ex-miners who knew what it was like to live and work in the area and who could respond to the particular concerns of those listening to them. By the time the London Lead Company established its hold on the site, these preachers had already begun to influence lives. The Company purchased the Miners Arms, for example, in 1823 – the year Anthony Race began his evangelising mission – but several rent reductions failed to halt a decline in business. In 1800, the miners of Alston Moor had been said to 'work hard about four days in the week, and drink and play the other three'. In the space of a generation, however, the spread of Methodism meant that the villagers had gained a reputation for efficiency, reliability, abstinence – and even virtue. The miners, it was reported, 'preferred books to drink' and the pub was rebuilt with an emphasis on accommodation for travellers rather than carousing.[6]

Nenthead was by no means the first village to have its roots in Nonconformist religion: by the beginning of the nineteenth century there was already a clear link between Nonconformism and experimental settlements. The idea of creating an entirely new community which could be run along independent lines and which could draw in like-minded residents had obvious appeal to those who had already broken away from the authority of the Established Church. If the traditional village was presided over by the parish spire, these new, potentially more egalitarian, villages were constrained by no such architectural reminder of privilege and hierarchy – they were not without a church, by any means, but they were attempting to reconfigure the role of worship in both the physical built environment and the personal lives of the inhabitants.

The earliest communities were founded between 1744 and 1780 by the Moravians, a German sect which claimed to be the oldest free church in Northern Europe. It took its ideals of community living from the model of the medieval monasteries, establishing seven settlements in Ireland and England, including Gracehill in Ballymena and Fulneck near Leeds. The Moravian villages were constructed according to a simple formula for neat and wholesome living. Based on a European grid plan which dated back to the Middle Ages, the settlements were designed with a modest church building at their centre, surrounded by the manse, brethren houses, communal houses for single men and women, day and boarding schools, a farm, shops and workshops. The burial ground, or God's Acre, was of particular importance, carefully planted and landscaped, and laid out with a strict symmetry. It was a tranquil haven at the heart of the village and a conspicuous reminder of life's transience. The last of the Moravian villages was established in 1785 at Fairfield, in Greater Manchester, a neatly paved enclave with tree-lined streets and tidy brick housing designed by Benjamin Henry Latrobe who later emigrated to America and worked on the Capitol building in Washington, DC. The population of 200 was served by an inn, bakery, laundry and farm, a dedicated fire service, night watchman and doctor. The members of the village received a wage for textile work or other manual labour, with all the profits feeding back into a communal fund.

Generally non-doctrinal in their attitude to religious belief, the Moravian villages were constructed on principles of cooperation, discipline, advanced education and brotherly harmony. They became known as oases of calm and civilised living, with attractive gardens and contented citizens existing in the midst of the growing urban slums of the early nineteenth century, and they acted as something of a tourist attraction: as the expansion of industrial Manchester gathered pace, for example, a constant stream of reformers made their way to Fairfield to marvel at what the Moravians had achieved; Robert Owen was almost certainly aware of the settlement and probably visited during the time he was employed at mills in the area.

Today, the sense of surprise and wonder still prevails. The Fairfield settlement is well preserved and although no longer directly under Moravian ownership it claims to remain 'a living and serving community', with housing rented out in order that 'the ideals of Christian living can be translated into reality'. I approach the village along Fairfield Road in Droysden, a typically soulless city street to the east of central Manchester, a rather ugly conglomeration of small feature-less Victorian terraced houses, worn-out shops, modern semis and supermarkets with vast car parks. The Ashton Canal which runs alongside for a while provides an odd, heady mix of run-down industry, derelict warehousing and wasteland with glossy new apartment housing and a view of the contemporary curves and spikes of the Etihad Stadium, the home of Manchester City Football Club. When I finally turn into Fairfield Square, the heart of the original Moravian community, it seems remarkable that such a place has survived the onslaught of Victorian industrial ambition and post-war regeneration, a tiny link to a brief moment of history that was to have lingering implications for lives throughout Britain for the next 200 years.

At Nenthead, the Quakers shared many common principles and approaches with the Moravians but perhaps the most significant was an emphasis on education. When the miners arrived to take their place in the new village, the London Lead Company had engineered effective control of three of life's most pressing needs: housing, food and money. But providing opportunities for decent schooling was considered equally as important as practical basic requirements – indeed, it was considered a practical basic requirement in its own right – and anyone coming to live in the burgeoning Nenthead of 1825 would have found that educational needs were also already taken care of.

The school pre-dated the construction of the new expanded village by some seven years. It was established before the Market Hall or the Ready Money Shop, before the development of family housing. Building commenced in February 1818 – along with another school at Middleton in Teesdale, twenty miles east towards Barnard Castle – to erect a simple, practical set of classrooms which would accommodate 200 children and, most importantly, be 'warmed by stoves'. The London Lead Company also subscribed to parish or charity schools in smaller hamlets throughout the district but when it opened in summer 1819 under the direction of a schoolmaster on a generous salary of £90 a year (with a £10-a-year bonus), the Nenthead school was the Company flagship. Both weekday and Sunday schooling were immediately made obligatory – at a cost of 1 shilling a quarter – for boys of between six and twelve years old and girls of between six and fourteen. It became a condition of employment that miners' children should attend school regularly as well as Sunday school every week.

This emphasis on compulsory education was a genuine innovation: Nenthead was the first place in the UK to make schooling obligatory. But it was by no means unique in its recognition that education should be an integral and valued part of everyday life. Rather it was part of a growing consensus on the important role schools could play in developing individual potential, social cohesion and economic growth. In 1802 the Factory Act, championed by Robert Peel, was defined as 'An Act for the preservation of the health and morals of apprentices and others employed in cotton and other mills and cotton and other factories'. Morals were best taken care of, it was decided, by a programme of education: the Act required an employer to provide instruction in reading, writing and arithmetic during at least the first four years of the seven years of apprenticeship, as part of the normal working day rather than in addition to it. While the term 'apprentice' might suggest young men on the cusp of adulthood, in fact many apprentices at this period were young pauper children brought from distant workhouses to work in the cotton mills; the education provision was a way of providing them with necessary basic skills.

Alongside the provisions of the 1802 Factory Act, there were a number of independent schemes aimed at putting education at the heart of the growing Industrial Revolution. 'Schools of industry' were set up by philanthropists and reformers to provide the poor with manual training and elementary instruction. One of the first of these opened at Kendal in the Lake District in 1799 teaching 'reading and writing, geography and religion' plus shoemaking to the boys and 'knitting, sewing, spinning and housework' to the older girls.[7] The system expanded, with the intention of providing a distraction for poor and vulnerable children who might otherwise be tempted to a life of crime, and in 1846 the government began making grants to day schools of industry towards the provision of gardens, trade workshops, kitchens and wash houses, as well as for gratuities to the masters who taught boys gardening and crafts and to the mistresses who gave 'satisfactory instruction in domestic economy'.[8] By the middle of the nineteenth century the system had been further formalised as a way of dealing with unruly or neglected children: the 1857 Industrial Schools Act allowed magistrates to remove potential delinquents from their homes and place them in a residential industrial school. In 1876, a further Act created day schools along the same lines.

In a rival system to the industrial schools, monitorial schools used monitors and standard repetitive exercises to drill basic reading, writing and mathematics into hundreds of children at the same time in the same room, under the direction of a single teacher. Again, practical activities included cobbling, tailoring, gardening, spinning, sewing and baking. The idea was developed independently within a few years by two reformers, both of whom were inspired by their religious backgrounds: Joseph Lancaster, a Quaker, joined forces with liberal Anglicans and some Roman Catholics and Jews to set up the British and Foreign School Society for the Education of the Labouring and Manufacturing Classes of Society of Every Religious Persuasion (the British and Foreign School Society) in 1808; Andrew Bell worked with the Church of England to create the National Society for Promoting the Education of the Poor in the Principles of the Established Church in 1811 in order to promote schools under the guidance of local clergy and constructed on the principles of Bible study, catechism and prayer-book services. For the next thirty years or so, until the early 1840s, monitorial schools proved a popular and highly influential form of education; in time the model was adopted throughout the world, particularly in the United States and India, allowing huge numbers of children to be educated and disciplined on an industrial scale.

Despite such innovations – and the introduction of the Parochial Schools Bill (1807) which in theory made provision for all working-class children – standards of education remained distinctly patchy: a report in 1816 examined 12,000 English parishes, and found that 3,500 had no school at all, 3,000 had endowed schools of varying quality, and 5,500 had unendowed schools of even more variable quality – most likely small 'dame schools' where elderly women taught basic skills and acted as childminders. Perhaps most importantly, both the industrial and monitorial systems promoted a model of education that took place outside the community, in a specialised schools 'bubble', rather than situating schools at the heart of village life. The first effort to really integrate schooling in a formal way into village communities was made by Robert Owen at his cotton mills in New Lanark: in 1816 he opened an Infant School, admitting children from the age of two, and offering instruction while their parents were working, although this amounted to a rather vague promise to provide 'whatever might be supposed useful that they could understand . . . singing, dancing and playing'. Owen's ideas were adopted in London by a group which established an infant school in 1818 – importing a teacher from New Lanark – and by Samuel Wilderspin (1792–1866) who developed a system of infant education along the lines of the New Lanark experiment.

The question of how best to organise schooling for older children was not seriously addressed until the 1820s when David Stow founded the Glasgow Normal School based on a system of classes, and promoted as addressing the 'Moral and Intellectual Elevation of Youth'. But his policy of dividing children into groups based on age required several rooms and several teachers and so proved expensive. 'All-age' schools, educating pupils from six to twelve years old, became more popular because they could work with a single teacher and one or two assistants, but little significant progress was made until the 1840s and '50s when Schools Sites Acts allowed for the purchase of land for school buildings and parliamentary grants for the education of poor children.

In the early years of the nineteenth century, the debate was not so much about how best to organise mass education but, on a more fundamental level, whether or not such a radical innovation was a good idea at all. Beyond the fells of Nenthead, there was widespread and hostile opposition to the principle of providing schooling for workers and their children. In 1807, during discussion of the Parochial Schools Bill, one commentator warned that if the poor were taught to do more than read the Scriptures they might be inspired by 'a disrelish for the laborious occupations of life' and so aim above their station.[9] Tory MP Davies Giddy went further. A proper education would, he claimed:

> be found to be prejudicial to their morals and happiness; it would teach them to despise their lot in life . . . instead of teaching them the virtue of subordination, it would render them factious and refractory . . . it would enable them to read seditious pamphlets, vicious books and publications against Christianity; it would render them insolent to their superiors.[10]

The apparently simple act of teaching children to read and write was placed in a wider context of social management; a free education was set in direct opposition to the desire to keep the poor in their place. Against such a backdrop of anxiety – with the wealthier and more established members of society desperate to cling to their privileged position of power – the introduction of compulsory schooling in a village of poor, working families such as Nenthead could be seen not only as an act of generosity but as a complex statement of radical intention and commercial ambition.

When I come to Nenthead this time I'm better prepared. I've packed waterproofs and woolly jumpers in anticipation of unseasonal Pennine weather; climbing out of Alston I'm determined not to be intimidated by the vast sweep of moorland. As it happens, there's a clear sky and the promise of a benign late-spring day: a pair of harriers dodge and glide in the warm air, violets and cowslips colour the fields and verges, an old man on a very old bicycle waves as he eases up the incline. There must have been days like this, a few of them, when the mines were working; days when it was a pleasure to be in a high, wild place, to have the sun on your back and the land stretching away, a sense of space to raise the spirits before crawling underground in the dark. I wonder if the memory of such days was any kind of sustenance when the winter closed in.

I begin my walk from the far end of the village, near the track that leads along the river to the mines. There have been all kinds of changes since I worked here. The old caravan has been cleared away and instead there's a proper visitor centre with signs and fences and a new heritage icon: a rusted old ore tub on wheels, stranded without track to run on, a sad remnant. The gates are locked and the centre is closed today; I later learn that the trust that runs it has gone into administration. Nonetheless, it's possible to see that the site has been spruced up: paths have been widened and tarmacked in places, rubble swept away; the layout of the buildings is clearer and the interpretation boards prominent. There's even a basic bunkhouse, apparently, in the old Assay House, the finest and best preserved of the buildings which still stands squarely, and rather grandly, at one side of the paved yard.

I stand by the entrance and peer through the vertical gaps between the planks of the gate, seeing everything in slices. I'm surprised at how familiar some of it is and for a moment I'm taken aback by the wash of nostalgia. I find that I'm sorry that the site has lost its ragged look. Twenty years ago, visitors (when they came) could experience an unreconstructed, un-reinterpreted past, abandoned but authentic, the strata of history a slight puzzle. They could see quite clearly that this was a difficult place, the human hold on it easily loosened. The ruins were stained, marred, ugly: they were witness to the sheer daily struggle of industry, the unglamorous toil that marked so many lives. It was possible, for a moment, to begin to understand what it meant to drive a shaft through rock 2,000 feet above sea level, to extract ore with the same intimate suffering with which you might extract your own tooth, to haul weight in the dark, to want something other than this with a dreary, unshakeable passion. Now, instead – when the gate is open – visitors can pretend to be miners, but outside, in the fresh air, crouching alongside the stream and panning for minerals. It's restorative, untaxing bank-holiday entertainment. Schoolchildren are encouraged to dress up, so that they look at themselves and their friends rather than at the scarred evidence of a complex industrial past. It feels to me that in the transition from one experience to the other the residual, spectral energy of the place has been diminished.

Turning my back on the mines I pass the Miners Arms and begin to make my way into the village. Here too, of course, there have been changes. The place is still dominated by the Lower Rampgill dressing floor, a huge flat area of land where lead ore was sorted from the rock. The ugly factory building that slumps at one end is also still there, more or less intact and used now as a vehicle depot. But across from it a small terrace of new houses has been built along the road, its red brick naked against the stone of the old terraces. Some of the wasteland has been landscaped and planted; there is a small section of new paving and a children's play area. The little village store with its bright awning and phone box has closed and there's a community shop instead, with a post office and a cash machine. I stare stupidly at the board propped outside, advertising ice cream. It's taking me a while to extricate myself from the distractions of a return; it's difficult not to see only the slight alterations here and there, the marking of small changes in village life – and my own – since 1992.

As I climb the hill, following some of the walkers' paths that criss-cross Nenthead, I'm distracted again by a remarkable display. In the garden of a nondescript modern bungalow there's a collection of models – a collection, in fact, of model villages. Miniature cottages, paths, gardens and churches have been built here out of local stone, clustered into circles cut into the lawn; there's a stately home with a dome – possibly Castle Howard – presiding over the most distant of the circles. Rooftops stand around knee height; church spires higher. The details of doors, windows, porches, verandahs, columns, water-wheels, mill chimneys and garden conservatories are all rendered with enormous care but the villages appear to be random collections of buildings. There is no sense of them being replicas of actual places, but rather they seem to bring together different styles, features and functions at the will of the man who makes them.

It's a bizarre outcrop in the hillside and, of course, the idea of a model village within a model village is too good to resist. There's an immediate, Russian-doll feeling of contrivance and neatness and seren-dipity. I can't find when the term 'model' was first used in relation to planned philanthropic settlements, but I do know that miniaturisation was a preoccupation of the nineteenth century. Miniature people in the forms of goblins and fairies captivated Victorian audiences. The first edition of Grimm's fairy tales was published in 1812. By the 1840s and '50s fairy painting, too, was becoming a distinct genre of art: the detailed, fantastical work of John Anster 'Fairy' Fitzgerald was first shown at the Royal Academy in 1845, coming to wider public view on the pages of the *Illustrated London News*; during the 1840s John Everett Millais produced a series of fairy paintings based on *The Tempest*. Increasing mass production allowed for miniature ornaments and household objects: miniature books attracted attention in the most fashionable of bookshops, while houses, in the form of doll's houses, were enormously popular, not just as playthings but as domestic ornaments. Doll's houses offered a managed world; they were subject to absolute manipulation by the owner who could order the life of the imagined family within – or at least its material expression – and control the boundaries of time and space in the small but perfect rooms.

In an age of often bewildering advancements in science, miniaturisation offered a means of escape and a way of asserting power. The doll's house is a complete, hermetically sealed place for the idealised family, untouched by the outside world and uncontaminated by intrusive demands. Rather like objects under glass in which the Victorians also delighted, it can be displayed in the parlour as an intriguing but unthreatening otherworld. Looking at the models laid out on the hillside, I begin to think about this process of miniaturisation in the context of Nenthead, a place which could be seen as distinct from the usual nineteenth-century pressures and concerns: an isolated settlement created by a Quaker community viewed as outsiders. I wonder how far the London Lead Company was setting itself apart here. I wonder if it's too bold a question to ask whether the real model village provided something rather like the miniature model village – a place to be contained and controlled; a place that looks just like its full-scale companion but which is at the same time subject to a different perspective; a trick of scale and belief.

The original model village at Nenthead – the full-size one – has been reworked and reconfigured since 1825. In places, only traces of the old buildings are visible. The Market Hall and warehouse have now gone, along with the Ready Money Shop. There is no sign of the square clock tower; the public wash house and baths alongside it have also disappeared although they remained in use until 1905, offering hot and cold baths and showers and providing housewives with sixteen wash tubs, boiling vats and steam-heated drying cupboards, folding tables and mangles – each woman would have an allocated wash day and for the price of a penny could guarantee taking home clean, dried and finished clothes by the end of the afternoon. The heavy machinery on the Rampgill Low washing floor, the wagon rails and crushing rollers as well as the magnificently named hotching tubs (effectively large sieves) have given way to parked cars and buses.

These changes have of course reshaped the village. In particular they have stripped away the obvious signs of industry on either a commercial or a domestic scale, leaving behind a place that is much less evidently self-contained. I doubt many of today's residents live entirely on what they can buy at the community shop; Nenthead today, like all other villages, is a place that looks beyond itself, to the supermarket and the petrol station and the cinema. But such changes can be distracting and deceptive. You could argue that Nenthead was always a place that looked outside the village boundaries to what was happening elsewhere; that despite the geographical remoteness, the poor road system and the absorbing demands of heavy work underground, Nenthead's nineteenth-century residents were both inspired and confined by the London Lead Company's national status, its commercial drive for international success and the Quakers' vision for a better world.

As I sit on the parapet of the stone bridge that crosses the Nent, the blockish Methodist chapel stands in front of me; terraces stretch away neatly to the left, the lump of the bus depot is almost out of sight behind. I realise that what I want to look at is not only what has changed but what has stayed the same, the many significant things which remain unaltered in Nenthead, and which have remained more or less unaltered since the beginning of the nineteenth century. And because this is a modest place, a place where radical ideas are plainly presented – a fervent reformer in Quaker clothing – the lingering evidence of the past and what it might all be about will take some teasing out. Nenthead does not advertise its identity in the quirkiness of roof lines or architectural decoration. It sits very quietly in the fold of the fells. The complexities of this remarkable village are well concealed.

The Reading Room, now the community shop, is a good place to start. It's a plain but attractive one-storey building with large windows, a flagged roof and an attractively curved wall where it bounds the rise of Vicarage Terrace. On the other side it's attached to a larger whitewashed house, Ivy House, originally the home of the mining agent. It's not a particularly imposing building, and the stone panel which reads 'Lead Company's Workmen's Reading Room' is weathered and easily overlooked. Like many of the remains in Nenthead, it appears rather ordinary; as the first free library in England it looks disappointingly insignificant, especially when you consider that this is the extended and improved version: the original 1833 room was rebuilt in 1855 and enlarged in 1859. Its position in the centre of the village, attached to the mine manager's house, is, however, a clue to the important place it was considered to occupy in the miners' lives – or perhaps the important place the London Lead Company hoped it would occupy.

It is clear from the records that workmen were encouraged to read from the very first days of the Company's operations. By 1800 regular grants were being given to district agents to allow them to buy books for the miners' use; in the 1820s this was expanded to the creation of libraries housed within the Company schools. These contained both literary and technical texts; evening classes were also held and might include chemistry and assaying work in basic laboratories. By 1850, the London Lead Company was subscribing to over sixteen libraries in the small settlements around Nenthead, including Garrigill, Lune Forest and Tyne Head, contributing more than £100 a year to the purchase of new books. Most of these libraries were well-meaning but rather ad-hoc affairs which relied on the enthusiasm of individuals but the Reading Room at Nenthead – along with two similar rooms constructed at Middleton-in-Teesdale and Stanhope – was an organised facility.

In addition to the school, the Reading Room guaranteed opportunities for a broad education for the entire village. The mines agent, Robert Stagg, was keen to show how such a policy could have an impact beyond the development of the individual: he wrote to thank his employers for their support and assured them that the provision of 'a respectable education' would 'lay the foundation for a radical and general improvement in the moral and religious habits of the rising generation' while 'giving more orderly and correct habits to the workmen at large'. The new educational facilities, he writes, 'can hardly fail eventually to prove beneficial to the Company'. He clearly articulates here what had perhaps before only been implicit – that in providing education for adults alongside the compulsory instruction for children the London Lead Company was consolidating an emphasis on 'moral and religious habits' and providing a means by which employers could inform, guide and control the lives of their workers. The intention was now clear – not only to provide a means of recreation for the miners but to provide long-term benefits to the Company.

Notes in the 'Report Book of Deputation' over the following years suggest that Stagg was quite correct in his assessment: the education campaign seems to have been remarkably successful in moderating behaviour. In 1830 the records noted that 'good conduct of the miners [is] very marked' and 'cannot be spoiled by the vile example setting by the Labourers in the South'. At Christmas 1838, despite the 'dearness of provisions . . . the conduct of the miners reflects the highest credit on them as men and Christians'. With such practical examples of good conduct on which to draw Stagg wrote to the Company again in 1847 revealing a little more about the values being promoted by the Nenthead system: adopting a congratulatory tone he explains that 'the total absence of rebellions and insubordinations of every kind' in the Company mines could be directly attributed to the work of the school and the educational improvement of the miners, which had ensured that 'chartism – radicalism – and every other abomination have for so very many years been strangers to the concern – and there does not exist today in the united kingdom a more orderly, industrious and contented body of workmen'.[11]

The Reading Room played a key role in the formation of such an 'industrious' workforce. The relatively short hours of work in the mines, and the long winter lay-offs when poor weather prevented work, meant that anyone with a taste for self-education could make time to learn. In 1789 the families at Nenthead were found to have among them 'twenty-six readers, six writers, and three arithmetical scholars'; in contrast, a report in 1861 found that the combination of formal schooling and access to the Reading Room had raised literacy levels in the space of a couple of generations.[12] It made special mention of the unusually high levels of learning throughout the district: 95.7 per cent of fathers could read and 90 per cent of mothers, with almost as many being also confident with writing.

When the London Lead Company expanded to take over mines throughout Britain, it quickly transformed small, ragged affairs into highly organised and productive organisations. It combined a fearless business approach with innovative techniques to exploit to the full each of the sites: the largest shaft in the Alston Moor fields is on Middle Fell, between the villages of Nenthead and Garrigill; it reaches 100 fathoms, or 200 yards in depth, a remarkable achievement which allowed access to new and profitable mineral veins. The Rampgill vein, at Nenthead, produced over 300,000 bings (a bing is 8 hundred-weight) of lead ore. In the 1880s, this was valued at £2 million – the equivalent of almost £100 million today. The London Lead Company did not exist for philanthropic reasons; it existed to make money. And it achieved this with great success.

The commitment to education at Nenthead and the surrounding fells cannot be divorced from this commercial context. Teaching children to read and write – and encouraging their fathers to study – was not simply an altruistic act. It's certainly true that the Quakers paid more attention to the principles of a general education than many of their contemporaries. Perhaps because they had themselves been excluded from the formal education system dominated by Church of England institutions they were quick to see the advantages of non-traditional schooling. The founder of the Society of Friends, William Penn, set out a vision for education in 1682 when he was on the brink of leaving Britain for America. In a moving letter to his wife, in which he outlined instructions for their children, he urged her to 'be liberal' in their learning, encouraging 'ingenuity mixed with industry'. In particular he recommended 'the useful parts of mathematics, as building houses or ships, measuring, surveying, dialing, navigation'.[13] As the Society of Friends grew, education became an integral part of the community, with schools becoming established in Quaker houses. By the end of the eighteenth century, attention was also being directed to schooling provision for those beyond the Quaker circle: as early as 1779, the Society of Friends established a school in London for girls and boys from the ages of seven to thirteen in an attempt to make learning accessible to less affluent families. But as Penn's emphasis on 'the useful' makes clear, the intention was not education for its own sake but teaching with a distinct practical application: the creation of a better workforce.

The question of maintaining and honing a skilled group of workers had exercised the London Lead Company since its earliest days. The founders immediately realised that if they were to transform the haphazard collection of mining sites – each with different habits and techniques – into a coherent and profitable business they needed to develop a professional and highly systematised method for organising the work and managing the miners. What emerged was an intricate hierarchy which relied on a system of 'overmen' and agents who were responsible for the work and safety of each mine and who acted as intermediaries between the men on (and under) the ground and the Company. But it was not just the structured nature of the system which was unusual – what made it particularly effective was that the management level was almost entirely drawn from the workforce. This allowed for the personal advancement of the most skilled men or those judged to be of best character: with diligence and determination it was possible to rise from miner to overman and then to agent, district agent and finally to superintendent.

The emphasis on internal promotion proved such a success that after 1820 no outside officials were brought into the Company; all of the men at managerial level had risen through the ranks on their own merits. This created a remarkable culture of loyalty and ensured generations of coherent work practices. But such apparent unity was not easily achieved in a business employing large numbers of workers in a variety of roles, from washer boy and smelter to assayer. Good behaviour and adherence to agreed working habits could not be assumed – instead it was enforced through regular inspection and diligent supervision. In a similar way to Robert Owen's village at New Lanark, the smooth running and steady profits of the London Lead Company depended on the efficient application of a culture of scrutiny.

A report of 1820 suggests such a policy proved highly successful. Before the introduction of the management system the miners had apparently been free to 'play tricks, and take advantage of all kinds'. The author was quite clear that what had caused a change in behaviour was 'the daily and hourly inspection of the overmen'. Such

frequent and conscientious attention by the managers had, unsurprisingly perhaps, put 'a final close' to all kinds of shoddy or lazy work
and, as the report noted, created a noticeably 'improved economy'
for the Company as a whole.[14]

A few years later, a traveller to the district was struck by the 'general
decorum and good behaviour' of the miners. On further investigation,
he discovered that this civil conduct was not so much a result of
natural obedience and good nature as of widespread fear of punish-
ment. The London Lead Company's system of internal reward and
promotion was matched at the other end of the scale with a strict
system of penalty: fines of up to 2 shillings were levied for swearing
or 'abusive language', wagers were discouraged with a fine of sixpence
and those who were found to have fathered a child illegitimately were
obliged to marry the mother or face immediate dismissal. Indeed, the
threat of being forced from work hung like a Pennine rain cloud over
the miners who were at constant risk of losing their jobs for a range
of reasonably minor offences: 'drunkenness and quarrelling are
punished by dismissal', the traveller noted.[15]

In much the same spirit, the Nenthead school opened in 1819 with
a structure of inspection already in place – overseen by a dedicated
schools' inspector – and a lengthy series of regulations governing both
weekday and Sunday education. Some of these rules enforced the
Quakers' commitment to strictly non-denominational teaching, with
no 'particular tenets of any religious sect inculcated on the Scholars',
but many others were concerned with monitoring and recording the
behaviour of pupils: there was an emphasis on time-keeping, for
example, and a requirement to maintain a 'journal of attendance,
progress and behaviour'. More significant than these regulations for
the smooth running of the school community, however, was the
emphasis placed on preparing – and in fact selecting – boys for work
in the mines. Poor behaviour in the classroom was clearly shown to
have a knock-on, lifelong effect: any boy applying to work for the
Company had to produce a certificate proving that 'he had been
industrious, and of good behaviour' during his years at school. If he
could not, then he was barred from working and forced to continue
to attend weekday school until such time as the superintendent felt
able to vouch for his character. Similarly, any boy failing to attend
Sunday school, or displaying 'disorderly practices' whilst there, could

be summarily dismissed from working in the mines. In this way, managers could effectively weed out troublemakers, or even those of a more independent turn of mind, long before they joined the work-force. The general importance attached to education in all the model villages and the early emphasis on establishing school buildings cannot be divorced, I think, from the impulse to establish a culture of scrutiny and control which we've seen here at Nenthead and at New Lanark. Schools were an integral part of the system of grooming generations of workers. Whatever the social, political or religious doctrines which ostensibly drove them, the effect was the same: providing a malleable workforce.

When I was working at Nenthead there was a tiny primary school here, just a house for a single teacher who took classes for half a dozen pupils in the downstairs rooms. They came on a field trip once or twice, crossing the river to see whether I had any information which could supplement the usual lessons. I used to think it was the perfect place to go to school, a kind of educational idyll. I had an idea that the children scampered over the moors all day chasing butterflies and learning the ways of the wild. I suspect the reality was very different: dull and isolated, the youthful relationships too intense and no way of being anonymous. I suspect, too, it was cold and leaky – the old blockish building was grey and ugly and has since been sold; the school has moved into what used to be the village hall, a chapel-like building on the hill.

Before I end my visit, I walk up to see what might be going on. Following the curve of the road, I pass behind the back of most of the houses, looking down on to the heart of the village. The unusual shape of the Reading Room makes it easy to distinguish; the roof of the Methodist chapel and the sheer bulk of the building mean that it, too, stands out. There is something pleasing about the way in which the original landmarks – the institutions which shaped this place – still predominate. A woman with a small brown terrier passes at a brisk pace and says hello, then looks back again, twice. Something about my slow progress seems to alarm her, as though the idea of someone idling here is sinister. This remains a place cut off, unused to casual tourists and *flâneurs*.

The school is quiet. There's nothing much to see – an ordinary village primary school with a concrete yard, bright drawings and project work visible through the windows, a single car parked by the fence. Turning, I come back along the path that takes me to the models laid out on the bungalow lawn. 'Model' villages. 'Model' making. A 'model' of behaviour. The idea of the model is ingrained in our concept of development and of education – it suggests repetition, imitation, example. But the potentially problematic nature of the term is also apparent in the difficulty I found in titling this book. Could I talk about model villages without readers conjuring pictures of Legoland? Is the idea of the 'model' now entirely subsumed into the concept of the miniature? And what about the creeping suspicion of obsession – of matchstick ocean liners and fleets of replica planes?

If it's impossible now to think of the model village without thinking of the obsessive and the miniature – the tiny, pristine walls, unpeopled landscapes and unhistoried communities of this other Nenthead on display in someone's garden – then I have to draw some comfort from the way in which changes in scale and perspective create critical distance: Swift's evocation of Lilliput was not cute and comfortable, after all, but a satirical attack made possible by the slippage between a world of real size and a similar but tinier one. His manipulation of scale allowed him to pose uncomfortable questions about the nature of humanity; it allowed him to make barbed comparisons between the miniature or gigantic fantasy worlds of *Gulliver's Travels* and contemporary Europe of the early eighteenth century. Perhaps, in the end, even full-size model villages have a similar effect and create a similar slippage, drawing us into the past while prompting us to reconsider the present. With Nenthead, this place in the North Pennines a long way from anywhere, the London Lead Company could be considered to have created a specimen in a glass jar, a Victorian doll's house, a model – a thing that could be held up for examination and speculation and intrigue. In this place, where landscape demands separation, there is a model village within a model village. What do you make of that?

3

Edensor, Derbyshire

I used to live not far from here. It's always felt like a place between – between the city and the country, between the unforgiving moorland and the pastoral valleys, between the past and the present. The limits of Sheffield butt into the uplands that lurch across from the west, uplands with simple, respectful names like 'Big Moor'. Gritstone edges slice through these moors, marking the boundary between hard geology and soft. Natural cairns and huge boulders push through the grass and heather, towering over the drop to the valley below; rock climbers rattle their way up the tricky faces to the paths at the top where families walk their dogs. And not quite obscured by all this, there are Bronze Age carvings in the rock, Iron Age settlements, stone circles and lone waymarkers, weathered now and undemonstrative, while hundreds of abandoned millstones lie scattered between the boulders or half-buried in the peaty ground, worked by hand a long time ago and still entirely unnatural. This harsh land was a place of industry, before the fast-flowing rivers converging on Sheffield washed the Industrial Revolution downstream. It was a place of work for men and boys quarrying stones, hacking them into shape and hauling them up to the top of the edge to be sent away to grind flour, lead ore, paint pigments, glass and apples for cider. It took one man and one boy one month to produce a pair of millstones.

Between the hills and edges of this place between, in the Derwent Valley – not many miles from Cromford – sprawls the Chatsworth Estate, home to the Cavendish family, the Dukes of Devonshire, since the sixteenth century. It's an estate of many and opposing histories, not all of them quite tangible. It's a place of construct and illusion, of change and permanence. And like all estates of such size, it's punctuated by a series of villages attached in one way or another to the big house. They cluster around the mansion like planets in a solar system, some close by, some distant, all dependent on the star at the centre. Closest to the house, Pilsley, Beeley and Carlton Lees – with their nursery-rhyme names – are still home to employees and pensioners. Further afield, Shottle is a village of estate farmers. The homes are solid and well planned, constructed in stone and spaced generously around village greens and wells; there are schools, churches and post offices, pubs and local shops.

These are ancient settlements, many of them dating back to the Domesday Book and beyond. They're part of the landscape. And for a very long time they have had a particular purpose: to serve the needs of the people who serve the Duke. They are all, in some aspects at least, model villages, constructed by a patron for his staff, farmers and families. Even today, in an apparently non-feudal age, they house some of the 600 people still employed by the Chatsworth Estate. I could perhaps have picked any of them for my study. But I'm only really interested in one of them. It doesn't look the same as the others. It's the odd one out in an estate which harmonises its signs and woodwork and buildings in an identical shade of dusty blue. It's the flouncy one, the show-off, the eccentric. This is one of the most remarkable and idiosyncratic workers' villages in the country, a picturesque experiment that is guaranteed to charm and puzzle us. This is Edensor.

Since I started work on this book, I've begun to notice remnants of model settlements all over the place: gatehouses with inordinately tall chimneys; little country dwellings with ornate detailing or black-and-white woodwork knitted across their frontages. In the village where my parents live, there's a red-brick cottage which is even called 'Model Cottage'. In recent years it's been extended so that it conforms more easily to modern needs, but what is visible to the passer-by is the original 1879 building designed by the architect John Douglas in an attractive warm orange brick. There are rows of narrow, arched, mullioned windows and decoration in white plaster which creates strong geometric patterns: diamonds running along the length of the external walls and squares at the gable end. There's a stack of elongated chimneys to create a focal point; a cobbled front yard, climbing ivy. It sits on a busy main road, a modest private residence, a handsome, rather than a pretty, building. It's not particularly celebrated. It's hardly even noticed, I suspect. But it brings home to me how widespread the fashion was for creating models of this kind; how strong a hold the ideal of the perfect village home had on designers, landowners, architects and indeed residents.

According to Gillian Darley in her extensive architectural survey, *Villages of Vision*, there are over 400 examples of these kinds of planned settlements across the UK. Many have now completely disappeared, subsumed by changes to the landscape: the Bedford Estate, for example, had one industrial village entirely devoted to servicing building work but this has since been cleared away. Others have been fractured and overwhelmed by modern building so that only traces remain, the occasional row of neat cottages or a square of industrial terracing. But nonetheless so many villages do still remain, in one form or other, that it's perhaps no surprise that my own path has crossed with so many. I've known Edensor on the Chatsworth Estate for over twenty years and it seems to me that here perhaps more than at any other model settlement you have a clear sense of the place as complete, untrammelled by urban additions, its original intentions undiluted. On my visits to some of the villages, I find I need to go through the process of unseeing modern clutter – it's rather like restoring a painting, taking off extrinsic layers in order to see more clearly the colour and form of what lies beneath. It's a process of trying to re-envisage old places as new ones, seeing them as they were when they were shiny and modern and perhaps as challenging as contemporary city housing estates. But here at Edensor the village sits confidently and cleanly in front of you. It becomes immediately clear that you've arrived somewhere that was intended to look like this. You can be seduced into thinking that only a little time has passed since the village was built and that the world is much as it has always been.

I'm standing on Edensor village green. The midwinter sky is already darkening and my photographs are blurry in the poor light. The desultory pop of intermittent gunshot, at a distance, signals the end of a pheasant shoot. Occasionally a car passes steadily on the road beyond the tall iron railings. Christmas lights twinkle in some of the trees, in windows and porches. Behind me, adjacent to the cattle grid, there's a battlemented gatehouse with an octagonal tower at one corner. Above the studded front door, a medieval cross is carved from the brickwork. The flagpole is bare. On the other side, across the green and the sweep of tarmacked lane, a large, square house faces out to the open parkland, weighted down by its balconied wooden porch and prominent blue eaves. It looks like a municipal building in a small Swiss town. The undecorated pine tree lodged in front of the first-storey door adds to the Alpine ambience. Alongside this imposing villa, its dressed stone shabby on one side, there's a smaller house, rather plain, but with exaggerated gables and impractically tall chimneys. It marks the far boundary of the village. A high kitchen-garden wall pulls away to bare trees.

The cluster of buildings elongates to both sides of me, stone cottages punctuating the cleft in the valley as it rises away to Black Firs Wood on the horizon. Everything is dominated by the church of St Peter's, set up on a knoll, its ornate spire too tall and heavy, greening with moss. The village feels solid, a genteel place, restful and untroubled. It's easy on the senses. At this hour of the day, with the dusk closing in, it makes me think of warm hearths, roaring fires, comfort; at this time of year, it conjures thoughts of Christmas cards, languid wassailing and lavish television adaptations of nineteenth-century novels. It's a lovely, romantic place to be.

It was the 6th Duke of Devonshire, William Spencer Cavendish, known as the Bachelor Duke, who was responsible for the Edensor we see today. He was twenty-one years old when he became Duke in 1811; charming, flamboyant and eccentric, prone to hypochondria and depression. He inherited not only 200,000 acres of land and the old Cavendish estates of Chatsworth and Hardwick Hall in Derbyshire and Devonshire House in London, but also – through his grandmother Charlotte Boyle – Bolton Abbey and Londesborough in Yorkshire, Lismore Castle in County Waterford and two more London residences at Burlington House and Chiswick House. He was an extraordinarily rich man and could afford to indulge an enthusiasm for collecting and entertaining: at Chiswick he installed a celebrated menagerie including a bull, a Neopolitan pig, a Peruvian llama and an Indian elephant called Saidi who uncorked the Duke's wine bottles with her trunk. He had the means to impose his vision on the ancient estates he'd inherited: he rebuilt the castle at Lismore, transforming it into a huge Gothic fortress with a medieval-style banqueting hall designed by Augustus Pugin, and he completely reworked the gardens and parkland at Chatsworth. He had the wealth to follow fashion – and to lead fashion – in the most extravagant ways: to build a unique Picturesque village at Edensor.

Shortly after inheriting, the Bachelor Duke appointed the architect Jeffry Wyatt, later Sir Jeffry Wyatville, to construct a new North Wing for Chatsworth House, as well as an Orangery and a garden Broad Walk. Wyatt also built a new carriage route that would show off the approach through the estate to best advantage. This required the demolition of the eastern half of the original Anglo-Saxon settlement of Edensor. Today there's just one remnant of this part of the village, a single cottage with a walled garden, marooned on the grazed slope above the river, parted from the rest of the village by the road. Popular myth would have it that the Duke took offence at the scruffy peasants visible from the main house and so razed their village to improve his view, but in fact, the demolition seems to have been an entirely prag-matic manoeuvre – a simple piece of road building. Nonetheless, it displayed quite openly the Duke's attitude towards the village: the ancient settlement could be swiftly and unrepentantly reconfigured to meet the demands of the new nineteenth century. Edensor did not have a right to its place on the land.

It was the 6th Duke's partnership with another architect and engi-neer, Joseph Paxton, which was to have most impact on Edensor, however. Paxton was extraordinarily energetic and ambitious. He arrived at Chatsworth on 9 May 1826 at half past four in the morning, having travelled all night from London, and described his first hours on the estate. He was twenty-three:

> As no person was to be seen at that early hour, I got over the green-house gate by the old covered way, explored the pleasure-grounds, and looked round the outside of the house. I then went down to the kitchen-gardens, scaled the outside wall, and saw the whole of the place, set the men to work there at six o'clock; then returned to Chatsworth and got Thomas Weldon to play the water-works, and afterwards went to breakfast with poor dear Mrs Gregory and her niece: the latter fell in love with me, and I with her, and thus completed my first morning's work at Chatsworth before nine o'clock.[1]

Even allowing for some personal myth-making, this is an impressive start to a career. Perhaps even more remarkably, Paxton's pace and enthusiasm never flagged. He and the Duke formed a perfect partnership, combining curiosity with vision; wealth with engineering and horticultural skill; flamboyance with practicality. Over the next thirty-two years they worked together to construct an exceptional legacy of ambitious buildings, ingenious hothouses, rare plant collections, innovative forestry and vast conservatories. At Lismore, Paxton took charge of the construction work, creating the imposing skyline of pale battlements and turrets still visible today; at Chatsworth, he designed the gravity-fed Emperor Fountain for a proposed visit of Russia's Tsar Nicholas in 1844, displaying a spectacular plume 264 feet high, the tallest in the world. Together the Duke and Paxton wanted things higher, grander, bigger; they wanted their ambitions on display.

The Chatsworth Estate already boasted all the natural elements essential to the Picturesque vision: streams, ponds and waterfalls, a meandering river, ancient trees, rocky hillsides. This, however, wasn't quite enough: over time, Paxton and the Bachelor Duke emphasised these features, adding rock gardens and pine forests, pathways and dells. In the midst of all this activity, the two men also turned their attention to Edensor, or rather to the western part of the original settlement which remained. By 1838, building work had begun to transform the village yet again. Paxton oversaw the work on behalf of the Duke, but construction was supervised by John Robertson, his assistant. This was not to be like the haphazard villages scattered elsewhere across the estate; it would be conceived in intricate detail to please the eye and humour the fashionable spirit. In September 1839, the Duke returned from a year in Europe to note jubilantly in his journal: 'Fine day. Happy village. New Cottages.'[2]

The British preoccupation with the Picturesque began in 1757, when Edmund Burke published his influential treatise, *A Philosophical Enquiry into the Origin of Our Ideas of the Sublime and the Beautiful*, in which he attempted to define what it was that made things beautiful. He argued that our responses to beauty were not necessarily rational, and that there was a powerful, emotional and instinctive reaction to a type of beauty which he called the sublime and which he suggested was as important as – if not more important than – the more intellectual and formal beauty his eighteenth-century readers were accustomed to. Burke's *Enquiry* attracted the attention both of prominent thinkers and of the more general public; it was widely discussed and it encouraged a number of published responses. In 1768, William Gilpin entered the cultural debate with his *Essay on Prints*, which made a case for a type of beauty that sat between the rational 'beautiful' and the emotional 'sublime' – and which he called the 'picturesque'. Gilpin was not the first to use the term, but in a series of essays over the following decades he brought it to the forefront of contemporary discussion by attempting to define and popularise a way of looking at landscape that, as the word 'picturesque' suggests, derived from the way we look at works of art. 'That kind of beauty which is agreeable in a picture,' Gilpin argued, was also exactly the kind of beauty we should be seeking out in the world around us.

Gilpin's ideal of the Picturesque was drawn from a particular kind of landscape painting. He admired the work of seventeenth-century artists Claude Lorrain (1600–82) and Nicolas Poussin (1594–1665), for example, and looked for certain characteristics in nature that might transform the scene into something like one of their paintings: ruggedness, irregularity, dramatic shadow and light effects. During the 1770s, Gilpin undertook a series of travels, recording his impressions and expanding his theories in response to his experiences on the road. In an essay 'On Picturesque Travel' (1792), he drew attention to the links between natural and man-made landscapes, urging those with 'the Picturesque eye' to seek out 'the picture, the statue and the garden' as all equally worthy of attention. The important thing, according to Gilpin, was 'the general idea of the scene' and its ability to 'make an impression'. In the most successful examples of the Picturesque, he claimed, 'we rather *feel*, than *survey* it'.[3]

Gilpin's travel writing was published at a fortuitous moment: British roads were being quickly improved to make journeys more rapid, comfortable and appealing. At the same time, the Grand Tour abroad was being forcibly curtailed by the upheaval of a series of revolutions in continental Europe. With traditional routes to classical sites and European capitals becoming uncertain and even treacherous, more and more English travellers were lured by Gilpin's descriptions of undiscovered but easily accessible British landscapes. Within a short number of years, there was a boom in tourists to areas which had, until then, been largely tranquil: Wales and Scotland, and the beauty spots we now know as the Lake District and the Peak District. By the end of the century, the Wye Valley had become one of the most popular landscapes to be 'discovered' by this new wave of tourists. The publication of William Wordsworth's 'Lines Written a Few Miles Above Tintern Abbey' in 1798 – with its descriptions of 'steep and lofty cliffs', waters 'rolling from their mountain springs' and the 'wild green landscape' – captured the romance of the place. The valley was soon welcoming so many visitors that eight boats a day were making trips up and down the river which meandered through the Herefordshire lowlands to the Wye Gorge; by 1850 more than twenty accounts of the Wye Tour had been published as well as many collections of engravings and paintings featuring the ruins of castles at Wilton, Goodrich and Chepstow. The driving force of this invasion, in the Wye Valley and across Britain, was Gilpin's ideal of the Picturesque, the search for a landscape which offered the variety and richness of the most revered works of art.

William Gilpin's attempt to define certain natural characteristics through philosophical discussion, and to create an elaborate aesthetic code, relied on rules of informality, disorder and naturalness. But it remained essentially a way of depicting nature in paintings, and drawing links between nature and art. Indeed, the instructions to artists about how to look at, and represent, a suitably Picturesque view were often explicit and stringent. Following Gilpin's advice, guide-books would identify 'Station Points' from which to draw, encouraging the use of Claude glasses, small pocket mirrors which framed and simplified the scene to give a painterly effect. The didactic tone and demanding italics of the Rev. R. H. Newell's *Letters on the Scenery of Wales* (1821), for example, was commonplace: 'Bring the Castle exactly *within the angle* made by the sloping hill and woody steep *before* it. Then ascend or descent [sic], til the *water* and *three* of the promontories appear above the castle.'[4] Such a rigid approach to the appreciation and representation of scenery was apt to become formulaic and it's unlikely that Gilpin's work would have led to the creation of anything like the village at Edensor.

The most striking first impression of Edensor is the sheer variety pressed into the dip of the land. The two linear streets which fork from the central green are studded with eclectic and eccentric build-ings. You're immediately struck by the sheer freedom and confidence of the design: on one side of you are some elegant Tudor features;

alongside there's a Mediterranean-style tower, and beyond that the castellated Gothic. Walking up the hill, you're confronted by a fine English farmhouse, symmetrical and sturdy. The only dominant feature is the heavy tower of St Peter's church – if it appears out of proportion, even out of place, that's because it is. The original medieval church was rebuilt by the 7th Duke in the 1860s, long after the rest of the village was completed. The new building was designed by George Gilbert Scott, who won the competition to design the Albert Memorial in London, and it glowers over the excesses of the early-century Picturesque vision like a disapproving and rotund old Queen.

A correspondent from the *Gardener's Chronicle* who visited Edensor in 1842 noted admiringly that it offered 'a perfect compendium of all the prettiest styles of cottage architecture from the sturdy Norman to the sprightly Italian'.[5] Today, the weathered homogeneity of the materials – largely local sandstone and grey roof tiles – and the ubiquitous Chatsworth blue in which all the woodwork, doors, fences and window frames are painted, can, at a glance, give an initial impression of uniformity. But it takes only the briefest scrutiny to begin to see the assortment of designs and exuberance of decoration employed here. Scattered in an appropriately Picturesque fashion, the buildings present a challenging variety. There's a confusion of detail; there appears to be no coherent plan. Edensor strikes the visitor as a complex and enthusiastic celebration of architectural form – or a muddle, depending on your point of view.

Edensor owes its variety to the preoccupations of the writers who followed Gilpin. This new wave of Picturesque thinkers was determined to move on from the simple and restrictive travelogue, and was considerably more active in its approach: if a scene lacked a bubbling stream, then a bubbling stream was to be diverted through it; if a view could be improved by a ruinous barn then a ruinous barn should be constructed. As Gilpin's ideas were taken and adapted, the emphasis moved away from the simple appreciation of pictorial landscapes towards the more complex process of designing, creating and adapting them.

This was much more to the taste of the Bachelor Duke. He and Paxton were active in their projects, pushing forwards, trying out new ideas; they were endlessly looking to improve. Their ambition and ingenuity achieved a great deal – it was rarely bettered by practical difficulties or physical obstructions – but such an approach is not without its darker side, of course. Such supreme confidence can be read as arrogance; such a brisk march into the future inevitably tramples on some elements of the past. The construction of the fashionable village which the Duke envisaged was not a straightforward matter of building a few houses and rearranging the landscape. The serenity at Edensor today conceals a history of tricky negotiations and unsettled lives, of manipulation and experimentation. It's not quite what it seems. Take something that seems simple, like its name. Because I used to know this area well, I also know that to call this village Edensor, as it is written, marks you out as an interloper. To all residents and locals, this is a place called Enza.

This may not seem a big thing. It isn't a big thing. On one level, the evolution of the village's original Anglo-Saxon place name over time reflects little more than natural alterations in speech patterns. Language, after all, revels in all kinds of common words which are pronounced quite differently from the way in which they're spelt: in English, *bought* pronounced *bawt*; *laugh* pronounced *larf* – or *laff*, depending on your heritage. Etymology is a discipline of change. But the way in which Edensor's name has been appropriated and transformed seems to me to be worth a brief consideration. It suggests a more radical process, a challenge to the identity of the village and its place in the world. I'm struck, for example, by the way in which such linguistic alterations seem to happen to places with aristocratic heritage: the Marquis of Cholmondley announces himself as the master of a (non-existent) place called *Chumley*; Beaulieu in Hampshire, the seat of Lord Montagu, has lost its French identity and become anglicised to *Beelee*.

In part this is because many of the country's oldest places are linked to ancient families and time has wrought changes on the buildings, the people who live there and the way in which we identify them. But it also seems to me that place names like Edensor have, over time, been honed to better fit the manner of a particular speech and the vowel sounds of a distinct class. It seems as though the change in Edensor's name is not simply a natural process but an imposition of a particular viewpoint and a particular way of speaking. Edensor is a village that has been moved, rebuilt, redesigned and re-presented to suit the imperatives of one family, and the wider demands of the ruling class to which the family belongs. If I'm looking at the way in which the buildings here have been developed and what their shape, decoration and location might possibly mean in a wider context, then it seems to make sense to think about the name. 'Edensor' is a slippery word. How it looks to the eye is deceptive. It is a linguistic trick. And in the same spirit, the story of the Bachelor Duke's Picturesque idyll is a story of an ongoing negotiation of location and identity, of purpose and status. It's a tale of a village that has been manipulated to impress and deceive and entertain; it's an account of ordinary dwellings transformed, like the word Edensor, to express ambition, authority and fashion.

The Edensor of turrets and Alpine roof lines and mock-Elizabethan features is heavily influenced by the work of one of Gilpin's successors, Uvedale Price. Price was from a wealthy Herefordshire family with links to fashionable Whig society and a long tradition of patronage to art and architecture. He published his *Essays on the Picturesque* in 1794 and used his estate at Foxley, close to the Welsh border, to experiment with some of his ideas on practical gardening and landscaping, creating an open-air 'picture gallery' which took visitors on a carriage ride around the area, stopping off at key views of the Wye Valley and the Welsh Hills. In particular, Price's essays were intended to highlight what he called the 'poverty of imagination' of landscapers such as Lancelot 'Capability' Brown and his followers. Price believed these high-profile designers were destroying beautiful landscapes with their insistence on a 'new manner . . . [in which] gardens differ very little from common fields'. He felt that the fashion for a monotonous natural look had gone too far, flattening out local distinctions and severing the intrinsic link between a particular landscape and the place in which it was situated. All the new parklands, he argued, looked the same. And indeed there was sound basis for his criticism: Capability Brown alone had transformed over 200 estates during the previous half-century, ripping up formal gardens and quirky features and instead imposing a potent and simple aesthetic that had quickly come to dominate landscape architecture. In place of ubiquitous open parkland, Price wanted variety and drama, celebrating 'those accidents of locality' which made each landscape special.[6]

Among the estates reworked by Capability Brown was Chatsworth. In the 1670s, the 1st Duke, William Cavendish, had rebuilt the Elizabethan house in the classical style, and constructed a garden to complement it, favouring the formal symmetry fashionable in France, Italy and Holland. In 1696 he unveiled the Cascade, a decorative water feature with a series of twenty-four steps and slopes built in stone and fed from a nine-acre reservoir dug into the moorland above the house. It was an accomplished and expensive piece of engineering: the distance of the fall between each step and the next was unique so that the sound of the water would change along its length. But six years later the Cascade was torn up and rebuilt, larger and steeper than before. The land was there to be shaped and tamed. Imposing built features into the natural form of the landscape was one way of making a statement about the wealth and influence of the new dukedom and a means of stamping a mark of personality on to what Daniel Defoe had described as 'difficult desart country'.[7]

This process of manipulation was continued by the 3rd Duke, who employed William Kent in 1743 to draw up improvements for the gardens – and yet another reworking of the Cascade – in a fanciful style at odds with the formality of the original seventeenth-century designs. William Kent was a pioneer of the naturalistic manner of landscaping; although his plans were never implemented, it was a small step for the 4th Duke, twenty years later, to call on the services of Lancelot 'Capability' Brown. By the time of the Duke's death in 1764, the parkland had been transformed by Brown's energy and the powerful shared vision of an idyll of rolling vistas and 'natural' features. A bridge was built so that visitors could approach the house from the most charming angle; deer and sheep were put to graze in what had been the meticulous parterre gardens; all but three of the original fountains were pulled out, topiary and terraces destroyed. An extensive campaign of tree planting began to change the bare hills behind and around the house into woodland, with the introduction of both native hardwood and more exotic species – catalpa, sassafras, hickory and maple – shipped from Philadelphia, USA, in 1759. The border between the garden and the landscape beyond was blurred as thoroughly as possible to create a vast genteel pleasure ground, a seamless vision of how the world should look if viewed through the eyes of an immensely powerful and wealthy eighteenth-century aristocrat.

After the dominance of the Brown approach to landscaping, the public was probably ready for a change of view. Just as Gilpin's travel writing had proved timely, so Price's essays seemed to strike an immediate chord with his contemporaries. Soon after its publication, several country estates began to experiment with the practical implementation of his ideas. One of the most elaborate and impressive of these landscapes was developed at Hafod, near Aberystwyth in mid-Wales, by Thomas Johnes, a friend of both Gilpin and Price. Johnes built a new house overlooking the Ystwyth Valley and implemented a range of innovative farming, forestry and gardening techniques. But in 1807, just over twenty years after it was erected, the mansion was destroyed by a fire which began in its celebrated library. Johnes's most enduring creations turned out to be the features he added to the natural attractions of the valley and its hillsides: following the principles outlined by Price, he developed a series of walking circuits, capturing a succession of tumbling streams and artistic views punctuated by rustic bridges, grottos, tunnels and waterfalls.

Even now Hafod is a magical place, a beautiful stretch of land with something to surprise and entertain around most corners. It's somewhere I've come to know very well, and it's the place where I most clearly understand what the proponents of the Picturesque were attempting to achieve. The landscape, sculpted and tamed and subtly manipulated, seems even now to be the archetypal British landscape. It does what many of us still believe a British landscape should do: it draws us but does not intimidate, it suggests wilderness while remaining comfortable, it distracts us from everyday concerns but does not terrify us with the prospect of oblivion. This is part man, part nature, side by side on good terms.

At the far point of the Gentleman's Walk – the Ladies' Walk is shorter and less strenuous to allow for the obvious constraints of dress and a weak constitution – there's a feature called the Cavern Cascade. You take a narrow path along the side of a tree-lined gulley, a stream running through beneath you. In all but the driest weather it's slippery, the water below churning among the rocks: I hope Johnes's gentlemen visitors had sturdy shoes. After a while you come to a bend in the path, and you turn straight into a tunnel hewn from the rock, about the height of an average early-nineteenth-century man. It's not quite dark, but it's damp and shadowy, and there's an unsettling sheen to the bronze stone. Once inside, your pace quickens, because it's a strange place to be and because you want to see what's at the end of the tunnel. And at the end there's a waterfall, an entirely natural cascade, dropping from the woods above into a small pool. You emerge almost underneath it, the light playing through the water, fracturing into moments of rainbow. You rejoice in the feeling that you've discovered a secret, a hidden place, even though the names scratched into the tunnel walls behind you confirm the passage of many feet over many years. You've fallen for the charm of the Picturesque.

Unfortunately, the stone in the tunnel has peeled off in layers, and so the marks made by many of the earlier visitors have fallen away, leaving evidence mostly from the past twenty years or so. But even though their names have disappeared, we know that visitors to Hafod were plentiful. News of Johnes's work travelled quickly to a public eager for Picturesque experiences and, despite – or perhaps because of – its isolated location, his estate rapidly became a celebrated tourist destination. His contemporaries were delighted by what he had achieved and generous in their praise. Perhaps most importantly, the estate was considered to illustrate Price's ideas quite perfectly, becoming recognised almost immediately as 'an exact translation' of the principles of the Picturesque.

From such successful landscape experiments, it was a small step to look at how people lived and how the right kind of human settlement might embellish a scene's natural advantages. Like Gilpin, Price admired the works of Claude and Poussin, but he also drew on Dutch and Flemish art – particularly paintings by Philips Wouwerman and Salomon van Ruysdael – to examine ways in which people might be incorporated into his schemes. These paintings showed figures in the landscape, country cottages, ruins and farms. They depicted villagers driving cattle alongside a church, or riverside castles in a romantic dawn. Price began to think about how buildings might be included in his ambitions for the Picturesque. In 1791, he launched his own practical experiment, offering the architect John Nash a commission to design a castellated Gothic villa on the shoreline at Aberystwyth, complete with octagonal towers and invigorating views of the sea dashing 'very finely against the promontory on which the ruin of the old castle stands'.[8] A few years later, in his second volume of essays (1798), he looked closely at 'Architecture and Buildings, as Connected with Scenery'. He began to formulate ideas about villages, and how they might look if they were to conform to the Picturesque ideal.

A detour: Blaise Hamlet, Bristol

I've come to Blaise Hamlet, in the shadow of Blaise Castle, about four miles from Bristol city centre. The village is hemmed in by modern estates and hidden behind a high encircling wall so that the stream of traffic passes without pause. I've performed a brisk manoeuvre in the car, cutting across the rush-hour queues, to park alongside the kerb, just outside the small iron pedestrian gate that I fear might be locked. It isn't. When I step through it's like a moment from *Alice in Wonderland* or Pullman's *His Dark Materials*, when an apparently ordinary entrance turns out to be a portal into a completely new and transformed place, where one world gives way to another. I expect elves or costumed Munchkins.

Instead, I cross a small grove of ivy and old trees and emerge along the side of a hedge on to an undulating green, unevenly shaped and studded with blossoming fruit trees. Dotted about its margins are nine cottages in a variety of odd shapes: bulbous or angular, squat or stretched, several of them cowering under heavy thatch, all weighted down by the sheer amount of detail stuffed into their design. I can see a deep niche in the front of the first building, with a white bench and an old plant of some sort – a vine probably – creating a natural entrance. There are narrow windows in the shape of an elongated cross; tall brick chimney stacks decorated with carved detail. There are pigeon lofts and tiled dormers. There's another white bench at the corner of one of the cottages, latticed and angular, overhung by a wide, curved eave and skirted by the narrow path; another long low bench fronts the cottage in the corner, partly obscured by scaffolding; another fits snugly into the gap between a window and a stone pillar; yet another hugs the curve of a thatched wall. I'm not permitted to sit on any of them.

What I can see here today at Blaise Hamlet is more or less exactly what was envisaged as the perfect Picturesque village, the result of the growing discussion about the ideal settlement. Following Uvedale Price's lead, the debate of the late eighteenth and early nineteenth centuries tended to yoke together two fashionable concerns: how to improve the practical, often poor, housing in which tenants and workers lived, and how best to indulge the vogue for the gentleman's retreat, known as the folly or cottage *ornée*. When a village was built to bring together these differing priorities in one place, what emerged was the quaint, elaborate and frankly bizarre settlement of Blaise Hamlet.

By the early nineteenth century, there was an increasingly powerful philanthropic impulse to improve housing for ordinary workers. It was a period of radical change, from the agricultural patterns of the past to the newer urban environments which were developing with the Industrial Revolution. At the same time, taxes and food prices were being driven up by the cost of the Napoleonic Wars, and by a series of poor harvests; this was followed in 1815 by the hugely unpopular Corn Law which aimed to keep bread prices high to protect the interests of British wheat farmers. In the factories and cotton mills, wage reduction and unemployment sparked the Luddite riots of 1811–12 and a series of marches, organised by radicals to draw attention to difficult living conditions.

But the threat of unrest was not confined to urban areas. In the country, too, a rapidly growing population and a reduction in the amount of cottage accommodation frequently led to the development of slums. Problems resulting from damp conditions and inadequate drainage and sewage were commonplace, and were exacerbated by overcrowding. Faced with the decline in living conditions, the Board of Agriculture issued a number of surveys during the years of the Napoleonic Wars which began to emphasise the value of decent housing as a means of social control in the countryside. Rural landlords were easily frightened by the prospect of discontent among their tenants which might in turn lead to a growth in radical politics and a more sustained challenge to their authority, and so the surveys encouraged them to make at least minimal improvements to the housing on their estates. Although the direct correlation between quality of housing and quality of labour did not gain full expression until the 1840s, many landowners were increasingly persuaded that a well-housed labour force would be in better health and therefore more efficient – as a result imposing less demand on the local poor rates. A combination of self-interest with a growing sense of moral responsibility began to force landlords to address the problem of poor housing: George Eliot's 'Study of Provincial Life', the 1872 novel *Middlemarch*, looked back to the late 1820s as a period when even small landowners such as Mr Brooke were compelled to redesign the 'pig-sty cottages' in which their tenants lived.

At the same time, the idea of the gentleman's folly had been popu-larised by the construction of Endsleigh Cottage, near Tavistock in Devon, in 1810 by the 6th Duke of Bedford, and the Prince Regent's Royal Lodge, constructed in Windsor Great Park two years later. The principle of the cottage *ornée* drew on the thatched roofs and quaint decoration of traditional buildings but transformed these into comfort-able villas fit for the aristocratic classes. Despite the financial impact of the Napoleonic Wars, these costly residences, scattered in the most secluded nooks of country estates, became enormously popular, catering to the whims of the wealthy who fancied living for a day as cottagers or having a picnic in a romantic setting. The cottage *ornée* was always a one-off creation, but as landowners started to look at the humble villages gathered on their estates, it began to seem possible to combine the cottage *ornée*'s emphasis on embellishment and architectural quirkiness with existing buildings to make them appear prettier. Even adding a few thatches here and there, or a lattice window, quickly helped mundane settlements conform more readily to the principles of the Picturesque.

During the eighteenth century a number of landowners had exper-imented with small model estate villages for their workers. In the late 1760s and early 1770s, a cluster of twelve plain sandstone estate cottages, designed by Robert Adam, was built at Lowther in Cumbria. At Milton Abbas, on the Milton Abbey Estate in Dorset, there is still a sinuous row of pairs of low thatched cottages running along the valley road, set back behind wide grass verges. Built in 1780 by Joseph Damer, Lord Milton, the thirty-six cottages were designed by Capability Brown and architect Sir William Chambers to replace the market town of Middleton which was demolished to make way for new parkland designs. But Blaise Hamlet was perhaps the first attempt to take the guidance on the Picturesque outlined by writers like Gilpin and Price and fully integrate it into a complete village.

Although there's a Gothic castle folly above the gorge at Blaise, the house is actually an eighteenth-century mansion built between 1796 and 1798 by John Scandrett Harford, a Quaker banker. A few years after completion of the main building, in 1802, Harford invited John Nash to design a dairy for the grounds of the castle. The extravagant thatched building which resulted whetted the appetite of both client and architect and they began work on a village of estate cottages.

When Harford approached him to work at Blaise, Nash was already well known and well established, not only as an architect, but as a member of a fashionable elite which clustered around Carlton House in London, the home of the Prince Regent. The clique was close-knit, ambitious, commonly associated with vice and extravagance and largely disliked. Nonetheless, it was also enormously influential and Nash was in demand. He was travelling extensively to keep up with the demands of a variety of commissions and working closely with an assistant, George Stanley Repton, the son of the distinguished eighteenth-century landscape designer, Humphry Repton. Both Nash and his assistant were enthusiastic advocates of the Picturesque.

Under pressure to deliver work for a variety of projects, Nash outlined his ideas for Blaise Hamlet in a rather brief and vague form before sending them to Repton who worked them up in detail and in turn sent them to Harford for construction. Such long-distance communication was inevitably fraught with difficulties and frustrations; at times Harford became infuriated by Nash's unwillingness to work on site. Despite this, however, the team worked remarkably rapidly. Fired by enthusiasm and the excitement of the pioneer, the village was finished by 1810, open for tenants to move in and for public viewing and admiration.

The cottages were a fanciful exercise in fashionable taste at a time when the financial demands of the Napoleonic Wars were making themselves felt at most levels of British society. The costs of the village had been estimated at £2,000 but by 1812 outlay had risen to over £3,000. It was intended for elderly members of the community, providing solid, spacious housing for those no longer able to work for a living and at risk of extreme poverty, but the level of expenditure suggested that this was much more than an experiment in social housing: aside from its role in sheltering vulnerable tenants, Blaise Hamlet was a perfect showcase of Price's dictums, a statement of aesthetic taste that both Nash and Harford seemed to consider worth the money. The cottages were scattered randomly in the landscape, each with a garden and hung with creepers, each conforming to the rules of irregularity and variety through a series of changing roof shapes (three in heavy thatch, six in tiles); tall, decorated chimney stacks; accentuated eaves; latticed windows. The village offered a loose interpretation of existing regional vernacular architecture, re-presented through the prism of the Picturesque. No opportunity to puncture clean lines was overlooked: 'so much depends on the lean-toos [sic] and sheds', Repton wrote to Harford.[9]

Blaise Hamlet is still inhabited today. The site is administered by the National Trust, which likes to emphasise the feeling of 'tranquillity and seclusion that remains'; it's a popular destination for contributors to Trip Advisor who report that it's 'a corner lost in time' and a 'hidden secret'. It's not unique but it was the first of its kind, and the most influential. The village of Selworthy near Minehead, for example, is a similar mixture of trimmed thatch and perfect lawn. Its yellow-tinted whitewashed cottages nestle in an undulating estate landscape also owned by the National Trust, and it boasts an award-winning tea rooms. But Selworthy was built in 1828 by Sir Thomas Acland, more than a decade after Blaise Hamlet; it stands as testament to the powerful impact of the first experiment. If we want to understand just what an effect the Picturesque movement had in the early part of the century, and how it changed the way people viewed themselves and their environment, then the clues should be in Nash's small cluster of cottages in Bristol.

Blaise Hamlet is a place that makes me feel queasy, perhaps because of the multitude of perspectives and focal points, or perhaps because the whole village feels somehow out of scale, as though a series of twee miniatures has been suddenly expanded. The ornament manufacturer, Lilliput Lane, which specialises in hand-painted models, 'from chocolate box cottages to homes of the famous and buildings of historical importance' (as its website says), has a Blaise Hamlet collection. I'm guessing it's at the 'chocolate box' end of the range; indeed, Blaise Hamlet is the apotheosis of the 'chocolate box' aesthetic. For those wanting to buy into this, the cottages are reproduced in tiny detail, ready to sit on the mantelpiece and bring a touch of Nash's Picturesque into the ordinary home. Here in the 'real' village, I'm subject to the unsettling feeling of having been thrust into this Lilliput

world, neatly hand finished but entirely out of context and proportion.
The effect recalls some of the oddness of my impressions at Nenthead
when confronted with the miniature village; it raises questions, again,
about the 'model' village's relationship to ornament and reproduction.

On a fine but chilly spring afternoon, as I work my way from
cottage to cottage to take photographs, I am undisturbed in this quiet,
enclosed world; I can see nothing beyond the walls which surround
the village; I'm kept apart from things outside, my view proscribed
and bounded. There are only two other visitors, a retired couple
lingering to examine a shock of early pink roses. They do not seem
to share my unease. I'm struck by the delight on their faces; there's
an uncritical and unconditional suspension of disbelief as they peer
over largely unclipped hedges to admire hidden doorways and
sprawling gardens. They happily ignore the albeit discreet evidence
of twenty-first-century living – plastic composters, cases of Stella
Artois and bags of bird seed stashed in a porch, a supersize packet of
Doritos pushed up against a latticed kitchen window. But I don't know
what to make of the place. It's less twee in real life than in many of
the images I've seen; it feels a more organic part of the landscape. It's
prettier than I expected. But it's still unsettling.

There's no escaping the fact that Blaise Hamlet is an oddity. And
it's the distinctive strangeness of the village that makes its lasting influence more interesting and complex. Having finished his work there,
Nash went on to some of the most influential commissions of his
career. His friendship with the Prince Regent, a wealthy and adventurous client, guaranteed him work on landmark projects to redesign
London buildings and public spaces in a way considered more fitting
for the period. He put forward ideas for a new park and street – Regent's
Park and Regent's Street – firmly rooted in the Picturesque model. The
canal required for the park's water source, for example, was to be
transformed into a landscape feature while fifty-six villas were to
be scattered across the open land, each with distinctive architectural
detailing and offering a different view to each of its residents. In some
ways it was an attempt to recreate the village of Blaise Hamlet in an
urban setting, with long rows of houses and apartments defining the
edges of the park, keeping the city at bay from the Picturesque idyll
within. In an act of blatant favouritism on the part of the Prince Regent,
Nash was appointed Deputy Surveyor-General and Comptroller of the

Board of Works in 1813, on the sudden death of James Wyatt. Although the post was temporary, the appointment placed him in a direct line of professional succession with Inigo Jones, Sir Christopher Wren, John Vanbrugh and William Chambers.[10] In the same way, it gave something of an official status to Nash's interest in the Picturesque.

Nash continued to work on a number of distinctive designs including those for the Royal Pavilion at Brighton, the remodelling of Buckingham Palace and the creation of the Royal Mews and Marble Arch in the 1820s. But his association with a debauched social clique and the controversial nature of much of his work ensured that he was frequently the subject of criticism and ridicule in the popular press. As the executive of so many royal projects he became the symbol of a spendthrift fashion – and, worse still, a fashion built on the false and the insubstantial. Stucco, one of his favourite materials, is a render used to cover the facades of brick houses so that they can be made to look like stone. Nash used the technique extensively on the exterior of terraces in London and the resorts of the south coast of England as well as on villas in the fashionable spa towns of Malvern, Leamington Spa and Harrogate. A verse in the *Quarterly Review* in 1826 voiced a growing public feeling that there was something tawdry and perhaps underhand about such a method, built as it was on illusion and impermanence:

> Augustus at Rome was for building renown'd
> And of marble he left what of brick he had found;
> But is not our Nash, too, a very great master? –
> He finds us all brick and leaves us all plaster.[11]

Despite such contemporary doubts, however, Nash's adventurous approach to building, his grasp of the essentials of town planning, and his advocacy of the Picturesque aesthetic, continued to have lasting influence. It's difficult to overestimate the impact of the experiment at Blaise Hamlet on nineteenth-century architects and aristocratic clients desperate to make a mark on the landscape and on fashionable society. Within a few years, a string of villages had begun to emerge, replicating the fantasy environment created by Harford and Nash. Nor was this a brief moment of enthusiasm. The influence of the heavy thatch and high chimneys lingered, and by the 1830s and '40s – thanks in no small part to the example set at Blaise Hamlet – the 'rules' for constructing villages along Picturesque lines seemed clear: it was generally agreed that the key elements were what Uvedale Price had identified in 1794 as 'intricacy, variety and play of outline'. The con- venient vagueness of this definition, however, allowed for all kinds of responses. Some schemes aimed to achieve the proper Picturesque environment through the arrangement of the buildings themselves in the landscape, others by the addition of architectural decoration – anything from expressive eaves and porches to elaborate chimneys – still others by a combination of both approaches. Neither could natural ornament be overlooked. The careful choice of appropriate trees and shrubs to punctuate the village was usually considered an integral part of any scheme, as was the planting of climbing roses, jasmine and other creeping perennials to soften the hard lines and pristine stonework of the newly constructed cottages.

In the early 1850s, Sir Morton Peto, a railway magnate and Liberal MP for Norwich, created Somerleyton in the grounds of his estate near Lowestoft: twenty-eight thatched and half-timbered cottages arranged around a village green very much in the style of Blaise Hamlet. In 1857, Jesse Watts Russell took advantage of the site of his estate in Dovedale in the Peak District, to create Ilam, nestled along- side the River Manifold with the green slopes of Bunster Hill rising above. It was a spot which travellers had long lauded for its charms: the playwright William Congreve reputedly took advantage of a pretty grotto there to write his 1693 play *The Old Bachelor* and during a visit in 1774 Samuel Johnson noted that it was 'the fit abode for pastoral virtue'.[12] With such natural advantages it was a short step to creating a Picturesque village: a collection of Alpine-style cottages with steeply tiled roofs, dormer windows and large gardens; a small school with a romantic turret.

In the second half of the century, enthusiasm waned as newer fashions came to the fore, but, nonetheless, a taste for the Picturesque continued to be influential. In the 1860s, Baroness Angela Burdett- Coutts, one of the century's leading philanthropists, eschewed the practical housing she'd been developing for the poor in Bethnal Green to create Holly Village, in Highgate, on the other side of London. Planned with the help of the writer Charles Dickens and designed by Henry Astley Darbishire, the village is entered through an ornate arch,

The entrance to Arkwright's mill, Cromford.

(*Above*) The rear of the mill workers' cottages on North Street, Cromford, with the original 'weavers' windows' now blocked off.

(*Below*) The village square, Tremadog, with the Town Hall behind.

Nenthead village when the author lived there in 1992; the Methodist chapel is on the left with the reading room across the lane to the right and the current school on the hill above.

(*Above*) Italianate-style villa at Edensor.

(*Below*) A winter's evening at Edensor village with the Stand just visible on the hill beyond.

One of John Nash's nine Picturesque cottages at Blaise Hamlet.

Salt's Mill at Saltaire.

Terraces designed by Lockwood and Mawson, Saltaire.

guarded by idealised statues of Baroness Burdett-Coutts, clutching a
pet dog, and her long-time companion Hannah Brown, holding a dove.
Expensive materials are much in evidence – fine-quality teak and
Portland stone – as well as a range of decorative carved details,
including human heads and small animals. Although there is more
than a hint of mid-Victorian Gothic about the place, the village follows
the pattern established by Nash: seven cottages and a gateway cottage
grouped around a green and embellished with barge boards, crenel-
lations, pinnacles, dormers, sculptures and the ubiquitous creeping
foliage, a rural idyll within touching distance of the expanding capital.

In his survey of British architecture, Sir Nikolaus Pevsner suggests
that Blaise Hamlet 'comes off because it looks so sweetly sham'. The
phrase 'sweetly sham' seems absolutely right to me. It echoes in my
head as I circle the tall sundial on one side of the village green,
watching the cottages come into view one after the other. What
Pevsner has captured is the unsettling paradox of liking – and wanting
to like – this idyll while having to recognise its trickery and insubstan-
tiality. There's an unarguable sweetness to being here, with the sun
dipping behind the high wall to add a rosiness to the view of neat
rustic living in subdued English shades. Yet I can't help but be
astounded by the sheer falsehood of the place. In the wide expanse
of Picturesque landscapes, rather than villages, I've not felt the
impact of contrivance so strongly. The pathways and bridges Johnes
constructed at Hafod to emphasise the natural spectacle of streams
and waterfalls seem perfectly reasonable; the occasional rustic bridge
or mock packhorse crossing are welcome human-scale interludes in
a monotony of hills. Even the Cavern Cascade has as much natural
charm as it does touches of the theme-park experience. But here at
Blaise Hamlet, the houses leave a different impression. It's something
to do with the enclosure of the space, carefully sectioned off behind
its wall. But more than this, I think it's because this is a place where
people live; it's very much a collection of homes. It suggests intimacy
and domesticity and family. And for me, the overwhelming and inescapable impression given by Blaise Hamlet is of lives being manufactured and manipulated.

   What on earth would it have been like to live here, when the village
was new? I think a long time about this. There's no way of knowing,

of course, and it may seem rather a banal question. But I'm not wondering about cooking arrangements or drainage: I'm wondering about the challenge to identity such a place might pose, and the assumptions inherent in the construction of this kind of community. It seems to me that the cottages on view are only part of the story here; a kind of illustration to a text. But the text, unfortunately, is obscured – although not lost. It can, I hope, be pieced together by considering what Blaise Hamlet might actually be 'about'. This is a risky exercise, I know. Can a cottage be 'about' anything more than its specific construction of timber and brick and stone? We could argue about the answer to this for many months; theorists have debated similar issues for several lifetimes. But I'm going to be reckless and make an attempt to suggest that the cottages at Blaise Hamlet might mean something about the culture from which they sprang. I'm going to try to articulate what living here might have been 'about'.

At the beginning of the nineteenth century, the age of Victorian Empire was still in its infancy. It was a time of rapid social and tech-nological change, of innovation and ambition. But alongside develop-ments in science and technology, which began to challenge views on everything from the nature of humankind to the time taken to travel from London to Birmingham, there was an increasing taste for nostalgia. Historical ideals, traditions and objects became more and more popular and the apparently unstoppable march into the future was matched by a growing reverence for the past. Walter Scott's tales of rural adventure, for example – which tapped into a recognisable, if unreal, shared history – were delighting the reading public; his home at Abbotsford, created between 1812 and 1832, was a high-profile show-case for antiquarianism. The enthusiasm for the Picturesque was very much a part of this romantic attachment to an imagined past.

Interestingly, as the century progressed, the principles of the move-ment were more often expressed not in relation to the Picturesque in its own right but as a contrast to the demands of an increasingly industrialised environment. Discussing the value of randomly scat-tering cottages in the landscape in 1842, for example, the Scottish architect, garden designer and botanist John Claudius Loudon asserted: 'Cottages crowded together in a continued row have too much of the appearance, and have in fact, many of the inconveniences and nuisances, of a dirty back street in a country town.' Streets, in the conventional sense, he claimed, were to be avoided at all cost: 'There is not a greater error in forming artificial villages than always having one side of the buildings parallel with the road.'[13]

Loudon's dismissal of the 'dirty back street of a country town' is revealing. By the 1830s and '40s, the Picturesque village was not simply following rules established by writers such as Gilpin and Price, but was actively defining itself against the conventions of modern urban living and, by extension, the social and economic pressures which created them. Picturesque villages like Blaise Hamlet might be seen as ignoring the realities of the world around them, creating little havens of peace and prettiness completely separate from the imperatives of ordinary nineteenth-century lives. In fact, I would argue that the constant attempt to reject the Industrial Revolution, its architectural expression in the streets of growing manufacturing towns, and even, as Loudon suggests, the poverty and inadequacy of the country town, is intrinsically a political act, a tangible, highly visible and defiant manifesto which tapped into deep-seated fears of change and progress. By emphasising the possibility of a different way of presenting domestic housing, the exponents of Picturesque villages were at the same time bringing to public attention the deficiencies of the urban models they were rejecting. Faced with an appealing vista of clustered cottages tucked into the landscape, tourists to Blaise Hamlet or Ilam or Edensor were being encouraged to make comparisons with less attractive places; their visit was as much about driving home messages about what was not wanted – the dirty streets that Loudon had criticised, or close-knit rows of industrial terraces – as about celebrating the detailed decoration above a window or a charming slope of thatch.

The continual influence of the Picturesque style was very much part of this rejection of what was viewed as a brutal, unhealthy urban aesthetic; it clung to a yearning for the idealised settlement of the past, along with its apparently more wholesome values. It was not just about building houses, but more fundamentally about attempting to recreate a lost spirit of community and rediscover the unidentified virtues associated with the homely rural village. The dismissal of practical urban layouts in favour of a romantic return to a more primitive and haphazard ground plan was, in turn, supposed to suggest a rejection of the urban industrial lifestyle and a recapturing of a time of peaceful, innocent and carefree living. Since Burke's influential treatise in 1757, there had been a tradition of associating aesthetic beauty with moral virtue and theological goodness. In writing and discussions about the Picturesque, this tradition was continued. Architectural decisions were repeatedly identified with moral principles; evidence of cleanliness and purity – both physical and moral – was frequently raised as evidence of sound building technique. Peter Frederick Robinson's Picturesque manifesto, *Village Architecture* of 1830, for example, was clear that almshouses should be constructed with concealed doorways in order to 'avoid the appearance of any uncleanly habits'. He presumably had in mind both glimpses of unwashed linen and the dangers of idle doorstep gossip.

With plenty of similarly unwholesome pitfalls to trap the unwary, there was a steady growth in the publication of pamphlets, treatises and pattern books to help navigate the most Picturesque way to a simpler, cleaner and prettier age. Those wishing to build a village were never without advice to help them unravel the nuances of the fashion. Such pattern books first emerged in the late 1770s: Nathaniel Kent's *Hints to Gentlemen of Landed Property* (1775) debated everything from the relative merits of natural and artificial grasses to the varying methods of cultivating hops and turnips. In the midst of discussion about different rental structures it also touched upon the ideal nature of estate cottages which might be 'appropriated to the use of labourers of the most industrious disposition'.[14] By the early years of the nineteenth century there was a flood of similar publications, usually discussing the latest refinements of style while offering a cursory nod to practical matters such as proper drainage. John Wood, the son of John Wood the Elder who was responsible for designing many of the Regency streets and buildings in Bath, entered the fray in 1806 with *A Series of Plans for the Cottages or Habitations of the Labourer* which offered landowners a range of designs from which to choose. A couple of decades later, in his *Essay on the Construction of Cottages Suited for the Dwellings of the Labouring Classes*, the Scottish architect George Smith began to explore more practical issues, including the advantages of semi-detached cottages: 'This species of cottage can be built cheaper than two single ones,' he claimed, 'and, in general, these double cottages are found to be warmer and fully as comfortable as single ones.'[15]

The fashion for poring over village details and comparing building design was by no means a purely British one. Across the Channel, innovative architects were also toying with the concept of the Picturesque village. In the early 1800s, the brothers François and Pierre Caccault reconstructed the village of Clisson in western France, modelling it on an ideal of Tuscan architecture. By the mid-nineteenth century a new pattern of suburban villages was beginning to emerge around Paris: le Vésinet was laid out as an integrated villa suburb in 1848, capitalising on the arrival of new railway links; on an even larger scale, the suburb of Levallois-Perret was developed from 1845 in a simple grid of streets which became an independent commune in 1866. Beyond Europe, too, the influence of the Picturesque was making itself felt. In the United States, one of the most celebrated publications was *Cottage Residences* (1842) written by Andrew Jackson Downing, landscape designer and horticulturist, and a friend and admirer of J. C. Loudon. The book was widely read and Downing's ideas copied over the following decades. Both the philosophies and practicalities of the European Picturesque were quickly adapted to the larger American landscapes and open spaces – and to the growing middle-class demand for exclusive, private estates.

The British taste for pattern books, however, appeared insatiable. It was not just those with direct responsibility for providing estate housing who snapped up volumes on Picturesque architecture. The books made popular reading; they were advertised in all the most influential newspapers and seen in all the most fashionable parlours. Many publications soon ran into several editions. With such a wide readership, architects and commentators were acutely aware of the intensity of public scrutiny, but inevitably many of them struggled to make their mark in the congested marketplace. As a result, they began to propose more and more outlandish ideas in the hope of attracting attention. As the years went by, the proposed designs became increasingly derivative, florid and impractical.

Perhaps the most ambitious of a series of ambitious projects was proposed by Peter Frederick Robinson in his *Village Architecture*, published in 1830 as a supplement to a pattern book of cottages called *Rural Architecture*. This was a source of authoritative advice to the 'scenic draughtsman' on everything from the 'old English character' of the ideal parsonage to, as we've seen, the 'uncleanly habits' unfortunately associated with almshouses. Described as 'Being a Series of Picturesque Designs for the Inn, the Schoolhouse, Almshouses, Markethouse, Shambles, Workhouse, Parsonage, Townhall and Church', the book included not only a wealth of adventurous individual drawings for these buildings but went as far as including a plate for a complete main street, 'a village street of ancient architecture', assembled by yoking together an unlikely variety of historical designs to create a fantasy idyll of rising and falling roof lines, unexpected perspectives and unspecific European quaintness.

The village at Edensor, constructed with the Duke of Devonshire's almost unparalleled wealth, is the only realised example which comes close to Robinson's eccentric vision. For most landowners such suggestions were simply too expensive to consider. Nonetheless, pattern books offered plenty of advice for those on more restricted means, often eschewing the difficulties of building new housing altogether in favour of proposing ingenious ways to add Picturesque decoration to existing cottages. In this way, fashion-conscious landowners could give the impression of following the latest trends at minimal cost and upheaval, grafting architectural flourishes on to steadfastly cheap and practical cottages. For those tempted to indulge a little further, many of the pattern books suggested adding one or two new residences built entirely in the Picturesque style, slipping them in amongst the older buildings to trick the eye into perceiving the entire village as à la mode.

This dilettante kind of Picturesque was adopted at Harlaxton in Lincolnshire by George de Ligne Gregory, who was, according to his contemporaries, 'a gentleman of about £12,000 a year' – a relatively modest amount. Despite his restricted income, Gregory was spending vast sums rebuilding fourteenth-century Harlaxton Manor in an extravagant Elizabethan style and filling its interior with 'objects of curiosity, useful or ornamental'. He had little money left to spend on the village. In an attempt to make the most of his funds, he took the original wattle-and-daub cottage buildings and re-faced them in red brick, adding embellished stonework here and there for extra effect: rounded pillars, overstated porches and verandahs. When Loudon visited in May 1840, he was delighted with the effect created by this architectural sleight of hand. He suggested that the improvements – even though they were almost entirely superficial – would both please the eye of the visitor and, more ambitiously, raise the spirits and elevate the morals of the fortunate inhabitant, transforming him into 'a reading and thinking being'.

Loudon's suggestion – that the prettification of Harlaxton might lead to the improvement of the villagers in other, more personal, ways – demonstrates how the preoccupation with people as well as their homes had grown by the 1830s and '40s into a fundamental element of the Picturesque village ideal. In order to create a coherent community which drew on a simple, nostalgic and rural approach to life, it was essential for estate owners to integrate their workers into the schemes for their cottages. Villagers clustered on the green or going about their business in colourful costume often provided the finishing touch to the pastoral idyll.

Price's 1794 essay had told his readers that the 'picturesque' in humans was 'to be found among the wandering tribes of gypsies and beggars; who in all the qualities which give them that character, bear close analogy to the wild forester and the worn out cart-horse, and again to old mills, hovels and other inanimate objects of the same kind'.[16] His comparison of the poor with inanimate objects such as 'hovels' and useless animals like 'the worn out cart-horse' might unsettle modern readers but his choice of description sheds a great deal of light on contemporary attitudes. Just as buildings could be manipulated to add appropriate colour and decoration to chosen corners of the estate, so too could the lower orders of humanity be called into service to add the final touches to the overall picture. These people, Price implied, had as little say in the matter as any of the ruins being rebuilt and reconfigured to improve the views.

The prospect of a human element to the scene apparently proved too charming to resist and the notion of incorporating villagers into the landscape quickly became popular. Human figures came to be seen as critical to the cheerful and industrious impression landowners were attempting to capture. One commentator proposed an innovative alternative to the ugly necessity of providing livestock fencing, for example: 'Instead of a fence, the children of some poor but worthy cottagers, prettily disguised as shepherds, might be employed to keep the sheep from straying,' he suggested. Loudon, too, was on hand to offer advice. He recommended 'always' including provision for 'children playing and villagers passing to and fro, to contribute to the rural effect of the scene'.[17]

When I read about this fashion for disguising cottagers' children and old retainers in attractive costume and setting them to perform for passers-by, I immediately think of another burgeoning activity of the early nineteenth century: the popular theatre. Edensor and Blaise Hamlet are in many ways perfect pieces of theatrical scenery, offering elaborate backdrops against which villagers can be seen to live out their lives. The nineteenth century was, of course, a century of spectacle. It would, in time, see some of the most elaborate displays ever staged: the Great Exhibition of 1851 in the glittering Crystal Palace and, a few years later, the 1857 Manchester Art Treasures Exhibition. People would become entranced by illusion and sleight of hand, flocking to the Egyptian Hall in Piccadilly to see the 'magic' created by a series of trapdoors and special effects. By the middle of the century, the seance was to become one of the most popular forms of private entertainment, intriguing the respectable middle classes with spirit mediums and Ouija boards. It seems to me that the Picturesque village is another part of this visually stimulating, visually deceptive world. Illusion and dissembling, escape and fantasy, entertainment and display were equally visible on the stage and around the village green.

At the same time as the Bachelor Duke and Joseph Paxton were constructing Edensor, the popular theatre was experiencing a boom. Restrictions put in place by the Licensing Act of 1737 meant that at the beginning of the nineteenth century 'proper' plays were officially only allowed to be shown at two London venues, Drury Lane Theatre and Covent Garden, known as patent theatres. But there were plenty of ways of escaping these restrictions, and other theatres began to create increasingly intricate and colourful concoctions, interspersing dramatic scenes with musical interludes and burlesque. Audiences loved these new theatrical extravaganzas. Melodrama was particularly popular, with its presentation of short scenes, rousing music, over-blown acting and simple morality. The Licensing Act was not discarded until 1843; in the meantime, demand for theatre became so great that the system of patent theatre simply became unworkable – theatres sprang up all over London challenging the rules, blurring the bound-aries between legitimate and illegitimate theatre and pandering to the apparently insatiable public taste for spectacle.

The early-nineteenth-century theatre was a pictorial affair. Increasing care was taken to create staging effects which emulated paintings, and painstaking research was done to ensure accuracy for historical settings. More and more, audiences expected a great deal to be achieved on stage, not just by actors, musicians and dancers, but by clever scenery, good lighting and spectacular effects. One popular device was the panorama, or diorama, which was unrolled from one side of the stage and rolled up on the other, so creating a moving landscape that was used to depict a journey, or a change of setting. Another innovation was the backlit scene: painted on to linen or muslin, these scenes were lit from the front to give one impression – perhaps of an external wall or a building entrance – and then lit from behind to give another picture entirely, perhaps the vision of lovers kissing or a terrible murder.

Realistic visual detail was increasingly valued. Scenes and settings were developed with meticulous care to convince a demanding audience. As early as 1804, the Court Theatre in Mannheim, Germany, experimented with joining several pairs of wings with doors and windows to create an environment which captured the detail of a domestic interior. This became known as the box set, and the fashion soon spread across Europe. By November 1832, one London critic was enthusiastic in his admiration for a production which made full use of the box set: 'The stage's more perfect enclosure fits the appearance of a private chamber infinitely better than the old contrivance of wings,' he wrote.[18] By the 1840s, productions at Covent Garden could boast a series of heavily ornamented and realistic room settings stuffed with actual furnishings and correct down to the detail of the door-knobs.

Acting, too – particularly in the early decades of the century – was closely connected to the pictorial. One of the traditions inherited from the eighteenth century was the notion that the body and voice of the actor had to be consciously beautiful. This sat well with the importance of the stage picture: the beauty of the scenery, the increasing emphasis on light and colour. The actor was to make himself a work of art, looking to ancient manuals and statuary in order to develop graceful attitudes. Even the most overwhelming of passions were made visual through a series of universally understood gestures and facial expressions: jealousy, anger or fear, for example, were suggested

by an acting 'picture' that audiences could easily recognise and interpret.

It seems to me that this preoccupation with picture-making in the
theatre, with illusion and spectacle, is part of the same impulse which
drove landowners to construct pretty villages and people them with
attractive occupants. The Picturesque village was about providing and
managing a scene, so that visitors – the audience – could understand
what they were seeing and enjoy the entertainment of it. It privileged
the visual over everything else, over social purpose or practical efficacy
or political statement. The landowners and architects who conceived
and built these places were, like theatrical companies, taking the
principles of the painter and infusing them with life, activity and
immediacy.

Back to Edensor

The houses at Edensor are not small creeper-covered cottages. They
are not modest shelters for wizened old retainers. They are substantially larger than any home I might afford in the area; more grandiose,
I suspect, than the properties in which many of us might reasonably
aspire to live. They are built to a good size in quality materials; there's
no skimping on the floor plans. There's something languid about the
relaxed way in which the houses are placed apart, each with an extensive garden. Rolling green banks – large enough to graze livestock –
separate one neighbour from the next; even the verges are expressively
wide.

The intricacy and sheer delight of the detail and decoration also
act as a constant reminder that this is a whimsical, lavish experiment
conceived as a showcase of wealth and status as much as a pragmatic
housing project. Even with the most ambitious of planning regulations,
modern buildings tend to impose the simple and regular; frivolous
architectural features are constrained by cost as much as taste. We're
accustomed to think of housing estates as expressions of conformity,
plainness and practicality. But here at Edensor, the emphasis is on
ornament and difference and extravagance. Windows come in all
shapes and sizes, from the mullioned bay to the Georgian sash. There
are dressed and carved stone lintels and sills; decorative niches, arches

and date stones. Wooden gables are sculpted; fences and porches are trellised and pinnacled. Iron railings, garden walls and gateways are designed with care, cradling the changing levels of the land, topped with an assortment of balls and turrets and pediments.

Modern residents, too, seem determined to maintain the individuality of their environment. Here and there house names have been given – I notice that all the signs are hand-painted, makeshift efforts on slices of untreated wood, a slate leaned against a gatepost. There's a quaint little table with a roof – rather like a large bird table – set up on the verge outside a rather grand house that has the air of a substantial parsonage or an Oxbridge college: a piece of coloured paper discreetly advertises home-made fudge. Just inside the entrance to the churchyard, as the path leads up towards the gravestones, there's a small wooden notice imploring visitors to leave 'fresh flowers only please'. It seems to me that the principles of the Picturesque are still being resolutely upheld here. The little signs and hand-made touches – the aversion to the modern detritus of municipal cemeteries – demonstrate the lingering power of the ideal from which the village (in its present form) sprang. Today's residents, it seems to me, are anxious to emphasise the enduring romance of this place, to continue to differentiate it from the ubiquity of the contemporary housing estate and to enforce its difference.

There's a view at Edensor that particularly interests me. It's not looking into the village from the roadway, or even looking up one of the streets. It's the view you see when you stand at the top of the village and look out, back in the direction of Chatsworth House. You can see down through the cluster of buildings, over the rooftops of the cottages around the green, the too-big church spire of St Peter's on your right. Beyond is a brief sweep of the park, then a wooded escarpment rising 400 feet and, absolutely in the centre of the view, poking up on the horizon, a small, odd-shaped tower with a grey roof and a prominent flagpole.

This is the Hunting Tower, or the Stand, a confection of windows and round turrets, topped with a dome. Built around 1582 for Bess of Hardwick, grandmother of the 1st Duke, it's older than the existing stately home. No one seems to know its original purpose: it may have been for banqueting or summer entertaining; it may have been used by ladies to watch the hounds hunting in the park below. It has a vague apocryphal connection with Mary Queen of Scots who was imprisoned at Chatsworth for a while. More recently, it's been lived in by estate staff and members of the Duke's family and is now let out as a holiday home. Apart from cottages that are part of the village itself, it's the only building you can see from Edensor. There's no view of Chatsworth House, which is obscured by the lie of the land. The stables and farm buildings, too, are hidden. What the attention is drawn to is this odd little folly puncturing the horizon.

Horizons make us lift our eyes and gaze out. They lure us. They seem to suggest possibility. Because they encourage us to move beyond what is visible and into a world of imagination, they've long been a popular subject for artists. A mark on the horizon – the Hunting Tower – is clearly differentiated from its surroundings, drawing the eye to a definite point in a larger view. When I'm standing enclosed by the Picturesque vision of Edensor, the 6th Duke and Paxton draw my attention not just to the buildings around me but to this mark beyond, old and ornate, enticing me from where I am. Knowing Paxton's reputation for remarkable attention to detail, I cannot think this is accidental: the village was designed this way, with the Hunting Tower framed so neatly by the placing of the buildings and the fall of the land. And so, as was no doubt intended, I stand for a while and look out, and I think about the view of this odd little tower.

It's partly a means of providing another attractive vista, of course, another folly to delight and entertain, a talking point. The Hunting Tower has been drawn into the Picturesque experiment here, creating a painterly backdrop to the village and further blurring the distinction between the old and the new, the village and the park, the built and the natural. It's another scene in the theatrical presentation of the estate. But the more I look at it, the more I'm struck by the complexities inherent in the apparently simple act of constructing such a view; I wonder just what's going on as the eye is drawn from the near to the distant and back again. Standing on a green bank in the darkening quiet, is this exchange between me and a point beyond me a significant part of my experience here at Edensor? Why does it seem to matter?

To begin to answer these questions, I need to think again about the period when Edensor was built. The 1820s and '30s were, of course, decades of change and development. Many ordinary lives were still rooted in traditional habits – the rhythms of rural life would probably have appeared unchanged for centuries to all but the keenest observer – but such apparently ageless tranquillity could not conceal the dynamic changes which were taking place in the towns and cities, in technological, scientific and medical knowledge, in social and political organisation. Such changes meant a significant shift in the way in which the world – personal and public – was presented, managed and understood. Many of these changes would be expressed over the years in the physical evidence of the model village, but of specific relevance to my present preoccupation with the Hunting Tower is a particular conundrum which exercised both the specialist and the popular mind more than ever during this period: how does sight work, what is it that we actually see, and how can we best understand the surprisingly slippery act of vision?

In the early decades of the nineteenth century, a new generation of scientists and commentators was debating the intricacies of the eye. Their work was challenging long-held opinions about the nature of vision; the discussion which emerged began to explore the relationship between the physical act of seeing and the subtle ways in which we perceive and interpret the visible world. This was a time when theoretical – even philosophical – principles of vision were being developed in conjunction with a technical evolution in optical and photographic equipment; when the understanding of what it means to look at something was being revolutionised. The Victorians were fascinated by the intricacies of sight and by the ways in which they might understand what they saw. They began to ask complex questions. How reliable was the human eye? What relationship did it have to the 'mind's eye' of imagination? Was one type of seeing more important than another?

These inquiries, and the debate around them, didn't emerge from nowhere. Observing the natural world, interpreting works of art, viewing gardens and landscapes – these activities were already recognised as complex acts of spectatorship that oscillated backwards and forwards between the subjective and the objective, often blurring the distinction between the two. One of the legacies of the eighteenth-century Romantic movement was a growing interest in the personal nature of sight, and the ways in which memory and experience

influence what we see. Romantic poets and thinkers had begun to
explore notions of infinity; they were interested in the difference
between 'real' vision and the more intense vision of the dreamlike
state. Poems of the period often featured motifs about sight or imagery
inspired by the various effects of light. Take a seminal poem such as
Wordsworth's 'Ode: Intimations on Immortality', published in 1807.
It opens with lines which bring together the natural world, the celes-
tial and the dream with language which focuses on visual effect:

> There was a time when meadow, grove, and stream,
>   The earth, and every common sight,
>   To me did seem
>   Apparell'd in celestial light,
> The glory and the freshness of a dream.

It closes by drawing directly on the eye as a metaphor for the setting
sun, and hence in turn some kind of watchful deity:

> The innocent brightness of a new-born Day
>   Is lovely yet;
> The clouds that gather round the setting sun
> Do take a sober colouring from an eye
> That hath kept watch o'er man's mortality . . .

The poem is just one example of a widespread fascination with the
boundaries between the inner and the outer self – and how our experience of vision might reveal or express these margins. In the early
decades of the nineteenth century, poets, writers, painters and thinkers
were exploring the links between the topographical, emotional and
psychological landscape and expressing their ideas in increasingly visual
terms.

   But this was not just a process of looking back to the late eighteenth
century. It was also about looking forward, examining new ways of
creating images and new ways of interpreting them. At the period when
Paxton and the Bachelor Duke were creating Edensor – during the 1820s
and '30s – other experiments were altering the way in which the public
began to view things. This was the time when J. M. W. Turner was
moving from traditional landscape studies towards the much more

subjective, imaginative style which impressed and disturbed contemporaries, and which we tend to associate with him today. It was the moment when the world's first permanent photograph was produced in France using pewter plates in a camera obscura, altering perceptions of the image and opening the way for new approaches to recording people and places, to scrutinising detail and to photographic art. Modern archaeology was uncovering buried sites for the public eye and, more importantly, examining them in an orderly, detailed way; Jean-François Champollion's investigation of the Rosetta Stone led to the first published translation of its ancient Egyptian hieroglyphics in 1822. The rage for tours and visits was encouraging more and more people to embrace the adventure of travel and see for themselves a variety of landscapes and viewpoints.

Medical knowledge, too, was moving quickly. Debate about the eye during the seventeenth and eighteenth centuries had been based on simple apparatus, often designed to intrigue and entertain – peep shows, magic lanterns, the Claude glass, viewing boxes. Even as late as 1800, there was little consensus about how the eye actually worked. The fact that each of our eyes sees slightly differently, for example, was widely recognised but it was not understood and was regarded as little more than a curiosity. Although elementary aspects of the mechanics of vision were known to eye specialists in ancient Babylonia, Mesopotamia and Egypt – and Aristotle had been fascinated by many features of perception – only the most basic of research had been attempted on the problem since the work of Claudius Galen in the second century; a number of popular theories were in circulation, including one that proposed that we only ever saw with one eye at a time. By the 1820s, however, there was a widespread desire for more accurate and detailed information, both in Britain and abroad. In 1823 the Scottish anatomist Charles Bell performed a number of experiments to examine the problems of conjoint vision and the consequences of voluntary and involuntary eye movement; in Berlin, Johannes Müller published two books in 1826 in which he gave detailed descriptions of eye movements; the New York Eye and Ear Infirmary was founded in 1820 to create an environment for anatomical study.

At the same time as such inquiries were gathering pace, there was a growing enthusiasm for more complex optical equipment to support and develop the advances in anatomy. Especially popular was the

stereoscope: an instrument which brings together the left-eye and
right-eye views into a single three-dimensional image, usually making
the image larger and enhancing the illusion of depth. The aim of the
stereoscope was to make the picture as lifelike as possible. The German
physicist Hermann von Helmholtz explained:

> These stereoscopic photographs are so true to nature and so lifelike
> in their portrayal of material things, that after viewing such a picture
> and recognizing in it some object like a house, for instance, we get the
> impression, when we do see the object, that we have already seen it
> before and are more or less familiar with it.[19]

While emerging photographic techniques largely preserved conventional perspectives and seemed to continue a tradition of pictorial
codes, the stereoscope eradicated the classical 'point of view' which
had been important, for centuries, to artists and observers, and so
offered a radical way of looking at things. It focused on detail, on a
single view – and attempted to make the picture tangible. (Indeed,
the rather disturbing physicality of the effect meant that in time
stereoscopes became popular for showing erotic and pornographic
imagery.) At the same time, it was quite obvious, of course, that the
thing made tangible, the 'real' object – the three-dimensional house,
for example – was a manufactured experience, dependent on a clever
manipulation of images and created by the interaction of the viewer
with a machine. Suddenly sight was confused and confusing. Things
and pictures of things were becoming conflated. Viewpoint was everything.

Such unsettling advances – such challenges to the old ways of
looking at things – emphasised the deceptive quality of vision and
provoked a rethinking of the nature of reality. The simple view had
become more complex. As the understanding of the eye and its functions developed, so too did a series of tricky questions which began
to address difficult ideas, both physical and metaphysical. How could
you be sure what was real and what was an illusion? What about the
slippery border between the two which was beginning to be disputed
by new techniques like photography? Perhaps most importantly, where
was the 'meaning' of a view located – was it intrinsic to the image
itself, or was it in the eye of the beholder? The fascination with the

practices of seeing was thus part of a wider questioning of the place and role of the individual. As optical knowledge developed, it was becoming clear that understanding the visual – or attempting to understand it – was also about understanding the self, and one's place in the world.

All of which brings me back to the Hunting Tower at Chatsworth. I think its location at the edge – yet, paradoxically, at the focal point – of Edensor is significant. I think it plays with ideas of space, with our perception of where we are, situating us both within the confines of this constructed idyll and outside of it. It makes us aware of our place in the landscape, and our smallness. This, of course, emphasises the size of the estate, and hence the power and scope of the Duke who owns it. But I think it's about more than a question of topography and feudal relationships. The Romantic ideal liked to conjure a sense of the diminutive human in front of the vastness and glory of the sublime; it questioned the human place in the landscape and our momentary personal appearance in a long continuum of time and tradition. I think the view of the Hunting Tower is intended to raise similar ideas; I think it is there to make sure we look out from Edensor and don't become too caught up in the small pleasures of architectural detail. I think it's part of the larger question raised by the village about the nature of what we see, about illusion and reality.

The architectural historian David Watkin claims that, for a century from 1730, the enormous influence of 'poets, painters, travellers, gardeners, architects, connoisseurs and dilettanti' ensured that 'the Picturesque became the universal mode of vision for the educated classes'.[20] It was only one way of seeing things, but because it was a way championed by the influential, the fashionable and the innovative it became the most accepted and authoritative way, it became 'universal'. As I stroll from one end of the village and back again, taking photographs and wondering about the quality of the fudge, the confidence in this universal mode of vision seems striking, even now. Edensor is a place of ambition, of course; it's also a place which asserts ownership. The matching Chatsworth blue paintwork identifies every building and feature with the family, the house and the estate of the social ruling class. The unity of the Picturesque aesthetic – despite the eclecticism of the architectural styles – grounds the village in the single, authoritative vision of the 'artistic' ruling class of poets and painters and travellers that Watkin has identified.

Model villages express the power of their owners in different ways. When an early settlement is razed to the ground to cleanse the landscape and to be replaced with something prettier, this is an expression of the absolute command of the landowner. When the poor and impotent are taken from their homes, or have their homes reconfigured about them, it is an expression of wealth and status and influence. In the following chapter, I'll explore Saltaire, a village that evidences the power of Victorian manufacturing and which is perhaps the most celebrated example of the complicated mid-nineteenth-century taste for autocracy and philanthropy. At Edensor, I would argue that authority is expressed in the way sight is manipulated; in the way we, as visitors, are presented with a determined view. By imposing a 'universal mode of vision' the Picturesque was also, of course, attempting to impose on the viewer the values and ideals of those who manufactured the view. Paxton and the Bachelor Duke seem to me to have been expert at manipulating what we see here, from the minutiae of architectural detail to the distant vista of the Hunting Tower. This is a place that displays personal taste with confidence; that compels us to engage with a particular fashionable outlook of the early nineteenth century. Any Picturesque village is, by nature, visually appealing, a masterpiece in scene setting. It entertains and deceives, exploiting techniques of illusion and spectacle. In conception and expression, Edensor is perhaps the most playful of the Picturesque villages, and playfulness, as we all know, is only possible from a position of power.

4

Saltaire, West Yorkshire

Bradford looks distinctly mid-Victorian. Descending towards the city from the surrounding moors there's a low mist, a persistent grey drizzle which darkens the sky and the stones. A new chimney, a sleek metal one, pumps out what might be mistaken for genuine nineteenth-century smog; a blanket of smoke hangs over the rooftops and leeches into the gaps between. The city must look very much as it did for travellers arriving on the steam train from London in the 1860s. It has the air of a film set, the sepia quality of an old photograph.

I hadn't remembered Bradford clearly. I hadn't remembered the yellow tones of the brick, which come as a surprise, or how very dominant the mills still are, their chimneys rising all around like determined blades of spring grass. It's an imposing place, a bold, defiant, robust place; it feels purposeful and confident, even now when its purpose is ambiguous and its confidence might be misplaced. It feels – and I reflect a long time before I concede that this is the apt word – masculine.

But I'm not here for Bradford. I follow the signs around the city centre and head north by a few miles to Saltaire. This is what I've come to see, of course: a beautifully preserved, 1850s village established for workers at the nearby Salt's Mill. How can I write a book about model villages and not discuss Saltaire? But its iconic presence as a mid-Victorian showpiece, an apparent expression of all that was best about nineteenth-century paternalism and foresight, is rather intimidating; I'm not sure where to start. I've been here before, several times – an art gallery has taken over some of the spaces where the looms once worked and there are shops and restaurants – but still it strikes me as a difficult place to know: its big, solid, confident architecture defies you to question it, to doubt or debate it. It's like the most respectable of Victorian gentlemen, commanding, slightly bullish and impeccably presented, any faults or idiosyncrasies efficiently concealed. As I make my way past the tall stand-alone chimney, with gun-slit openings and disturbingly extensive cracks in the brickwork, I wonder whether it will be possible to see beyond the village's undoubted aura of assurance and self-possession.

In 1801, the population of Bradford was 13,000. Half a century later, the 1851 census recorded a population of 103,000. Based on the textile trade, the city's growth had been rapid and formidable; it had quickly become a place of industrial prosperity and commercial ambition, of poverty, exploitation and slums: working conditions were so poor that life expectancy was between eighteen and twenty years.

Titus Salt was a man who had seen Bradford grow. Born in 1803 in Morley, near Leeds, by 1824 he had become a junior partner in his father's wool-stapling firm, Daniel Salt & Son. In the early 1830s he became interested in the use of alpaca hair spun with cotton or silk to produce a durable, lightweight worsted and the success of the experiment meant that business thrived – by the middle of the century Salt had five separate mills and had become the largest employer in Bradford. Elected mayor in 1848, he tried a variety of inventive methods to improve conditions in the city: he employed the Rodda's Patent Smoke Burning and Fuel Saving Apparatus, for example, in an attempt to reduce pollution. But the Bradford smog was not so easily defeated and in around 1850 he decided to uproot his entire business to a cleaner, more sanitary environment, buying land three miles from Shipley, in a moorland cradle served by major communication links: the River Aire, the Leeds and Liverpool Canal and the Midland Railway. He employed local architects, Henry Lockwood and Richard Mawson, and on 20 September 1853, Salt's fiftieth birthday, the new mill was declared open. Producing eighteen miles of worsted cloth a day on 1,200 looms tended by 3,000 workers, it was the biggest factory in the world, an expression of intrepid industrialisation and faith in a prosperous future.

Salt's full motives for moving out of Bradford are not entirely clear. Much has been written about Saltaire – it attracted enormous attention when it first opened in 1853 and has continued to do so ever since – but Salt himself tended to be diffident about his role and he never wrote about his ambitions; we can only speculate about his intentions. It was true that the new site enabled him to consolidate all his business in one place, which made economic sense; it also provided a striking visual statement of wealth and power to match any in Victorian Britain. But Salt clearly intended something more. As a deeply religious man, his attempt to create a healthy environment for his workers was apparently grounded in humanitarian concern and a genuine desire to find ways to improve the lot of ordinary families. The decision to move into the countryside was a question not just of expediency but also of philanthropy; it was not simply about the mill but also about the village built around it and the entire community it sustained. As with Robert Owen at New Lanark, however – and most other village founders – questions of expediency and philanthropy are difficult to unravel; impulses are often murky and intentions ambiguous.

I can't help but begin with the mill. It is enormous and contradictory: grandiose certainly, but with architectural restraint; overbearing yet oddly inviting; inhuman in its scale and symmetry, but dependent on activity, noise, and, above all, people. It has unmistakable dramatic presence. Walking in its cobbled yards I'm immediately reminded of my own insignificance, my smallness in time and space. It rises pale and stately like the most impressive of palaces; close up it wraps, maze-like, around me. It is both the most straightforward of constructions – a series of straight lines and repetitions – and the most complicated of buildings, seducing me with moments of unexpected perspectives and displacing me with its suggestive Italianate demeanour. When I stand overlooking the canal which cuts between Salt's Mill and the adjacent New Mill (built for Titus Salt by Lockwood and Mawson in 1868) I feel suddenly as though I might be in Venice. It's a bizarre illusion, partly evoked by the high close walls alongside the canal, the small, low bridge in the distance and the ornate chimney visible beyond which is modelled on the church of Santa Maria Gloriosa dei Frari in Venice, but partly also evinced by a less physical sense of place – a spirit, if you like – an implicit vitality and mood.

I spend a long time exploring the mill as best I can now that it has been divided up and portioned out to twenty-first-century businesses. There are few quirks. The building is organised and orderly. It's the scale of the place which leaves an impression, the sheer size of the now unfilled spaces, the yards and stairwells and vast floors where the looms worked. The Spinning Room, for example, is much as it was when spinning stopped here in the 1970s. Known as 'the Lobby' it is a light, cold space 168 metres long; when it was built in 1853 it was a thing to marvel at, the longest room in the world, a fearsome place in which to work. Today all the machinery has been removed and there are just odd bits and pieces protruding from the walls, hooks and bars hanging from the ceiling, fading layers of old paintwork and – am I imagining this? – the smell of lanolin.

Stepping away from the factory, I climb a short flight of narrow steps on to the railway bridge. A train rumbles by on the track beneath – Saltaire is still a working station on the Airedale line connecting Bradford, Leeds and Skipton – and from here the autumnal tones of the mill brick blend harmoniously with the leaves just beginning to turn yellow on the trees. There's a row of allotments alongside the railway line, dug-over plots, fruit trees and glasshouses, tidy and crowded, well loved. They were part of the original plan for Saltaire, a means of dividing the noisy, dirty work of the mill from the cleaner domestic streets and a way of providing food; they clearly continue to flourish. Turning opposite these, I make my way into the village. I'm following the official trail as marked on the leaflet handed out by the tourist office; I'm not sure why – something about the place encourages conformity – but it does give a sense of approved purpose, even pilgrimage, to my wanderings.

The cottages knit neatly together in a grid of terraces, like a good weave – the intention was to use the land efficiently to house as many workers as possible. They draw me up the slope, each terrace leading tantalisingly into another, always offering the promise of something new. I begin to veer from the walk marked by pink arrows on my map. These streets are lived in: they're packed with parked cars and 'For Sale' signs; the small gardens bloom with roses and hydrangeas. When I pause to take photos I feel slightly self-conscious. But it's worth pausing. When I look closely, I notice some unusual features about the terraces, and I realise that they are not all the same. In some, three-storey houses rise in the middle and at the ends, like hardbacks in a row of slighter paperbacks. It gives the impression of a battlement or a rampart, although there was no military intention: the larger buildings were simply designed to provide lodgings for single workers; the smart cottages between, with arched ground-floor windows and front gardens, were the spacious homes of 'overlookers', the foremen who ran the factory floor. It's a repetition of the motif of scrutiny so evident at New Lanark – encapsulated here in the designation of 'overlooker' – but the foremen's watchfulness extended even beyond the factory floor: they could now, from their homes too, keep an eye on the antics of potentially disruptive singletons. Their cottages hem in the lodging houses, physically buttressing them, keeping them upright in all senses.

Other streets are less elegant. Here, there are no gardens; the cottages are plainer, smaller, with regular square windows. But even so, there are some nice touches: the natural slope of the site, for example, means that on several streets, houses on the top side have two solid steps down from the front door to the pavement; on the lower side, the front doors are level with the street. There's no status implied here – it's simply a demand of the landscape – but there might have been: the village is graded throughout, manipulated to reveal and consolidate rank. At the very edge, with what would have been views over open country, there is a row of handsome semi-detached villas, spacious and airy; the smallest, most cramped cottages are in the central terraces, with views only of each other.

At the end of almost every street, there's a shop building, a genuine corner shop with a large ground-floor display window. These are mostly boarded up now; they are the only buildings in Saltaire not in use. As the area around Titus Salt's original village grew more and more urbanised, these shops became increasingly redundant. Commerce here, like elsewhere, has regrouped, becoming detached from its original intimate relationship with the home. Saltaire village is now just a tiny network of streets within the huge West Yorkshire conurbation; it's less than five minutes' walk from here to the main Bingley Road, lined with high-street names and independents, chemists and butchers and cup-cake emporiums. But the old shops still retain the whisper of their former glories: the stonework of their frontages is painted in bright colours, blues and pinks, faded now and peeling; the original owners' names can just be made out, stencilled on to the walls in black lettering; here and there traces of advertisements remain visible. One of the most interesting of these abandoned shops is at the corner of Upper Mary Street and Titus Street. I stand a while alongside, attempting to decipher the writing on the raised stone lintel – 'J. Armitage, Bootmaker'. Despite my best efforts, I can later find out nothing about him.

As I continue I become aware – almost without noticing – of the continual presence of the mill. Although it sits at the foot of the hill, below the level of most of the village, it is nonetheless oddly visible – and even when it is not actually apparent, the huge space it occupies seems somehow palpable. Sometimes it's just the chimney seen at a distance, glimpsed from the corner of the eye as I turn into a different street; sometimes it's a part of the main building itself, solid against the misty moors. It is inescapable, entirely dominant, and in its omnipresence, Salt's notion of paternalism is built into the fabric at Saltaire. The relationship between the mill and the village reconstructs the relationship of father and child: the larger, stouter, more imposing building stands at a discreet distance from the smaller domestic streets but keeps a vigilant eye on them. Like Captain von Trapp lining up his offspring at the start of *The Sound of Music*, the mill lines up its dependants for protection and inspection. In the physical identity of this most Victorian of model villages, the ideals of paternalism on which it is founded are constantly represented and reiterated, marked out on the ground by the architectural constructs and the spaces between them.

The paternalist vision of the workplace as some kind of mutually beneficial project between a fatherly owner and the employees in his care influenced a generation of Victorian industrialists, becoming, as the nineteenth century progressed, a lauded model throughout the country. Examples such as Robert Owen's mills at New Lanark – and especially the mid-Victorian village at Saltaire – were widely recognised as creating an acceptable way of managing the demands of the Industrial Revolution. Indeed, the idea still affects our view of the nineteenth century: the picture of the kind-hearted industrialist providing for his workers in the midst of terrible poverty and miserable conditions remains a mainstay of a particularly nostalgic, sepia-coloured image of the period. The very phrase – paternalism – has warm, family, fireside overtones.

In many ways, Saltaire's paternalist framework appears to bring the village closer to pre-industrial feudal models of society than the cut and thrust of laissez-faire economics that governed many nineteenth-century factories. The paternalist system could easily be presented as the fulfilment of a social contract between master and worker, lending the whole business a distinctly moral tone and concealing entrepreneurial ideals under the guise of the gentleman. In providing housing and basic facilities for those who laboured on their behalf, the factory owners were drawing on a feudal tradition that stretched back centuries. Just as the mills and factories of the Industrial Revolution were becoming larger and more impressive than many of the stately homes across the country, so the new industrialists were stepping into the shoes of aristocratic families to create a modern version of an ancient system of patronage. The embellished workers' cottages at Edensor and the neat terraces of Saltaire are not so far apart in spirit: both can be seen as expressions of the same impulse to consolidate hierarchy and emphasise the gap between the rich, benevolent father figure and the poor scurrying workers at his feet.

But by the mid-nineteenth century, when Saltaire was built, feudalism had had its day as the driving force underpinning British habits and philosophies. *The Economist* magazine, founded in 1843 and acting as a powerful advocate of laissez-faire capitalism, summed up newer modern attitudes in its simple response to the problem of famine in Ireland in 1847: 'It is no man's business to provide for another.'[1] This hands-off dictum seems at odds with Titus Salt's attempt to take care of most aspects of his workers' lives, from bathing to schooling, but in fact there is more common ground between the two approaches than might appear at first sight. By taking charge of their own 'personal' communities along the lines modelled at Saltaire, factory owners were able to prove to the government that they could manage industrial premises and their workforces without any meddling from the state: it reinforced their role as independent entrepreneurs, allowing them to defend the basic principles of free trade and unfettered industrialisation. By establishing that business could be entirely managed on a small scale – down to the most incidental of workers' needs – they could keep unwelcome large-scale intervention at bay.

*

The paternalist approach was not just about the father, however – it also needed the workers to play their role as the extended family; it relied on the villagers seeing themselves as an extension of, and subservient to, the factory owner's authority. Paternalism is a two-way relationship which functions as much because of the commitment and belief of those at the bottom as because of the ambition of those at the top. Most of us in twenty-first-century Europe would chafe under the restrictions of such a system, but while the growth of trades unions and individual rights did begin to challenge old structures of authority from the middle of the nineteenth century, the truth remains that in the domestic cottages at Saltaire, the traditional ideal of the family held sway, with the working father at the head of the household and his wife and children ordered below. The family man's role was one of protector and caretaker – the family replicated the wider paternalist approach but on a smaller, simpler scale: 'The factory paternalist shouldered the responsibility for the welfare of his employees while the respectable working man shouldered the respon-sibility for the welfare of his family and – through co-ops, friendly societies and trade unions – for the welfare of the community as well,' explains one cultural critic.[2] The paternalist framework apparently suited everybody – or at least the male 'everybody' – by bolstering ideas of patriarchal dominance, helping to define male respectability and keeping the family (in its widest sense) intact and functioning efficiently.

But the question has to be asked: how did women fare in this system? How did female workers at Salt's Mill identify themselves within this male-centred framework? And how did women feel about the everyday business of living in Saltaire?

The role of the female mill worker is an intriguing and compli-cated one. In many ways, the mid-century, when Saltaire was built, marked a turning point in attitudes: in the 1830s and '40s, during the early days of the industrial factory system, the mill girl was the epitome of the modern working woman, financially independent and adopting a role alongside her male counterparts in the public life of the village. She was commonly included in strikes and protests: of the 18,000 workers who went on strike in Preston in 1853–4, for example, 11,800 were recorded as female. In light industries, such as textile manufacturing, women made up as much as three-quarters of the workforce. But the second half of the century saw this change – the ideal of the home took hold and working-class women began to see the little cottages of the mill town as a retreat from the terrible demands of factory work rather than as an expression of domestic constraint.

Elements of this transition are reflected in many of the novels of the period. Before the mid-1840s, several popular books provided descriptions of the lives of factory girls, although few of these are well known, or even remembered, today: Charlotte Tonna's *Helen Fleetwood* (1839–41), for example, tackles both the evils of child labour and the role of the female factory hand, making a case for legislative reform; Frances Trollope's *Michael Armstrong, the Factory Boy* (1839), again attempted to highlight the miserable lives of children working in the mills but also features working-class female characters, including Fanny, a girl who is rescued from the worst excesses of factory labour. The book also argues that individual philanthropy, of the Titus Salt type, was simply inadequate in the face of mass poverty and overwhelmingly poor conditions.

By the middle of the century, the industrial novel was becoming more mainstream and many of the writers we recognise more readily today were tackling industrial themes, but the characterisation of the working woman was not clear-cut. Both Charlotte Brontë's novel *Shirley*, published in 1849, and Elizabeth Gaskell's novel *Mary Barton*, published a year earlier, explore the condition of working-class families in factory towns: *Shirley* is set in Yorkshire in the 1810s, while Gaskell's book looks at Manchester around 1840. Both authors use the idea of the factory girl to suggest some of the new opportunities for ordinary women made possible by the Industrial Revolution – but neither of them has a factory girl as heroine. In *Mary Barton*, Mary is apprenticed to a milliner – a more genteel profession – because her father disapproves of mill work for women; mill girls are only shown coming and going on the streets. In *Shirley*, the girls who make up most of the workforce in the local mill are mentioned only in passing. Similarly in Dickens's *Hard Times*, another mid-century novel (1854), the story of the death of an injured factory girl was removed from the book before it was published and by 1866, when George Eliot's *Felix Holt, The Radical* came out, working-class women are hardly present at all in the narrative. Despite women's prominent real-life role in factories, there was an increasing reticence about showing their activity to the public.

The ambivalence about the working-class woman in these novels points to the change that was taking place. As the century progressed, the idea of the factory girl was seen to pose an increasing threat to social order: in the ever-growing towns, as more and more female workers were taken on, it was no longer possible to overlook the working woman, or present her as nothing more than an odd temporary quirk of industrialisation. Women were coming and going on the streets in their work clothes, fulfilling their shifts, managing machinery – they were visible and numerous. By the 1840s, there was obvious unease about the situation and a desire to prevent women becoming permanently comfortable in their working role. The political establishment, middle-class moralists and working-class Chartists were all turning their attention to the potentially transgressive nature of the factory girl and joining ranks to argue that working women should be taken off the factory floor and returned to the home. Popular novels, despite their campaigning role, often reinforced these attitudes: although Frances Trollope spent a month in Lancashire mills researching *Michael Armstrong*, witnessing the lives of factory women at first hand, the book finally succumbs to accepted romantic ideals, marrying Fanny off to a middle-class suitor, and removing her to a safe distance – physically and morally – from the scene of her shameful early life.

This development was partly due to a growing realisation of the terrible conditions many working women were facing. In 1842, for example, the Children's Employment Commission on Mines extended its inquiry from children to their mothers, and for the first time revealed some of the hardships endured by female miners: its paper included graphic woodcut illustrations and led to an emotional parliamentary debate in which members voted to ban women from underground labour and re-classify them as children, so that they could be protected from the worst jobs. It was a ground-breaking decision that in time would lead to changes in working conditions for men as well as women, but its easy assumption that women could be regarded as children suggested that the move was not just a matter of safeguarding women's physical health: it conveniently placed female workers back down the order of a patriarchal system, denying them an adult – and a sexual – identity.

As this decision suggests, the change in attitudes towards working women was about more than poor working conditions and concern for female health: the impulse to return women to the domestic sphere grew out of increasing fears that the working-class girl was getting above herself in all kinds of ways. In particular, she seemed to be threatening to burst out of her accepted sexual role into a new world of licence and promiscuity. By the mid-century, the early view of the female industrial worker as a wholesome family woman helping to shape the changing workplace had given way to a more troubling image of an unconventional, sassy and liberated bawd of questionable morals and challenging opinions. Whether such a change was really taking place hardly mattered – what was important was the perception that the working woman was out of control and threatening the approved way of doing things. The middle classes, in particular, were growing in confidence and influence during the mid-century, benefiting from the increasing wealth in urban areas and establishing themselves as the main force in municipal life: middle-class opinion mattered. And the middle classes were increasingly uneasy about the prospect of unmanageable working women who might undermine the stringent dictates of Victorian respectability.

The very fact that a woman had to leave the home to make a living in the factory was increasingly seen as an indication of poor moral choices, even though many had no choice at all – other than to give up work and starve. At the conclusion of both *Shirley* and *North and South*, the heroines return to their families, unable to support themselves independently and reinforcing the notion of home as the proper place to be, the role of wife and mother as the proper one. By the end of the century, novels were going a step further by presenting the working woman as intrinsically damaged and corrupt: George Gissing's *The Nether World*, published in 1889, is set in the working-class London district of Clerkenwell and offers the reader a tour of sordid endemic poverty and domestic violence. Gissing's working women are ground down by their situation, unable and unwilling to make the effort to escape it:

See how worn-out the poor girls are becoming, how they gape, what listless eyes most of them have! The stoop in the shoulders so universal among them merely means over-toil in the workroom. Not one in a

thousand shows the elements of taste in dress; vulgarity and worse
glares in all but every costume . . .

While class was certainly a factor in determining attitudes, it's worth
noting that the disquiet about single women was not confined to
views of the working class: single women of marriageable age were
perceived as a growing social problem in mid- and late-Victorian
England, whatever social background they came from. The issue was
tackled by, among others, William Rathbone Greg, who founded
Quarry Bank Mill at Styal in Cheshire and who published an essay in
1862 with the provocative title, 'Why Are Women Redundant?' Greg
looked across the social strata and included the aristocracy in his statis-
tics which showed that '[t]here were, in England and Wales, in 1851,
1,248,00 women in the prime of their life, i.e. between the ages of
twenty and forty years, who were unmarried, out of a total number
of rather less than 3,000,000'. He was clear that the financial means or
class status of the woman made little difference – no matter what the
personal circumstances, Greg warned that such a situation threatened
economic and political stability as well as personal happiness: he
predicted a miserable life of 'celibacy, struggle and privation' for those
who failed to find a husband quickly and suggested shipping the single
women en masse to the British colonies 'in at least 10,000 voyages' so
that they could link up with the single men forging an empire and so
reintegrate themselves into acceptable social structures.[3]

In such a climate of panic, where even middle- or upper-class single
women were seen as a threat to decent society, working-class women
in the mills and factories were, of course, especially alarming. As a
result they came to be increasingly presented as desperate and transgressive, not only unnatural in their prioritising of work over family
but in their appetite for drink, entertainment and, especially, sex. The
perception of the factory girl as unruly and debauched quickly gained
ground, supported by a substantial body of work from influential
commentators. In his study *The Condition of the Working Class in England
in 1844*, for example, Friedrich Engels offered a damning verdict on
the nature of the working woman: 'The collecting of persons of both
sexes and all ages in a single work-room, the inevitable contact, the
crowding into a small space of people, to whom neither mental nor
moral education has been given, is not calculated for the favourable

development of the female character,' he explained. Mill girls, Engels claimed, were 'in no position to understand' respectable domestic work, used indecent language, and were likely to be sexually corrupted by both dissolute colleagues and powerful mill owners. He quoted one 'witness' from Manchester who asserted that 'three-fourths of the young [female] factory employees, from fourteen to twenty years of age, were unchaste.'[4]

Titus Salt's ambitious clean-living settlement at Saltaire was intended to provide just the kind of environment to counteract such unfortunate activity as Engels describes; smog and ill-doing were to be blown away by fresh winds from the moors. Today, however, it's difficult to recapture this sense of Saltaire as a new venture, set apart from existing habits and structures: the village tucks so neatly and discreetly into the wider conurbation that it's hard to see it as distinct or separate. Open land is no longer visible; the moors have long been built over and the park at the foot of the village, across the river, is concealed by mature trees and the mill itself. Saltaire is now a place surrounded by shops and traffic and urban habits; it's now peopled by working women going about their business without too much opprobrium being heaped upon them.

Walking along its streets, I'm constantly trying to remind myself of what was *not* here in 1851; my exploration of these villages is as much about unseeing what threatens to clutter the original ideals and intentions as about seeing the architectural forms which express them. Salt's village was intended to be remote and hygienic, located a safe distance from the environmental and moral corruption of Bradford – I try to strip away all the roads and houses and factories that have since intervened to conceal this intention. Recent critics have been at pains to show that Saltaire failed to provide a real solution to the relationship between employer and worker for the very reason that its site was so much more healthy and isolated than the typical industrial site – it provided an escape from, rather than an answer to, the problems of urban industrial society – but that does not, or should not, detract from the hope and optimism on which Saltaire was founded, a place conceived to provide not only industrial profit and work for a community, but new clean domestic structures in which to live.

When I come to the top of the grid of original terraces, I turn left on to the busy Bingley Road, then cram in a few hundred yards of twenty-first-century high-street commercialism before turning downhill along Victoria Road. This long, straight street plunges back into Salt's vision, running the length of the village, not quite at its centre, but linking the river, factory and station with the housing. As befits a street named after the Queen, this is where the stately buildings congregate, the architecture intended to impress and even intimidate. It's also a shopping street, with well-preserved frontages and tasteful awnings. There is a sense of arrival, even today; in the village's heyday this effect would have been even more pronounced, shops, businesses and meeting rooms sitting alongside civic buildings, the school, hospital and almshouses. This was a bustling, purposeful thoroughfare, a thriving hub of personal and business life.

The buildings along Victoria Road took some time to design and construct. Most of them are later in date than the original cottages: the school opened in 1868, as did the neat quadrangle of almshouses; the imposing Victoria Hall opposite opened three years later, offering residents a library, dance hall, lecture theatre, billiards room and gymnasium. These are buildings which reflect the civic aspiration of a place which, for over a decade, had been heralded as a model of entrepreneurial astuteness and paternalist munificence. The plainness of the early domestic terraces gives way here to decorative detail: ornate stonework, colonnades and arches, pinnacled chimneys, a whimsical bell tower. The Salt coat of arms is much in evidence and there are lawns and flower beds, specimen trees and four wonderful reclining sandstone lions, licking their paws in imperious nonchalance. A report in the *Building News* in October 1869 told how the lions were originally intended for Trafalgar Square in London, but after finishing the designs and preparations, the sculptor, Thomas Milnes, had the commission snatched from him and given instead to Sir Edwin Landseer. Titus Salt stepped in to rescue the project and the four beasts – intended to represent Vigilance, Determination, Peace and War – now lie greening under the spruce and sycamores which line the pavement. They are remarkably expressive and natural; I spend a little while admiring them and wishing they were not so hidden by the drooping branches.

The lions and the coats of arms and the general feeling of pomp root this part of Saltaire firmly in a context of mid-Victorian civic pride and confidence. It looks very like the centres of the large, successful Victorian cities – Sheffield, Birmingham, Preston – with their emphasis on public space and public buildings, on asserting confidence even in the face of terrifying working practices and city slums. Victoria Street displays itself openly to the world, and so in turn displays the philosophies underpinning the entire village. It's a kind of marketing tool, presenting Saltaire as a bright, noble and permanent solution to the problems of nineteenth-century industrialisation. This feeling becomes particularly strong when I discover that Titus Salt had even greater plans for the public face of his village: in a remarkable feat of ambition, he manoeuvred to bring Joseph Paxton's huge Crystal Palace from London as a centrepiece to Saltaire, dismantling it and transporting it in pieces when the Great Exhibition had finished so that it might become a futuristic factory building.

Salt had exhibited his textiles at the Great Exhibition; his alpaca worsted, in particular, attracted attention, drawing praise for both its light, soft qualities and its rapid dominance in the marketplace: 'The trade has sprung up within a comparatively short period and progressed with a rapidity and success unparalleled in the history of manufactures,' enthused one commentator.[5] But in addition to hearing his business commended and admired, Salt – like many of his contemporaries – had clearly been dazzled and seduced by the experience of the Exhibition itself, by its grandeur; by the exuberant circuses and tightrope walkers; by the dog, pigeon and flower shows, the reproduction dinosaurs and the fountains in the park with 12,000 jets of water; and by the sheer sensual onslaught of 100,000 objects on display. These included a massive hydraulic press designed by Stevenson, an expanding hearse, folding pianos, a Sheffield 'sportsman's' knife with eighty blades, a carved ivory throne, a white marble statue of a naked Greek Slave secluded in her own red velvet tent, huge malachite vases twice the height of a man, a lump of gold the weight of a woman, the famous Koh-i-Noor diamond, silks, stained glass, stuffed animals, buttons, nails and balls of thread – which was all aside from the spectacle of the visitors themselves, a vibrant, excitable mixture of people of all classes from all over the country eager, as *Punch* magazine memorably noted, to 'push and pant, and pinch their way amongst each other' for the best view.[6]

The Crystal Palace: an icon of mid-Victorian England. Salt's object of desire is a fascinating one. The building was not only an architectural wonder of its time, but it also captured most acutely the period's delight in commodity and its display: the brilliant extravaganza of the Great Exhibition had, just a few years before the building of Saltaire, put under one roof the most fashionable and impressive of objects; it had linked scientific, national and personal progress directly to industry and the making of material goods to sell. It had brought the world from Persia to Prussia, China to Bolivia and America to India under a great glass dome – under a giant display case – and represented it as a place for buying and selling. The Exhibition was a confusion of invention and nostalgia, of modern gadgets and ancient treasures, impossible for visitors adequately to comprehend or describe, but all underpinned with the unremitting sense that whatever you wanted should surely be available to be bought and owned, to improve the quality of your life and to make you a better person. The abundance on display created a sense of promise, of wealth and surplus, improvement and progress, of the unlimited potential of manufacturing and the infinite robustness of Victorian productivity. The Crystal Palace was a palace of commercialism to rival any twenty-first-century shopping arcade.

Titus Salt was among the many employers who arranged for his workers to visit the Great Exhibition, and later shows such as the 1857 Art Treasures exhibition in Manchester. Such a magnanimous gesture provided an opportunity to show off his own status, to make a mark among fellow manufacturers, and to reward and inspire those who made his wealth possible. This was not a quiet day out for a few favoured employees but a parade, a communal celebration and, in some ways, an advertisement. The workforce 'all dressed in their Sunday best . . . [arrived] in three special trains', reported one newspaper: 'The fine brass band belonging to the establishment accompanied the first two trains, and the Saltaire drum-and-fife-band the last . . . They were accompanied by their generous employer, Mr Titus Salt, who paid all expenses connected with the trip.'[7]

The momentous expedition offered many ordinary workers a glimpse of a much wider world than they were accustomed to, and a memorable day out with their friends. But after their return, those who had seen such beautiful and marvellous things for the first time had plenty of opportunity to reflect on the objects, and what impact such things might have on their own lives. The abundance of wallpapers, textiles, carpets, clothing and labour-saving devices on display seemed designed to prompt them to imagine how the perfect home might look – and how manufacturing could help achieve it. The Great Exhibition was not just a distant phenomenon, a showcase of the unattainably magnificent, but also a place where ordinary people could find things they liked and aspired to own. It demonstrated how they could decorate their houses comfortably and conveniently and – more significantly, perhaps – it suggested that objects could transform their lives in more subtle ways, asserting their taste, education and social position, and offering a means of self-expression.

Joseph Paxton, too, was eager to use his experience of building the Crystal Palace to improve the homes and lives of those who visited. He spoke frequently about ways in which his design could be adapted to develop innovative housing techniques. While there remained something of the visionary eccentricity evident in his village at Edensor, his message was also a distinctly practical one: he presented the principle of assembling buildings from prefabricated sections as a cost-effective means of construction, for example, and he advocated adapting the light and ventilation systems to create healthy, airy environments. Such proposals prompted *The Economist* to look forwards to the clearing of the slums and the development in their place of 'the light and elegant, the cheerful and airy, the cheap and wholesome style of the building of the Crystal Palace'.[8] In such a way, the Crystal Palace promised to link commercialism with practical philanthropy. It indicated that beyond the pageant, there might be the possibility of social change. Both the building and the objects within it seemed to suggest the prospect of an improved way of living that was shinier and brighter and somehow inviolable.

Unfortunately, Titus Salt's plans for the Crystal Palace fell through. He was outbid by a consortium of eight businessmen who moved the building to Sydenham Hill in south-east London, where it was re-designed, extended and rebuilt as a permanent venue for exhibitions. But I try to imagine what Saltaire might be today if Salt's scheme had come about and the Crystal Palace had survived here. It's a building which seems to have only the most tenuous relationship with the idea

of a factory – at the Great Exhibition it showed a plethora of manufactured goods but in an environment completely divorced from the
noise and dirt of the manufacturing process. One recent commentator
has emphasised how the architecture created a rarefied atmosphere
'of aesthetic and linguistic contemplation', flooding objects with light
and presenting them authoritatively classified, as untouchable in the
vast galleries as they would be in a museum, or even a church or
cathedral.[9] The Crystal Palace at Saltaire would have been a factory
Utopia, an ethereal place of light and air, of permanent spring, entirely
at odds with the daily grind and physical misery of working heavy
machinery. Looking down to the mill site, I wonder what it would be
like, this glasshouse by the river, at once High Victorian and timeless?
Would it rise shimmering from the valley or would it have proved
impossibly impractical, its glass smeared now, darkened and smashed,
the thing little more than a broken-down old greenhouse? I find I'm
sorry not to have had the chance to find out; I'm astounded by the
ingenuity and daring of such a scheme, and by the self-assurance of
a man who could conceive of it.

I'm not the only one to admire Salt's vision: the Saltaire project
captured the imagination of all those who were involved in its
construction. William Fairburn, Salt's civil engineer, described the
huge mill with wonder, as a 'palace of industry', while the Mayor of
Bradford, who spoke at the opening in 1853, also had palaces on his
mind: Titus Salt, he declared, had created 'palaces of industry almost
equal to the palaces of the Caesars!'[10]

This repetition of the notion of the palace – and the reference to
Roman authority – returns us to our discussion of the complexities
of paternalism; it reminds us again of its relationship to the feudal,
aristocratic and even royal structures of the past. The palace was no
longer seen just as a place of idleness or fashionable entertainment
but now, as Fairburn recognised, also 'of industry'. Work – industry
in all its senses – was important; it created the conditions for progress,
for wealth, for power. All the elements which were once centred in
the royal palace were now transferable; they could find a fitting place
in the great mills of northern towns. The sense of what and who
ruled in the national interest was changing, and the architectural
splendour of Salt's Mill was making these changes manifest.

Salt's desire to bring another palace, the Crystal Palace, to Saltaire was not inappropriate. The Great Exhibition was about industry and commerce, trade and profit, identity and internationalism – the word 'palace' was now being used to help define (and perhaps contain) the most powerful forces of the mid-nineteenth century. And here at Saltaire, those closest to the project were recognising the influence of the new industrial elite by referencing the most visible legacies of the old elite – the huge, expensive, expressive palace. Salt and his colleagues were the new industrial royalty, with the power and responsibility this suggested; they were adopting structures and words that summoned the greatness of the past ('the palaces of the Caesars') to locate themselves in a new ambitious vision for the future.

A siding: Swindon Railway Village, Wiltshire

I've come to Swindon. I've come on the train, because that seems the thing to do: this is a town built by and for the railways. When the construction of a new London–Bristol route was approved by Parliament in 1835, the chief engineer – Isambard Kingdom Brunel – began to buy locomotives from various makers for the Great Western Railway. It quickly became clear that the project required a central works where the hotchpotch of engines could be standardised and repaired. In 1841 the GWR directors agreed to develop Swindon, then a small hilltop market town: 'What were then green fields are now covered with a flourishing town and works of enormous magnitude, from which engines, carriages, and waggons required for working the two thousand five hundred miles of the Great Western system are supplied,' boasted Brunel's colleague, Daniel Gooch.[11]

In time, the new town came to have all the usual facilities: shops and a hospital, a church and school, a park and public baths, a mechanics institute and a covered market. But what I've come to see is the terraces. I've seen terraces before, of course; lots of them. Saltaire is a criss-cross of terraces; I could have stayed at home to see terraces. But there are few finer examples than those here, built as housing for the railway workers and constructed to a good enough standard to warrant the higher rents charged to skilled engineers.

I wander up and down what is now the 'Swindon Railway Village Conservation Area', a local authority designation that should protect the 1840s settlement from inappropriate development. Beside the railway line there are old industrial buildings, some reused, some abandoned and semi-derelict: there's a small industrial unit with a car repair shop and a furniture maker's. At the height of the GWR age, the works at Swindon was vast, employing 40,000 workers and covering over 300 acres, 73 of which were undercover. Much of this industrial majesty has gone; the most impressive of the original buildings now is a collection of stone blocks in varying heights, with rows of small windows. It looks very like a mill; there's a new roof, the slates reflecting odd moments of blue sky above, and the stonework has been cleaned. This was the GWR general offices, and appropriately is now the archive building for English Heritage.

But what I'm drawn to is not these symmetrical works' buildings, for all their solid industrial glamour, but to an odd feature, a tower: a tall grid of discoloured iron topped by sheets of corrugated metal and a large square tank or box – this turns out to be the GWR water tower, built to store water for the works and its steam engines. As I come nearer, I see that the wall in front of it is a swirling sea of blues and greens, waves of painted colour completely concealing the stonework and creating an illusion of vibrant movement. This sweep of graffiti art acts like a stage, holding up the decrepit construction above, which – for all its rusted iron and smeared concrete – is a wonderful thing. It seems right that such a landmark should be lauded and the graffiti is the perfect way of drawing the eye, counterpointing the pale skeleton above rather than distracting from it.

I continue on beyond the water tower, towards the other side of the site where I come to a park, flat and featureless except for some fine old trees; it could be any municipal park – there's nothing Victorian about it. Worse still, one side of the open ground is buttressed by a low 1960s building in dirty pinkish stone and concrete, its flat windows showing off the strip lights within: this is the Territorial Army building. Someone should knock it down – perhaps the TA could make it the focus of an exercise – because it intrudes rudely on St Mark's church, a fine example of Victorian Gothic designed by George Gilbert Scott and built in limestone from public subscription. The vicarage along-side, in spacious grounds which lead away from the churchyard, lost part of its curtilage to the Territorial Army as long ago as 1871.

And so I've done the tour of the industrial and municipal sights and

I've come to the domestic streets – the terraces. Laid out in a strict grid pattern centred around a square, these are built from locally quarried 'Swindon' and Bath stone, some of which came from the two-mile-long Box Tunnel which Brunel drove through Box Hill to take the line onwards towards Bath. The cottages are mostly plain but each street has its own subtle individuality – some of the facades facing the railway are decorated with Jacobean and Elizabethan motifs, for example, because the GWR liked to impress travellers passing through on its trains. And each of the streets bears a name derived from the stations on the railway route to Bristol: Exeter, Taunton, Oxford, Faringdon. They are wide, avenue-like; the impression of space is reinforced by generous front gardens, the pale stone frontages offset by lawns and small trees, clipped hedges. There's the water tower again, rising above the rooftops and tall chimneys, a spectre from the old railways.

This is, like all terraced communities, a place of linear perspectives and repetition: side alleys and back alleys, wall ends and corners, windows and doors identical. This always pleases me: there's something comforting about it. But today my overwhelming feeling is one of disappointment. Because this is a messy place, too, its rhythms disrupted, discordant. I walk from tarmac to concrete paving slab to brick, modern materials crumbling and uneven underfoot, upsetting my stride; there are road signs and markings everywhere, too bold and numerous, drawing the eye from the lines of housing; litter stuffs the drains and rubbish is piled against the walls and kerbs; the trains have given way to cars and the roads are busy with fast-moving traffic; the terraces on the eastern side are blunted by newer, taller buildings, hotels and office blocks which loom from the town centre. It's noisy and anxious and there's a sense in which the tight grid of terraces is out of place and redundant, standing obstinately in the way of modern, everyday Swindon like a dam in the gushing river of urgent daily life. And this seems wrong. Because the terraces were, of course, very much about modern daily life; here in Swindon, as elsewhere, they were the expression of practical domestic living, of getting on with home and work, family and neighbours, making a way in the world and making ends meet.

Just as the working man was essential to sustain the patriarchal structures controlled by factory owners like Titus Salt, so the working home was integral to the idea of a re-envisaged social community with the industrial master at its heart and head. While old-fashioned palaces like Chatsworth might have chosen idiosyncratic housing plans, these were the exception: the new industrial palaces chose to base their demesne on a sober, orthodox and regular pattern – the terrace.

The practicality and cost-efficiency of the terrace layout had obvious appeal for industrial investors, even those of the most philanthropic turn of mind, and most nineteenth-century planned villages used the terrace as their starting point. Terraces allowed large numbers of people to be housed in a relatively small area; they could be constructed quickly and easily with a simple one-brick-thick wall throughout, and, as we've seen in Swindon, they could be left plain or given some architectural flourish, depending on financial priorities. But terraces were not, of course, unique to model villages: they were (and still are) everywhere. Mill and factory towns across the country grew from the backbone of the simple terrace; whole cities developed from the basic idea of packing houses in lines and then arranging those lines into the most functional of patterns.

Terraces had been a feature of English architecture since the eighteenth century – think of the crescents of Bath and Buxton built in the 1760s and 1770s, or London squares such as Grosvenor Square and Bedford Square, and you have a clear picture of the best of British terraces and their Jane Austen-like gentility. These Georgian stalwarts retained elements of the European palace with its classical proportions and straight lines; they were refined and stylish developments, largely designed for the nobility or the rising middle classes, recalling royal prestige in their imposing size and regularity. With an architectural sleight of hand, a row of houses on one side of a square could be made to look like a single impressive residence and each individual family could bask in the illusion of inhabiting a huge city mansion. As the fashion developed, the emphasis came more and more to be placed on symmetry, binding together a row of houses as tightly as possible to give an impression – an illusion – of sameness. Architects were anxious to ensure a smooth, continuous surface, with each house bonded as securely as possible to its neighbour and the facing brick or stone laid uniformly along the length of the row. This created what one architectural commentator has identified as 'both self-contained houses and palatial unity'.[12]

In Europe, cities and large towns tended to evolve on the model of blocks of flats rather than terraces. No one seems to be able adequately to explain why the British custom developed so differently: it seems to be partly to do with higher land prices in Europe, but it appears also to have been a matter of taste and habit. In Britain, particularly in major cities, blocks of flats were often intended either for the very poor, or the very rich. Neither the lack of privacy at the cheapest end, nor the complicated bespoke layouts at the most expensive, suited the influential middle classes.

In addition, most English towns differed from their European counterparts in the distinct separation of work and home: by the middle of the eighteenth century very few merchants still lived above their shops, for example, while in larger cities like London, there was enough space to allocate discrete areas for trade, markets and workshops. This meant that the main streets and squares could be given over to residential building, and each residential area could begin to develop its own identity dependent on those who lived there. The distinction was largely, of course, based on class – unlike many European city dwellers, the English tended to dislike mixing several classes in a block of housing – and as time went on, middle- and upper-class districts became notable for their commitment to the urban terrace.

By the beginning of the nineteenth century, the most fashionable had moved out of the city entirely, preferring a detached country residence – and the terrace idea was beginning to be adopted in a different context altogether, as a solution to the housing crisis brought about by the Industrial Revolution. But the change of focus from the genteel to the working-class actually made very little difference to the basic structure of the terraced house: most adhered to a simple plan of two rooms on each floor, one front and one back, with an entrance and staircase to the side. While the depth and height of the houses could differ, there tended to be very little variation in the width; whether designed for a doctor or a mill hand, the terraced house was, in essence, the same. This made it simple and convenient for the surveyor, the estate manager and the builder since the same plot could be adapted to different sizes and markets. Individuality could be marked, if required, on the outside, in decoration and flourish, bow and bay windows, roofing materials and garden plans allowing for thousands of variants to the basic scheme, often with a regional character.

By the end of the nineteenth century, most English families lived in a terrace, whatever their background or status, using the streets between as promenades and meeting places. The idea of the home became inextricably linked with the picture of a row of houses, each self-contained but also linked to those either side in a gesture of community spirit. Such a picture suggested simplicity of design and living, the perfect conjunction of personal space with neighbourly warmth, a refinement of the domestic ideal to its basic components. But just as the imposing Palladian terraces of London or Bath had created an illusion of much grander, palatial developments, so the smaller urban terraces of industrial centres like Manchester and Bradford set up illusions of their own: what seemed to be a neatly defined home for a single nuclear family was often, in fact, little more than a cramped, crowded lodging house, shared by two or more families, packed with paying boarders, shift workers coming and going at all hours. Noise penetrated between the walls from one family to another; neighbourly companionship became intrusion. Just like its eighteenth-century predecessor, the mid-nineteenth-century terrace appeared to provide the perfect impenetrable facade, but all it was doing was concealing the fractures in an unstable ideal of home life.

In Swindon it's beginning to snow. I make my way through the traffic, past a disused nightclub and into the heart of Emlyn Square, originally planned by Brunel as a wide, open high street which would create a central promenade between the two sets of residential terraces. Now it's cramped, its original spaciousness lost to more recent buildings and overshadowed by the rather bizarre Mechanics Institute building, an unappealing concoction of gables and turrets in an uncertain mix of styles, with a plain tower behind like a remnant from a sturdy Norman church. To one side of me, there's a very large wall. It runs along the length of two streets, facing the cottages; it's punctuated by window openings, some arched and some rectangular, but none-theless it's a monolithic presence, an obvious barrier.

I begin along the length of the wall in search of an access point. It's a particular quest: I'm looking for the entrance to an underground tunnel which ran below the railway lines and connected the village directly to the GWR works. I'm expecting something cramped and perhaps dark; I have a picture in my mind's eye of an entrance to the mine adits at Nenthead, a low stone archway, partly obscured. When I find the tunnel entrance here, I'm surprised by its grandeur. There is nothing of the sheepish underpass about this: it's a proper point of arrival, an imposing stone portal under a wide gable. Furthermore, after a moment I realise that it's in the centre of the village. It stands where another monument might have stood in another village – a well, a sundial, even a church – at the point where the inhabitants come together, in the most visible communal place. This tunnel entrance makes the link between domestic and working life plain and tangible; it acts as an icon for the village, reinforcing the idea that this is a place dependent on work, a place yoked actually and metaphorically to the railways.

The snow falls more heavily, but slowly still, reluctantly. I head towards the streets furthest from Emlyn Square. The outer terraces face the modern world, but as I walk further into Brunel's vision, the past closes more tightly around me: on the inside of the grid pattern both sides of the street are lined with terraces and I can see only the length and breadth of the 1840s village. I take Bathampton Street, which leads at the far end down to the park, the other end closed off by the back of the old Mechanics' Institute. The sight lines are short and closely defined but when I shuffle round the corner of the pavement, I can see the water tower again, from a new angle. It seems to stand very close to the final house in the terrace, overlooking the road junction, the strangest of sculptures. Like the mill and its chimney at Saltaire, it's a constant landmark, a perpetual reminder of the purpose of this place, a beacon signalling the power of the railways and those who own and manage them.

The further I come towards the park, the quieter it is. The fading of the traffic noise and the dim light and the falling snow suggest a kind of timelessness, illusory but seductive. The terraces line up solidly on either side; a robin sings, the quiet seeming more dense when it stops. Suddenly the frustrations and iniquities of modern Swindon seem distant. My feelings of unease sink away and instead I feel warm and rather nostalgic for a moment, as though I've wandered into the feel-good set for a Hovis advertising campaign.

It's not just the wet, uncertain snow that creates this snug Christmas-card effect: a village designed, like this one, as a model of good-quality, spacious terracing indulges shared cultural memories; it provides a kind of accepted and acceptable version of home – a child's drawing of home, if you like – substantial but not too pretentious, neighbourly, compact and tidy, symmetrical, with chimneys and solid front doors. It sits us down at the fireside of past lives and helps us eavesdrop, momentarily, on what might have mattered to them.

The ideal of the home conjured by the industrial terrace is not as straightforward as it might seem, of course. As I walk around Swindon, the railway is inescapable; it's the railway which makes and defines the village – and which brings us back to the worker. The families who lived in the new terraced housing were, by and large, working-class families but the construct of the home was, by and large, a middle-class one. The implications of this difference are enormous.

Dorothea Brooke, the heroine of George Eliot's magnificent 1869 novel, *Middlemarch*, is a reformer with a particular taste for housing projects: she attempts to improve the miserable lot of the tenants on her uncle's land, and she spends happy hours with her rich neighbour and brother-in-law, James Chettam, sketching out improved housing schemes: her highest praise for the rather gormless Chettam is that he is 'very good about the cottages'.

Alongside the fictional Dorothea there were plenty of real-life women of the gentry and upper middle classes experimenting with better housing. In the 1850s and 1860s the sisters Georgina and Mary Talbot created a village in Dorset for the poorest residents – the unemployed and destitute. They contracted as many workers as possible to clear land for farms, cottages and almshouses, subsequently charging a modest rent of around 4 shillings a week to families who took up residence. The village had no industrial or estate purpose but was simply conceived to ameliorate the lives of the most miserable.

At Ford in Northumberland, Louisa Beresford, Marchioness of Waterford, also threw herself into the task of providing decent housing during the 1860s; much more uniquely, she spent twenty-one years painting the interior of the village school by hand, using the children and other villagers as models for a set of biblical scenes. As a young woman, Louisa was tutored by Dante Gabriel Rossetti and John Ruskin; it is likely that she modelled for several of the Pre-Raphaelite circle including John Everett Millais. She was married in 1842 but her husband, Lord Waterford, died in a riding accident in 1859 when Louisa was forty-one years old and childless. The following year, she began to decorate the schoolhouse, painting life-size watercolours on sheets of paper which were then applied to canvas and mounted on the walls.

The murals run along the length of the building, showing everything from Moses being set adrift in his basket to the young Jesus Christ engaging in debate with the elders of the temple. The school is now known as Waterford Hall. I first saw the paintings there when I was about sixteen years old: in those days the building was deserted and a little shabby; it smelt stale and forgotten. Even at that age, Louisa Beresford's decoration struck me as rather an uncomfortable achievement. Like the remarkable tapestries worked by Mary Queen of Scots during her long years of imprisonment, the intricate paintings in an out-of-the-way schoolhouse have an air of confinement and frustration about them. In the years since my first visit, the building has been refurbished. It's much more cared for, less mouldy; there is a display of Louisa's sketchbooks and an admission fee. But the feeling of discomfort remains: stepping inside draws you into a striking but ultimately disturbing mid-nineteenth-century construct of womanhood – the remarkable energies and sustained dedication of Louisa Beresford are expressed in a rather clumsy and ultimately pointless piece of interior design. It's a situation recognised by George Eliot: despite her enterprise and good intentions, Dorothea Brooke's fate is not unlike Louisa Beresford's, her activity ultimately confined to unrecognised acts of charity: 'Many who knew her, thought it a pity,' Eliot remarks, before adding, 'But no one stated exactly what else that was in her power she ought rather to have done.'

The relationship between woman and home in the mid-nineteenth century was a complex and ambiguous one. It's not, of course, a coincidence that actual women like Louisa Beresford and fictional heroines like Dorothea Brooke both directed their attentions to the village, to cottages and living conditions, schools and almshouses. The village, particularly when it was an integral element of a country estate or an industrial enterprise, could be regarded as an extension of the family; realising small-scale housing projects was therefore an apt and proper use of female talents within a suitably domestic context.

The ideal of the woman in her household was sustained at the highest levels of British life: after her marriage to Prince Albert in 1840, Queen Victoria quickly became established as an icon of domesticity and motherhood; she epitomised a female identity constructed around a respectable family life. For her subjects, Victoria's marriage came to be seen as the ideal of marital harmony and propriety; her family embodied the idea of an intimate domestic unit. Seen by many as the 'mother of the nation', Victoria offered a striking model of femininity grounded in maternity and – despite her public role – settled at the domestic hearth. Her devotion to God, her nation and her husband exemplified the virtuous woman, busy, able and upright, expressing herself in the service of others.

The anxious middle classes rapidly adopted the royal model. Popular literature and novels, as well as advertisements in magazines and newspapers, reinforced the notion that the home was the woman's domain, a place where she could perform her duties to her family and by extension to society as a whole. The role of the mother became loaded with symbolic meaning; she was increasingly portrayed as emotionally fulfilled, happily swapping a productive role outside the home for a reproductive role within it, affirming her identity through constant attendance upon infant children. The unmarried or childless woman was to be pitied – and was apt to be labelled abnormal or even immoral.

The quiet, passive ideal woman pictured by middle-class commentators was characterised in a long poem called 'The Angel of the House' by Coventry Patmore, first published in four instalments in 1854 and reworked and extended over the next eight years. Patmore was inspired to write his poem by his wife, Emily, whom he believed to be the perfect Victorian woman – his 'Angel' was meek, charming, graceful, sympathetic, self-sacrificing and above all pure. Although at first the poem did not receive much attention, it became increasingly popular as the century progressed; the perfect domestic woman came more and more to be associated with Patmore's heroine who was 'all mildness'. In the end, the poem's influence was so powerful that the angel of the house continued to hover over the home well into the twentieth century, presenting a tenacious view of Victorian womanhood. Later female writers railed against the repressive ideal in an attempt to break down the notion of the perfect woman and in 1931 Virginia Woolf wrote with evident frustration that 'Killing the Angel of the House was part of the occupation of a woman writer.'[13]

As befits a place overseen by angels, the mid-Victorian home became a haven, a heaven, discrete from the uncertain world of work. While men were taking their place in the public sphere of business and politics, the female sphere came to be increasingly defined as private and domestic, protected from the potential corruption of outside influence. Those who could afford to, dressed the home with plush fabrics, heavy curtains and soft furnishings, emphasising the cosiness of the domestic space and cocooning the family from the world beyond. Fashions in clothing also asserted the woman's distance from the grubby, practical demands of the workplace: the middle-class woman in a wide crinoline and tortuous corset became a walking symbol of the wife and mother, with attention drawn to her hips, buttocks and breasts and her costume making any strenuous activity more or less impossible.

The female ideal was underpinned by a wealth of popular literature which gave women advice on how to run the household and their role within it: Mrs Beeton's famous *Book of Household Management* remained a best-seller for fifty years after it was first published in 1861; Charles Eastlake, Keeper of London's National Gallery, published *Hints on Household Taste* in 1878, warning women about the dangers of 'silly knick-knacks which too frequently crowd a drawing-room table'.[14] The relationship between the appearance of the home and the moral stature of the family who lived there was constantly explored by writers: in *Pendennis* (1850), William Makepeace Thackeray goes to great lengths to describe Lady Clavering's rooms because her choice of objects for display carries a moral message. The dining room, notes Thackeray, is 'very chaste . . . that being the proper phrase', while in *Wives and Daughters* (1864–5), Elizabeth Gaskell makes frequent comparisons between Mrs Gibson's less-than-genteel past and her predilection for surrounding herself with tasteless 'objets d'art'.

For all their attempts to create a refuge from external forces and a family retreat, middle-class women were much more active than we sometimes imagine. It's easy to picture them sitting in the house all day, taking tea and fainting under the pressure of tyrannical underwear, but in fact many women took a lively role within their own circles. Although they were bound by the obvious restrictions of the period, many managed to forge a life outside the home, developing interests in art and philanthropy, music and politics. The domestic ideal was, to some extent, a female as well as a male construct: it allowed women to create their own space, a manageable environment in which they had power, a role in which they were respected and a social place they could manipulate.

But the perfect home was also, in many ways, a sleight of hand – middle-class women simply did not have time to idle their days away with piano recitals and embroidery. Maintaining a neat and well-managed household required hard physical labour, from fetching and boiling water to scrubbing floors and labouring over time-consuming meals. Only the richest households could afford more than one servant, and so it usually fell to the woman of the house to take on many of the daily tasks. It is when we remember this, perhaps, that we become most acutely aware of the class implications of the domestic ideal: in order to maintain a good home, women had to be rich enough either to employ many servants or to stay in the house all day in order to clean and manage it. As soon as the woman was required to go out to work to earn an income, the model irretrievably broke down. How could a woman who worked long shifts at Salt's Mill also find time to do all the strenuous household chores and fulfil her role as nurturing angel?

Despite this conundrum, many working families still aspired to the same persistent ideal of home as those higher up the social ladder. The idea that women's duties should be completely focused on the family hearth – the fixed centre of domestic life – was so firmly rooted that many families would do anything to protect her place at home. To make this happen, working women often chose to take jobs which could be fitted around domestic chores, however uneasily – most frequently this amounted to needlework tasks, like stitching together pre-cut garments. The income from this work was not regarded simply as pocket money; the wages were usually essential to supplement what was being brought in by the husband or father. But the labour was typically very poorly paid and extremely demanding. While from the outside the family maintained the fiction of the leisured woman tending to her home, seen from the inside such work amounted only

Miners' cottages skirting the green at Creswell.

'The Model',
Creswell.

(*Above*) Cottages at 14–16 Church Drive, Port Sunlight, designed by Grayson and Ould with the initial L for Lever in the ornate decoration.

(*Below*) A seat in the bridge over 'The Dell' at Port Sunlight, designed by Cheshire architect John Douglas.

The bridge and cottages
at Port Sunlight.

The Town Hall at Portmeirion; in front, a bronze statue of Hercules by William Brodie (1863) and to the right Angel Cottage, built in a traditional West Country style in 1926, the first cottage designed for Portmeirion by Clough Williams-Ellis.

(*Left*) The *trompe l'oeil* mock copper and sandstone turret hiding a chimney at Portmeirion.

(*Below*) A view of Portmeirion village with the pink Gothic porch from Nerquis Hall visible in the bottom left.

to long hours of drudgery for small reward. The campaigning American journalist Sarah Hale noted in 1867, for example, that to make an average shirt by hand required 20,620 stitches; at a rate of thirty-five stitches a minute, a competent seamstress could not hope to complete a shirt in less than ten to fourteen hours.[15] Since most women had to interrupt their work to tend to children, prepare meals and do the essential laundry, in practice finishing a shirt could take much longer. In addition, the seamstress had to provide her own cotton and thread as well as candles for working through the evening and night; she was usually forced to negotiate her rate of pay with a middleman, accept a punishing system of fines and deductions and collect and return her work on foot. As the *Hampshire Telegraph* pointed out:

> The best workers cannot obtain two shillings a week, though they work early and late, and the fact will scarcely be credited that a dozen of seamen's shirts are made for ten pence! And even this price has been known to be withheld on the alledgment [sic] that the work is bad; at these prices the wretched females cannot earn more than two pence a day . . .[16]

With a foot-powered sewing machine, working at 3,000 stitches a minute, a seamstress could improve production, completing a shirt in about an hour, but the hire of the sewing machine could be as much as 2s.6d a week, making it beyond the reach of many workers unless they were able to club together with family and friends.

As the poorest women struggled to make ends meet while sustaining the illusion of an ordered home life, the middle classes stepped in to provide advice. Wealthier women, particularly in urban areas, were keen to be seen to help, sponsoring kindergartens, leading temperance campaigns and lecturing working-class women on hygiene reform and cleanliness. Their practical intervention was often accompanied by a religious message, underlining the apparently inseparable relationship between moral uprightness and the well-run home. Living under such scrutiny, working-class women could hardly escape censure. The poor sanitation and overcrowding of working-class areas in industrial centres meant that disease was rife and infant mortality rates high, but rather than attack the fundamental root of the problem, it was all too easy for middle-class philanthropists, doctors and government inspectors to label poor women as irresponsible and careless, bad mothers and neglectful wives who were incapable of fulfilling their proper domestic role.

Saltaire again

I've left the official walk suggested by the tourist board leaflet and headed off up alleyways. I'm standing at the bottom of a reasonably wide flagged path which slopes gently upwards from the direction of the mill. On one side there are the tall backs of some of the larger buildings on Victoria Street; on the other, the gables of several terraces are stacked in neat horizontals and what I see is the harmonious visual rhythm of duplication: identical wall ends with their stumpy chimneys, matching windows, row upon row, the undemonstrative repetition of careful brickwork. Even from the back and sides, the terraces are handsome and precise. From all angles, they present a considered picture of the home, and seen together there is something fortress-like about the terraces: they line up like town walls – from any one point you can see nothing but another terrace, another row of cottage frontages – protecting the citizens of the village from corrupting forces beyond but also blocking the gaze of those who would try to see through the defence to the realities of domestic life within.

While the cottages at Cromford were built with top storeys to accommodate home working – wide openings offering light to those poring over textiles – the homes here, constructed almost half a century later, seem more concerned with concealing economic necessity and instead reinforcing a sense of contained, predictable and manageable family life. All model villages display the qualities which their founders held most dear, and which they believed would help forge a different future. Here at Saltaire the defining characteristic is the solid, unimpeachable, unquestionable faith in the family unit, expressed on a small scale by the rows of self-contained cottages and on a large scale by the powerful presence of the mill.

As I continue up the back of one of the terraces and turn again across the grid of streets, moving from the private to the public face of the housing, I become aware of all the street names. They're painted in bold white letters on dark blue panels and they're fixed at the end of each row so that they're very visible, both individually and as a set; I can read down almost the entire line to the streets at the very edge of the village. I walk slowly, reading each of the names affixed to the terraces that turn away to my left; then I return on the other side, reading the new set. At first I assume the names are typically regal: I see Mary Street and Edward Street and George Street. But then I notice an Ada Street and a Helen Street, a Fanny Street and an Amelia Street – these are much more familial, informal names without, as far as I'm aware, obvious links to the House of Hapsburg or the great European monarchies. This is a surprise. In such a place of solidity and convention it's an unexpected quirk. I wonder what's going on here. What are the names? Do they mean anything? Is there a hierarchy implied, the residents of stately William Street outranking those of the more homely Jane Street?

My tourist board leaflet has the answer, an apparently simple one: the streets at Saltaire are named after Titus Salt's children. There are one or two exceptions, most notably those remembering the architects and Victoria Road, the imposing main thoroughfare. But the cluster of streets running north to south at the centre of the town bears the names of Salt's six sons and five daughters, arranged in loose alphabetical order from Ada to Whitlam. Across and between them, from east to west, runs the backbone of Titus Street. When I look at the layout on my map I'm reminded of the branches of a family tree, or the diagrams in my old schoolbooks which purported to explain the process of smelting pig iron and its visual affinity to a farrowing sow. The terraces run down from Titus Street like children hanging to their fathers' coat-tails: it's a pattern which emphasises parenthood, family and the home.

In 1859, around the time Saltaire was constructed, a Scottish reformer with the deceptively cheerful name of Samuel Smiles published a modest book entitled *Self-Help; with Illustrations of Conduct and Perseverence*. It discussed the importance of the common man, and the essential role he could play in shaping a better nation through his actions: 'Even the humblest person, who sets before his fellows an example of industry, sobriety, and upright honesty of purpose in life, has a present as well as a future influence upon the well-being of his country,' Smiles explained. With such consequences in mind, he urged his readers to improve themselves in all possible ways through study, discussion and prayer, but most crucially through work: 'For all experience serves to illustrate and enforce the lesson, that a man perfects himself by work more than by reading,—that it is life rather than literature, action rather than study, and character rather than biography, which tend perpetually to renovate mankind.'[17]

As the title suggests, Smiles's book counselled self-reliance and individual responsibility. He held up two industrialists, Josiah Wedgwood and George Stephenson, as models of determination and stability, but he did not suggest his readers should aspire to emulate such great men too closely; instead he discouraged the working man from aiming above his station, advising him to be content with his material lot. The inevitable frustrations and difficulties of everyday life, Smiles suggested, should not be seen as miseries from which to escape, but as a welcome spur for the development of sound moral character:

> The common life of every day, with its cares, necessities, and duties, affords ample opportunity for acquiring experience of the best kind; and its most beaten paths provide the true worker with abundant scope for effort and room for self-improvement. The road of human welfare lies along the old highway of steadfast well-doing; and they who are the most persistent, and work in the truest spirit, will usually be the most successful.[18]

Smiles's unglamorous dissertation on the value of application and diligence was published in the same year as Darwin's revolutionary treatise on evolution, *On the Origin of Species*, and John Stuart Mills's ground-breaking philosophical essay, *On Liberty*, but its old-fashioned message proved surprisingly popular with readers. By the time of his death in 1904, over a quarter of a million copies had been sold in Britain, and the book had become a best-seller in Europe and Japan, although it's difficult to know how many of these readers were genuine working men and women – at whom the lessons were ostensibly aimed – and how many were comfortable middle-class commentators content to admire everyday struggles from a distance: in many ways, Smiles's argument that people were divided into the deserving and the undeserving – the rough and the respectable – appealed to the ruling municipal hierarchies because it shifted responsibility for inequality and suffering from economic or political action to individual moral choice.

Whatever the complexities of Smiles's readership, his confident promotion of 'application and perseverance, resolute will and purpose, and almost sublime patience' came to be read by many as a manual for working-class respectability – in particular, it was influential in defining a working-class male sense of self, a role and purpose for the working man in the new environment of the industrial city. Over twenty years after the publication of *Self-Help*, Daniel Merrick, the leader of the Sock and Top Union of Framework Knitters based in Leicester, took Smiles's principles as the basis for a novel, *The Warp of Life* (1876), set in a hosiery factory. The story contrasted the lives of two workers. Bill Crabtree drank and left his children unfed and uneducated; more seriously, perhaps, he 'lived in a house not a home'. By contrast, Samuel Wright was industrious and thrifty, a teetotal Methodist, whose children were clean and cared for and whose home was 'a picture of happiness'.[19] The book was overtly moral in tone, promoting the intrinsic value of self-improvement, venerating the home and making the case for a dignified and independent working class who could be trusted to act honestly and rightly if they followed simple rules of behaviour.

Saltaire is built along strong Smilesian lines: dominated by the mill, which signals all too clearly the value of work, its most striking buildings are given over to the notion of public self-improvement; the neat terraces are an icon of working-class respectability. It is the Samuel Wright of villages: an upright, conscientious and sober portrait of Victorian living. It's a place which seems to capture the Smilesian masculine spirit of industry and morality, and where both male and female identities are manipulated to fit the unforgiving demands of the mid-nineteenth century.

I end my visit here where I began: at the mill. The thick, persistent drizzle has turned the yards shiny and darkened the stones. It seems more than ever a solemn place, self-consciously sincere. Looking back towards the village, I have a suspicion that this careful knot of simple houses has evaded my best efforts at understanding it. With its pattern of defined terraces and its unspectacular architecture, it seems undemanding, even forthright, but the complex and shifting idea of home which hovers over all the model settlements is nowhere more evident than here at Saltaire. The village sits in a paradox – it is at once a forward-thinking powerhouse of industry and a symbol of undefined nostalgia, where unrealisable personal and family values are celebrated, idealised and re-presented. But it is singularly impressive, nonetheless, and like Salt's employees at the Great Exhibition, I've had a good day out. So I wait for the car windows to de-mist and I drive away, the mill and its village unmoving behind me, gradually disappearing into the urban sprawl of the West Yorkshire conurbation and the low cloud sinking off the moors beyond.

5

Creswell, Derbyshire

A biting east wind sweeps across the flat farmland of Nottinghamshire, very little getting in its way until it comes here, to Creswell at the north-east corner of Derbyshire. I'm in the middle of a large stretch of open playing field, a huge oval which inclines slightly towards the wind; it's almost featureless – there are just a few bare trees, some very straight tarmacked paths and an old-fashioned children's play area with metal swings which I know, just by looking, will crunch your hands with cold the moment you touch the chains. This is coal country – the Midland coalfield, of which this area is a part, stretches from Nottingham in the south to Bradford and Leeds in the north, running into the Pennine foothills to the west and the North Sea to the east – and surrounding the field are the rows of houses which make up the village, known simply as 'the Model', constructed in 1895 by the Bolsover Colliery Company.

The nature of the rock here – the wealth of the deposits – is the sole dictating factor in the formation of the community. Indeed, so rich were the coal seams, so extensive the mining and so large the workforce that planned villages punctuate the area, clustering particularly in South Yorkshire, their names recalling many of the major collieries – and their renowned bands: Grimethrope, Goldthorpe, Maltby. Less than ten miles away from Creswell, the Bolsover Coal Company invested in another village, New Bolsover, which was completed in 1896, nearly two hundred houses for miners and colliery officials that was also, in a depressing lack of imaginative spirit, christened 'the Model'. It sits rather precariously at the foot of the slope below the fairy-tale ruins of the twelfth-century Bolsover Castle; its red-brick terraces, like the ones at Creswell, also surround a green – a large rectangle this time – and peer out over a windswept view. Both villages were an expression of the Company's success – it supplied the evocatively named Bolsover 'Kitchen Cobbles' or 'Hard Nuts', coal from a compact top seam that burned long and freely with a minimum of ash, making it enormously popular not only with British consumers but in Russia, Norway, Sweden, Italy and Germany.

The village at Creswell has something of the maze about it. It consists of two rings of parallel terraces, their back yards facing each other with a narrow road between. One set of cottages fronts on to the green; the other looks towards what would have been the pits, spoil heaps and brick yards but is now waste ground or newer housing. Because of the geometry of the place, the inner ring of terraces is, of course, smaller than the outer one, and so the paths which cut through from the green to the world beyond are narrower at one end than the other, splaying outwards at an angle. When I arrive at the perimeter of the Model, by a row of shops, it's only the ends of these alleyways that I can see. They are just gaps in the rows of featureless brick walls but they are enough to draw me towards them and then on, into the grassy interior. Perhaps because of the roundness of the place, the broad oval of the design, the process feels somehow intestinal, even womb-like; there is certainly a sense of being enveloped, taken from the ordinary life of newsagents and chip shops and passing buses, and held apart.

As the alleyways narrow towards the centre of the village, funnelling me in, I'm more and more enclosed by the walls on either side; sight lines are truncated and I can only see more walls, the suggestion of a back yard. I suspect, for a moment, that it might be a dead end. Today, with clean brickwork, new paving, bollards and street furniture, neat yards and quiet streets, the anxiety this experience inspires is fleeting; I encounter no more than a split second of doubt before coming out again between the rows of cottages where the view widens and I can see the yards with their washing lines and trampolines and Union flags. But ten years ago, the Model at Creswell was semi-derelict and a byword for urban decline. The closure of the mines in 1991 and the subsequent unemployment and poverty meant many of the houses became empty. The alleyways that on my visit are something of a game – thrusting me into new parts of the village from a new angle – deteriorated into havens for addicts and vandals. Until its regeneration in 2004 Creswell felt abandoned, a failed experiment. The paths were best avoided, especially after dark; this was not a place you wanted closing in around you.

Ironically, when the Model at Creswell was conceived it was with the express intention of creating a safe haven, developing an open, welcoming pattern of housing. The straight terraces of Saltaire and Swindon were reimagined for a new generation and a new aesthetic. Down the road at Bolsover, the layout remains linear, the terraces slotting into a square, but here at Creswell the architect, Percy Bond Houfton, used the concentric circles to mark out a spacious environment with an expansion of the traditional village-green idea at its heart. The curves make a difference; the place feels generous and unconventional; the village is immediately appealing.

Creswell was the first in a number of planned settlements designed by Houfton, each experimenting with the use of open space: the most self-consciously 'rural' of these was probably Woodlands, near Doncaster, which was built in the early twentieth century for the miners at Brodsworth Colliery and which, as its name suggests, attempted to create a countryside environment in the heart of the black industrial coal lands. At Creswell, Houfton's layout is more formal – the green has the air of a municipal park rather than a natural feature – but his belief was clear enough: the integration of open space in and around the cottages would, he hoped, inspire good behaviour and community spirit: 'There is no reason why the miners should not have a village where three things could exist successfully,' announced Emerson Bainbridge, the founder and chairman of the Bolsover Colliery Company. 'The absence of drunkenness, the absence of gambling and the absence of bad language.' As at Nenthead, and most other planned villages, this sense of community was further engendered by the provision of wholesome family entertainment. 'The village has its own school, its institute and workman's club,' *The Times* reported approvingly. '[It has] a bowling green, cricket and football grounds and a brass band. And there are nursing, dress-making and ambulance classes, Boys Brigade, Cadet Corps and Boy Scouts.'[1]

As one reads the list of healthy activities on offer, and the unabashed moralising tone of the founder's vision, it can seem that little has changed during the seventy years or more which saw the building of New Lanark, Nenthead or Saltaire and this new reincarnation of the Model at Creswell. On one level, of course, this is true. There are common themes which emerge time and again. Employers and philanthropists were fully aware, for example, of the brutal conditions associated with mine working and naturally did their best to alleviate the emotional and physical effects of hard labour in an unhealthy environment. So the provision of allotments – as both a source of fresh food and a wholesome pastime – was a priority at Nenthead, Creswell and Bolsover, and at most of the similar villages established by beneficent employers in mining districts. At Nenthead, all the cottages were provided with generous amounts of land – some were even built as smallholdings – and sixteen acres of allotments were available at rentals of a few shillings. Dr W. Ewart, the London Lead Company's resident surgeon at Middleton-in-Teesdale, reported with evident sympathy on the effects of underground conditions, dust and lead poisoning in his recommendation that gardening should be widely encouraged:

> A healthy young man enters upon work in a lead mine; in a few years he begins to experience some degree of difficulty in breathing . . . he goes on working with increased shortage of breathing, expectoration and failing strength. His appetite for food is impaired, what he takes for breakfast is frequently vomited as he walks to work . . . He has great languor and frequently fits of severe coughing and evidence of imperfect oxygenation of the blood in the blueness of the lips etc. He may have got to forty-five years of age; he is low in strength, and compelled to give up work and stay at home a worn out miner. But even at home his health cannot be restored. The poor worn out miner soon dies exhausted.[2]

Similarly at Bolsover, each house was provided with an allotment of 600 square metres, rented at 4 shillings a year, in an effort to stave off 'the dyspnoea of old miners', anything from 'the infarction or stuffing of the lung tissue with foreign matter' to 'gradual degeneration and obliteration of blood vessels'.[3]

In the provision of primary household needs, too, the villages in Derbyshire suggest a continuum with the London Lead Company's energetic commitment to providing basic supplies at a fair price. At

Creswell and Bolsover the miners had reasonably easy access to market towns like Worksop and Chesterfield: the problem was not affordable food but, on such exposed sites, keeping warm. The colliery, of course, had plenty of coal – in an ingenious recycling system it installed a miniature railway at both villages, drawing coal by horse directly from the mines and delivering it in tubs along the backs of the houses from where it could be easily piled into cellars. On their return journey, the tubs provided an efficient means of removing night-soil waste which was taken from the cottages and sold to local farmers for fertiliser.

While many of the basic daily concerns had remained the same over the course of the nineteenth century, however, it is in the smaller detail that we begin to see difference, glimpsing something of the changes over time to people's lives, preoccupations and priorities. There is something other than the resolute modesty of Nenthead, for example, in the buildings here at Creswell. I emerge from one of the alleyways alongside a set of six houses with a Dutch-style roof line; across the park there are two terraces of cottages with high gables interspersed with a Georgianesque row, flat-faced and plain-roofed but marked by two small circular windows. There is variety and architectural ambition; there is ornament, discreet and undemonstrative, but nonetheless evident, and in these moments of decoration and diversity, we begin to perceive a vision that implies something more than simply providing practical homes for workers. This is not the sturdy philanthropic vision of Saltaire; this is a place that has witnessed fifty years of challenge to mid-nineteenth-century ideals and is beginning to look towards a new century. Just as the eccentric Picturesque at Edensor had given way, only two decades later, to the resolute Victorianism of Saltaire, so I think the village here shows how architecture was evolving again to reflect a change in mood and lifestyle.

Creswell was constructed at the high point of the Arts and Crafts movement. The 'Arts and Crafts' term we now use was not coined until 1887, but the ideas emerged first in the 1860s and by 1895, when work began at Creswell, they had become an accepted and influential part of cultural and political life. The middle classes in particular – the architects and reformers and philanthropists who drove the development of model villages – had come to embrace the combination of design aesthetic and social crusade which the movement embodied.

Drawing on the writings of the artist, critic and commentator John Ruskin, as well as the concerns of the Pre-Raphaelite Brotherhood – particularly its preoccupation with medieval art and culture, and its attention to natural form – the first identifiable Arts and Crafts group came together in April 1861 to form the company Morris, Marshall, Faulkner & Co. Created by William Morris, Ford Madox Brown, Edward Burne-Jones, Charles Faulkner, Dante Gabriel Rossetti, P. P. Marshall and Philip Webb, each of whom held a £21 share, the intention was to create a business which rejected machine-produced styles and instead turned attention to a range of craft techniques for making stained glass, wallpapers, fabrics and carpets with artisan methods. Many of the decorative patterns were adapted from natural forms, often using bold colours, and emphasis was placed on the unique qualities of the particular material being worked. Some products were even left purposely unfinished in order to allow the relationship between the material and its decoration to be evident and to create a certain rusticity.

The work caught the popular mood and 'the Firm', as it became known, quickly came to reflect the preferences and intellectualism of the socially mobile middle classes. During the 1850s and '60s there had been a growing reaction against 'vulgar' decoration as well as increasing discussion around the thorny question of what might constitute good taste. Manuals appeared, urging people to reconsider the displays in their homes and what these might say about them. Domestic ornament, it was suggested, was no longer just a private choice – what your home looked like and how you chose to decorate it had wider implications. In *Our Mutual Friend*, published in 1864–5, Dickens poked fun at the 'hideous solidity' of the objects in the homes of the newly rich, where objects were valued only on account of their financial worth. Furthermore, the book suggested that a lack of taste corresponded to a certain shadiness of dealing and moral inadequacy:

Mr Podsnap could tolerate taste in a mushroom man who stood in need of that sort of thing, but was far above it himself. Hideous solidity was the characteristic of the Podsnap plate. Everything was made to look as heavy as it could, and to take up as much room as possible. Everything said boastfully, 'Here you have as much of me in my ugliness as if I were only lead; but I am so many ounces of precious metal worth so much an ounce;—wouldn't you like to melt me down?

So widespread was the discussion about taste and ornament that it preoccupied several government select committees and prompted the founding of the South Kensington Museum (later the Victoria and Albert), which opened in 1857. Its first director, Henry Cole, was charged with reforming public habits, guiding consumers away from what was regarded as the bad taste of flounce and ornament towards an appreciation of better design and materials which, in turn, implied a simpler, more honest way of life. Cole boasted that he would change the face of British manufacturing by turning the public away from its previously mistaken preferences and instead creating a market for a more approved type of object: 'They will go to the shops and say, "We do not like this or that; we have seen something prettier at the Museum,"' he explained, 'and the shop-keeper, who knows his own interest, repeats that to the manufacturer and the manufacturer, instigated by the demand, produces the article.'[4]

Morris, Marshall, Faulkner & Co. found a niche for itself in this ongoing debate and climate of design reform. It offered the kinds of designs which appealed to those attempting to live by the new 'rules' of taste. At the 1862 International Exhibition in South Kensington, the company took two large stands amounting to almost 900 square feet of display space: one stand was a mishmash of stained glass, bits and pieces of embroidery, painted tiles, a washstand and bedstead, a sofa and copper candlesticks, while the other included a decorated cabinet designed by Webb and painted by Morris with scenes of St George and the dragon. The effect was striking but slightly bizarre: 'We were naturally much ridiculed,' Morris admitted.[5] In general, however, the work was well received. Both stands received medals of commendation, and it quickly became clear that the company had made a commercial breakthrough.

Perhaps by chance, Morris and his colleagues had alighted on what were to become cult motifs of the period – sunflowers, herbals, blue china – and within a few years business was flourishing. By the end of 1861, the company employed twelve workers, including boys from the Industrial Home for Destitute Boys on Euston Road. Commissions for stained glass alone rose from five in 1861 to fifteen in 1863, and there was plenty of work in decorating new churches. By 1864, the company had outgrown its original premises in Red Lion Square and had acquired new workshops at 26 Queen Street, and within a couple of years, two prestigious secular commissions further established the company credentials – to redecorate the Armoury and Tapestry Room in St James's Palace and to create the 'green dining room' at the South Kensington Museum. Both projects brought the distinctive designs more openly to public attention with their colourful, intricate, highly stylised explorations of natural forms, panels of fruit and flowers, painted floral ceilings and tiles entwined with leaves.

The change of emphasis from the ecclesiastic to the secular also corresponded with a restructuring of the company in the mid-1870s, when a bitter and protracted disagreement over share dividends led to the dissolution of Morris, Marshall, Faulkner & Co. and the birth of a new business, under Morris's sole ownership: Morris & Co. Morris turned his attention over the next few years to the dyeing of fabric and the production of textiles and carpets, exploring techniques for vegetable dyeing and studying the secrets of the silk trade in Leek, Staffordshire. Designs for block-print wallpaper began to accumulate during the mid-1870s; in 1879 he established a tapestry workshop. The popularity of the Morris & Co. work continued to grow, and was soon represented in commercial enterprises: in 1875, the opening of the Liberty & Co. store on London's Regent Street, for example, helped popularise the Arts and Craft aesthetic, bringing it firmly into the retail market and within the reach of the mass of middle-class buyers.

The ideas of the original group of Arts and Crafts pioneers spread, accumulating nuance and variety as new generations of artists, architects and designers came together. During the 1880s a number of Arts and Crafts groups were formalised: the Century Guild was created by the architect A. H. Mackmurdo in 1882; the Arts Workers' Guild was founded in 1884, quickly accumulating a distinguished and influential membership of practitioners, educators and reformers. In 1887 the Arts and Crafts Exhibition Society, with Walter Crane as its president, began to develop a series of shows in prestigious London venues. But this was not only a movement for the fashionable capital: by the beginning of the twentieth century, when Creswell was being designed and built, 135 separate Arts and Crafts movements had been established across Britain, and the Arts and Crafts ideal was being discussed throughout Europe and America.

The Arts and Crafts philosophy was an holistic one: it attempted to draw links between the quality of design and a more general quality of life. It was an argument John Ruskin had taken up in the mid-century when he advocated a rejection of modern ways of mass manufacture and soulless living in favour of a return to an emphasis on individual skilled labour, through which, he believed, the working man could find happiness and a certain moral rightness. In *The Stones of Venice*, an influential publication of 1853, he attacked the dehumanising effects of industrialisation:

It is not, truly speaking, the labour that it divided; but the men:— Divided into mere segments of men—broken into small fragments and crumbs of life; so that all the little piece of intelligence that is left in a man is not enough to make a pin, or a nail, but exhausts itself in making the point of a pin or the head of a nail. Now it is a good and desirable thing, truly, to make many pins in a day; but if we could only see with what crystal sand their points were polished,—sand of human soul, much to be magnified before it can be discerned for what it is—we should think that there might be some loss in it also. And the great cry that rises from our manufacturing cities, louder than their furnace blast, is all in very deed for this,—that we manufacture everything there except men; we blanch cotton, and strengthen steel, and refine sugar, and shape pottery; but to brighten, to strengthen, to refine, or to form a single living spirit, never enters into our estimate of advantages. And all the evil to which that cry is urging our myriads can be met only in one way . . . by a determined sacrifice of such convenience or beauty, or cheapness as is to be got only by the degradation of the workman; and by equally determined demand for the products and results of healthy and ennobling labour.

Ruskin's impassioned writings were at the heart of the Arts and Crafts campaign; his eloquent arguments were taken up wholeheartedly by Arts and Crafts followers in their insistence on the importance of the designer-craftsman, not only in rejecting the mass-production techniques and pollution, the squalor, monotony and dehumanising

conditions of industrialisation, but in establishing communities which
might suggest a more wholesome and sustainable way of living. The
mid-1870s saw Britain slump into an economic depression which was
to last until the end of the century, causing widespread unemployment
and hardship. It is no coincidence that this is the period which saw
the Arts and Crafts flourish – it was essentially a protest movement:
its early members were politically active; the formation of the many
companies, guilds and groups was as much to suggest the possibility
of a new social order as to propose particular design techniques; the
emphasis on creating small co-operative groups of workers was
intended as a direct critique of a centralised state system which
was more concerned with protecting the interests of wealthy capital-
ists and property owners than in promoting human welfare.

There were so many members of the Arts and Crafts movement,
with so many varying priorities and demands, that it's difficult to
define it by any single political aim. As with any community of this
kind, it was not necessarily a cohesive body of members; people were
drawn to it from a spectrum of ideologies and it was not without its
inconsistencies and contradictions. Despite what Ruskin and Morris
said about working creatively, for example, the making of wallpapers
by hand was a laborious, unpleasant and repetitive task. Nonetheless,
the link between Arts and Craft design and left-wing politics was clear:
Morris was friendly with both the Marx and Engels families, and he
became increasingly politicised as he grew older. At the end of 1884
he helped found the Socialist League, a mix of intellectuals and self-
taught workmen which came together to oppose capitalism, the Sudan
War and the threat of conflict between the UK and Russia. In
November 1887, he joined 100,000 other radicals, socialists and anarchists – joined in a loose coalition called the Law and Liberty League
– to march on Trafalgar Square in protest at the ongoing unemployment crisis, and in the vague hope of triggering revolution. In response
to the threat, the police 'charged in among the people' in an attack
described in *The Times*, 'striking indiscriminately in all directions and
causing complete disorder . . . the spectacle was indeed a sickening
one'.[6] In the fighting both protesters and police were injured, and the
event became known as 'Bloody Sunday'. Morris's contingent was
attacked on the way to Trafalgar Square, their flags and instruments
taken; thus deprived of a rallying point their party disintegrated.

Three years later, when Morris was fifty-six years old, he came to reinterpret his experiences in *News from Nowhere*, a combination of romantic idealism and revolutionary realism. Constructed as the narrative of a dream, the book has a floaty, visionary quality to it, describing a communist Utopia marked by a respect for simple craftsmanship and taking place in an imagined Britain of 1952 – but the fantasy world Morris creates is also firmly rooted in violent working-class revolution, a 'civil war' of hand-to-hand battles, disobedience and strikes which brings about the destruction of the established order:

> A sort of irregular war was carried on with varied success all over the country; and at last the Government, which at first pretended to ignore the struggle, or treat it as mere rioting . . . made a desperate effort to overwhelm 'the rebels', as they were now once more called, and as indeed they called themselves. It was too late. All ideas of peace on a basis of compromise had disappeared on either side. The end, it was seen clearly, must be either absolute slavery for all but the privileged, or a system of life founded on equality and Communism. The sloth, the hopelessness, and, if I may say so, the cowardice of the last century, had given place to the eager, restless heroism of a declared revolutionary period.[7]

With its language of class struggle and its vision of a fair future, *News from Nowhere* reflected the growing role of the Arts and Crafts movement as a voice for change during a period when workers' voices in general were becoming more clearly heard. With the end of the Chartist movement in the mid-nineteenth century, the fight for basic rights had been taken up by the steady growth of the trades union movement. The second Trades Union Congress, held in Birmingham in 1869, claimed to represent a quarter of a million workers, most of whom were skilled craft workers. Two years later the Trade Union Act began to give trades unions some legal recognition and the election of 1874 returned two miners' leaders to Parliament as liberal MPs. During the 1880s, unskilled workers also began to form new, often more militant, unions – the National Union of Gas Workers and General Labourers was founded in 1889; the General Railway Workers' Union in 1890 – pressing aggressively for change along socialist lines. The Arts and Crafts took its place amongst this growing body of active left-wing organisations campaigning for fair wages, tolerable living conditions and respect for working families.

The Arts and Crafts' emphasis on creating better ways of living – from more tasteful parlour decoration to more inclusive and equitable communities – inevitably came together in the designing and building of houses. Architects had been active in the movement since its inception, and the emphasis on environment, craftsmanship and detail lent itself to experiments with domestic spaces.

In 1875, twenty-four acres of land in West London were acquired by Jonathan Carr, a cloth merchant. After a false start with architect Edward William Godwin, he turned to Richard Norman Shaw to develop the estate of Bedford Park, a series of red-brick Queen Anne-style houses surrounded by gardens, open space and mature trees to give an impression of a rural idyll just thirty minutes from the City of London by steam train. Although it was originally intended simply as an estate, with up to 600 houses, Carr soon decided to add a church, an inn and shopping streets, creating an artificial, rather self-conscious 'village'. Bedford Park became the first garden suburb, a blueprint for a mix of pleasant housing, wide tree-lined roads and public gardens that would become an increasing feature of the expanding cities during the early part of the twentieth century, and which owed much to the influence of the Arts and Crafts movement. In 1901, a cooperative came together to begin work on building Brentham Garden Suburb in Ealing, West London; in 1906, Henrietta Barnett – founder of the Whitechapel Art Gallery and Toynbee Hall – began construction of a garden suburb in Hampstead on 243 acres of land acquired from Eton College; the following year the Oldham Garden Suburb was developed, linked to Manchester by a new tram route; Wavertree Garden Suburb in Liverpool welcomed its first residents in 1910, offering them, as one newcomer explained, 'an opportunity of securing at least a share in the advantages which as a rule are obtainable only by the few wealthy enough to be the individual owners of lawns and gardens'.[8]

These garden suburbs, as the name makes clear, were not villages. They were part of the city: with few shops, pubs or services, and no industry to offer employment, they made no attempt to be self-sufficient. The properties were usually offered at modest prices, but nonetheless residents were rarely industrial or manufacturing workers. They were more likely to be drawn from the increasingly confident lower-middle classes: the accommodation at Bedford Park, for example, was roomy (sometimes with as many as seven bedrooms) and fetched a rent of around £40 per annum. But garden suburbs did share with the planned villages an emphasis on community, a commitment to the use of good-quality materials and a pioneering sense that they were making better lives. They proved particularly popular with adherents to the Arts and Crafts movement who were keen to live in an environment which displayed their ideals so openly in the design of the houses and the interplay between home and garden. At Bedford Park, Jonathan Carr consciously set out to attract a particular kind of 'artistic' resident – so much so that one complained the experience was like living in a watercolour – and his efforts seem to have been successful: a survey of those who moved to the estate during its first twenty-five years found that of the 168 people living there, forty were artists – including John Butler Yeats, Lucien Pissaro and Ruskin's protégé, Thomas Matthews Rooke – sixteen were architects and nine were actors and musicians. (The lifestyle also seemed particularly popular with the armed forces: forty-three of the early residents were army officers.)

As cities grew, flourishing under a late-nineteenth-century regime of foreign trading and financial speculation overseas, so too did the opportunities for the Arts and Crafts. The movement prospered in urban centres with the growth of exhibition societies, art schools, workshops and architectural experiments: in Birmingham, the School of Art developed into an influential advocate, many of its teachers and pupils becoming leading exponents of the style; the Manchester School of Art also promoted the Arts and Crafts philosophy – the detailing on the school's building by W. J. Neatby is a fine example of distinctive ornamental natural forms – and Glasgow became a renowned Arts and Crafts centre, creating its own style inspired by the work of Charles Rennie Mackintosh, Herbert MacNair, and Margaret and Frances MacDonald.

But in some ways, the Arts and Crafts movement was divided, lured by a sophisticated profile in the cities while at the same time nurturing an unshakeable belief in natural materials and a preoccupation with rural life. Despite its influence in the new buildings and garden suburbs of the country's most active urban centres, the ideal remained, at heart, one of peaceful country living sustained by a nostalgia for local craft traditions. In 1874, when the success of his design company seemed secure in fashionable London, William Morris wrote of his longing to leave the 'sordid loathsome' city for life 'among gardens & green fields'. C. R. Ashbee, whose Guild and School of Handicraft had workshops in London's East End and a retail outlet in stylish Mayfair, nonetheless claimed that 'the proper place for the Arts and Crafts is in the country . . . away from the complex, artificial and often destructive influences of machinery and the great town'.[9]

Encouraged by such sentiments, many of those who were drawn to the ideals of Arts and Crafts made the move into the country, and the growth in the cities was equalled by the development of energetic rural communities. The aim was not to impose a style upon the countryside, in the manner of the Picturesque, but instead to rediscover what was already there, focusing on what were considered the authentic, intrinsic charms of rural living – vernacular building styles, traditional crafts, old-fashioned habits. Many of the most enterprising forms of the movement had links with particular localities: in the Cotswolds, for example, where William Morris had his country house at Kelmscott Manor, there was a lively group of advocates; in the Lake District, where Ruskin had spent the last thirty years of his life, several schools and workshops developed a distinctive 'brand' of Arts and Crafts fully expressed in the house and gardens at Brantwood which were designed by Baillie Scott.

It's not surprising that many of the philanthropists who were interested in creating villages should have been drawn to the influence of the Arts and Crafts movement, with its sense of social purpose and a distinctive design aesthetic well suited to domestic building. A village experiment promised to bring together the artistic and the political, each group of cottages suggesting both the beautiful and the radical. Many of the model villages built towards the end of the nineteenth and into the early twentieth centuries incorporated elements of Arts and Crafts, to a greater or lesser extent depending on location, budget and individual taste. They sat somewhere between the two axes of the movement, between the urban and the rural, between city fashion and independent working community. Often the evidence is small: at Bolsover the Arts and Crafts touch consists of little chains of daisies carved into the tight red brickwork along the house fronts. The modest rows of flowers seem to have little impact on a place that is still poor and workaday. Bolsover is a village where boys ride hard on pedal bikes on a schoolday, heavy brown dogs pull at chains and the flag of St George is much in evidence. It's not in any way a middle-class place, or obviously inspired by aesthetic values, and yet the daisies are there, a charming decoration and a nod to lives beyond those evident today.

Here at Creswell, the Arts and Crafts influence is more fully developed and subtly invasive: it manifests itself in the curve of a roof line or the brickwork detail above a window; it's visible in the touches of styling that disrupt the expectation of the everyday and industrial; it is certainly implicit in the sense of space, and in the attention given to parkland and gardens, bringing the ideal of the rural cottage to what would have been a blackened colliery site. But perhaps the best evidence of the intrusion of Arts and Crafts is in several small, now rather nondescript, features – the carved stone inscriptions marking the entrances to disused public buildings: the shabby, boarded and unloved library, hall and clubhouse.

These modest panels are worn and flaking, almost lost in the semi-dereliction of broken tarmac, peeling brick and untidy wiring. Sandwiched between a door and a window or, in one case, inserted at knee height beside a short flight of concrete steps, they are discoloured and patchy, the relief work hardly visible from some angles. I walk across the scruffy car park in front of the public hall several times before they attract my attention. But their neglect is a shame because the slight decoration on these unassuming signs rejoices in unabashed loops of acanthus and whorls of fern while the lettering is entirely evocative of the Arts and Crafts movement, recalling the wonderful typefaces William Morris designed for his Kelmscott Press.

Aside from the displaced elegance, there's an oddity about these inscriptions: the 'e' is missing from the end of the word 'entrance' which reads, in capitals, 'PUBLIC HALL ENTRANC', the whole surrounded by a wreath of carved leaves and topped by a crest. The missing 'E' doesn't appear to be the result of a clumsy repair and I stand for a while and consider the reading and writing skills taught in the Bolsover Colliery Company schools. I wonder if some clerk of works failed to notice the mistake. Then, briefly, I imagine a very particular thief chiselling the final letter away, to complete a word of his own perhaps, a word that lacks an elegant, curvaceous capital E. It's a disappointment to realise that the two 'L's of the word 'HALL' in the line above have also been manipulated, the second tucked into the angle of the first, smaller and slightly elevated. It becomes clear that the wreath was carved first and whoever came along to add the letters into the space inside simply ran out of room. It's a blunder, recorded for posterity. Perhaps no one could be bothered to start again. Perhaps Emerson Bainbridge, the Bolsover Colliery Company director, decided that he'd invested enough money in his village already and refused to have the panel remade.

However it has come to endure, this tiny mistake, this odd detail, seems to bear witness to much about the nature of a village like Creswell, and its relationship to the earlier overtly industrial model villages of Nenthead or Saltaire. While Houfton, the architect, integrated elements of Arts and Crafts design into the form and layout of his cottages, the lasting impression here is of a tough, working village, a place in which the decorated entrance panels to the hall are an afterthought, a hopeful gesture towards something other than the mining which dominated lives. Creswell is an in-between village. It doesn't show a full commitment to design ideals but it does attempt to rise above the pragmatism of the earlier model-village experiments. It is in essence a series of ordinary terraces and yet it attempts to camouflage this routineness with the occasional panel of nicely wrought Arts and Crafts lettering. When this goes wrong, however, it's not important enough to put right. The miniature train worked effectively and efficiently to deliver coal and take away sewage – this is what was significant. It did not matter if the Arts and Crafts flourishes were inaccurate and skewed.

This ambivalence is part of the central irony inherent in Creswell – that the Arts and Crafts movement, which was anti-industrial and anti-capitalist at its roots, should be adopted by a company which was dependent on, and complicit in, heavy industry: the Bolsover Colliery Company was in the original 'FT 30', an index of stocks which has since been superseded by the FTSE 100. The fact that architects and founders saw no antagonism between their business priorities and the philosophical ideals they were apparently embracing in the model village is an indication of just how complex the economic appetite had become by the end of the nineteenth century, how inescapable the commercial world and how powerful the grip of commodities on ordinary lives. In the early century, we see little attempt to mediate or camouflage the industrial. These early villages are presented quite openly as industrial constructions, clusters of cottages built in response to the needs of the mines or factories and in the same solid, practical pattern as the assay house or the company offices. By the end of the century, however, this clarity has become obscured. The coal miners' cottages at Creswell are tweaked to suggest something 'more' than a basic place for workers to eat and sleep. The Arts and Crafts touches are aimed at creating a sense of value and belonging; they make prosperity visible, drawing attention to the success of the Bolsover Colliery Company and the comfortable living conditions of its employees. They add flourish and superfluity.

What we can see in the architectural differences between Nenthead and Creswell is complex. In two windswept villages, perched above mineral deposits of exhausted wealth, we can see the change from early-century confident – even optimistic – industrialism to a style which, at the threshold of the twentieth century, is anxious to throw off the taint of industrial squalor and brutality and instead suggest something newer, more pleasant and more modern. With its Arts and Crafts detail, Creswell presents visitors with visible evidence of ambitious social ideals and aesthetic sophistication. It seems to be distancing itself from the poverty and severity of the mid-century towns: the configuration of the cottages around the huge oval green creates an immediate impression of comfort and progress. On closer inspection, however, the smaller details are unconvincingly achieved: there is, after all, a carved stone Arts and Crafts plaque with a missing 'E', badly done, unfinished. The village seems ill at ease with the trappings of its not-quite-industrial identity, like an old miner uncomfortably trying out new clothes. Despite its attempts at modernity and aesthetics, Creswell is ultimately a mining village, created by and dependent on industrial profits, solid and rather remote – and not enormously removed from Nenthead, 140 miles further north and conceived almost a century earlier.

Perhaps we've almost come full circle. Like Cromford, Creswell demonstrates ideas in transition, not quite thoroughly worked out or accepted. A century has passed, and again we're at a point of change.

Just as Cromford led us from the rural structures of the eighteenth century into the industrial hierarchies of the nineteenth, so Creswell is reshaping Victorianism for the twentieth century. It's a place which begins to query what comes after the certainty of nineteenth-century industrialisation, and which poses the question in the fabric of the village. At Port Sunlight, in the next chapter, we'll see evidence of the Arts and Crafts ideals worn more comfortably; there the rather reticent architectural expression seen at Creswell gives way to a more undisguised celebration of style and form, with patent flourishes more thoroughly integrated into housing schemes. But what interests me here is the sense of transition, the tentative reworking of the idea of home. I'm charmed by Creswell's shyness, its unwillingness to fully let go of tried-and-tested industrial habits and yet its evident belief in newer possibilities. The smog of the coal mine and the brilliance of the Arts and Crafts ideal are both important to this place, a village which seems to express the contradictions of a period in which people have grown accustomed to living with mass manufacturing and the comparative wealth it allows, while wanting something more, or other.

6

Port Sunlight, the Wirral

A freezing day in November; a bleak day, impenetrably grey and wintry. I approach across the flat land of the Wirral through industrial estates and unremitting series of traffic lights; past shopping centres and refineries. The village I've come to see is concealed by the accumulations of modern commercial life and when I turn in from the main road, the sudden arrival is a surprise: broad avenues and long vistas, peaceful village greens, trees organised into disciplined copses that draw in the eye. Because of the forgiving contours of the land, the industrial detritus beyond is completely invisible; it's easy to believe that I've been transported many miles into the ancient tranquillity of rural Cheshire.

Port Sunlight is engineered to suggest space, to promise (although not reveal) wide horizons. But paradoxically, there's also an impression of enclosure, created at least in part by the same uneasy sense of artifice that marked my visit to Blaise Hamlet. I recognise the unsettling feeling of having stepped into a beautifully crafted video game or film set: the perimeter of the village is arranged with blocks of houses all presenting their faces to the visitor; the corners are connected by walls which prevent views of anything out of place. I suspect that at any moment the illusion might be shattered by the arrival of canteen lorries, an elaborate explosion, a high-speed car chase.

But nothing happens. Like many of the other model villages I've visited, this is a quiet place; it seems hardly lived in, or perhaps tentatively lived in, as though the powerful architectural identity of the village is too overbearing. The streets are more or less deserted; there's no traffic. The only signs of life are a young woman walking a small dog – on the lead – and a man sweeping leaves from the rose gardens.

He's wearing a uniform marked 'Port Sunlight Garden Estate and Museum'. Just because he's there, doing something, I'm drawn to him, and I begin by crossing to the gardens and walking up the straight path between the straight flower beds. There are no blooms to see, only the meticulously turned and weeded earth. I go on towards the war memorial at the far end. Designed by Sir Goscombe John and installed in 1921, the monument is described by Pevsner as 'a rare example of a war memorial which is genuinely moving and which avoids sentimentality'. It's sprawling and elaborate, a wide circle of steps converging on a group of figures in animated poses: women and a great many children as well as armed soldiers crouching, their weapons poised, pointing directly at me or at the enemy just behind me; its theme is 'defence of the home'.

It seems fitting that the memorial should celebrate a halcyon ideal of home and family in a place which presents a multiplicity of versions of 'home', an unsettling kaleidoscopic display of what the idea might mean. Port Sunlight is a place of architectural medley and experiment; it reinvents the physical appearance of home on every street and at every corner: this is the miscellany of styles at Edensor on a much larger scale. The Arts and Crafts influence is strongly present – on my right, there's a line of gabled cottages with low eaves and country-style windows – but there's no single dominant design: already I've seen red-brick houses, not unlike town vicarages, with diamond-paned bay windows and geometric stone detailing; curved, Dutch-inspired roof lines which recall the terraces at Creswell but which are here larger and bolder, decorated with ornate white plasterwork; a large, dumpy, detached home with heavy battlemented gables and an odd little round tower; I've seen the Elizabethan, the Georgian, the Victorian. Port Sunlight is a place of infinite variety, and obvious confidence. On one of the streets, in the small window of a rather plain grey pebbledashed terraced cottage, someone has hung a small 'Home Sweet Home' decoration, but it seems rather lost and somehow poignant, a feeble attempt to capture an ideal of home in this place of inconsistency and variance.

Walking on beyond the war memorial and the gabled, red-brick Lyceum Theatre with its squat clock tower, I come to 'the Dell', a sunken strip of mature shrubbery and trees. It's an unspectacular, undemonstrative patch of land, a hybrid of municipal city park and the conventional landscaping of a minor country estate. Its single interesting feature is a sandstone bridge, pinkish in tone, arching from one grass bank to the other. It is weathered and suggestive, recalling ancient packhorse routes, hidden railway cuttings, or perhaps the meeting of old roads over an important waterway.

But the bridge is not very old: it was created in 1894 by the Cheshire architect John Douglas – the same who built the Model Cottage in my home village – who also designed several blocks of houses here and the Lyceum alongside. It's only been in place a little over a hundred years. And in 'the Dell' beneath there's no idyllic bubbling brook or slumbering blue river – just a concrete path. The path meanders as though it might be water. From a distance its flat greyness is deceptive; I half-suspect there might actually be a stream there. But this is an illusion. It's a very ordinary path. Here on the bridge, as elsewhere in the village, there's a fairy-tale element to what I can see. I'm asked to suspend disbelief, to enter into the spirit of the place, to look at the concrete path and see a stream. This is a village of ornament: turrets and towers, fancy metalwork, ornate stonework, decorative drainpipes, impractical bridges. It rejoices in a flourish over a doorway, or a flighty fan of roof tiles, anything to hold back the flat land beyond, industry stretching away along the banks of the Mersey, factories and refineries threatening to encroach on this calm, precise fantasy of rural life.

And that's the second thing I notice about the bridge. At one end it's firmly rooted in the village: there's a small round stone bench built into the parapet from which you can look out over the attractive collection of architectural styles and wide lawns at this side of the community, the old trees, the winding driveways. But a few steps away on the other side, walking over the steep stepped hump with my back to the church and the school, the library and art gallery, the neat houses, there's a different world. On the other side of the bridge is the factory wall. It's fronted by an open tract of land, tarmacked today and full of workers' parked cars. The wall is neither particularly high nor particularly ugly. In fact the brick archways and roundels are rather pleasing; they lend it the elegance of a fine nineteenth-century railway station. But it marks the boundary between romance and pragmatism, between the dreamy serenity of the village and the brutal cut-and-thrust of Victorian capitalism.

This was the bridge that took workers to their sweating, stinking, treacherous jobs boiling, mixing and manipulating chemicals and oils. It detached them from the unique environment of the village and joined them to the hundreds and thousands of other labourers in the north-west of England and beyond struggling with the dirty, dehumanising and dangerous processes of British manufacturing. The bridge spanning the pastoral promise of 'the Dell' in Port Sunlight yokes Victorian nostalgia, romanticism and idyll to the political, social and economic realities of early-twentieth-century manufacturing.

Port Sunlight was built by William Hesketh Lever, later Lord Leverhulme, to house the workers at his soap factory. The son of a Bolton shopkeeper, Lever had a modest education and worked for twenty years in the family grocery business before establishing Lever Brothers with his younger brother, James, in 1885. He was thirty-five years old, and ambitious; a man of contradiction and paradox. He came to own a number of luxurious and glamorous residences, but preferred to sleep in the open air, constructing special 'incomplete' bedrooms to make this possible. He was driven by both the business-man's will to succeed and the religious creed of the Congregationalist Church, of which he remained a lifelong active member. He was dictatorial and also enormously generous, a ruthless autocrat and visionary philanthropist. He objected to charity as 'the mother of pauperism' but believed in the principles of social justice.

Just as Titus Salt was compared by his contemporaries to Roman generals, so Lever was compared to Napoleon: in 1905, the landscape architect Thomas Mawson claimed Lever was 'a veritable Napoleon' not only 'in his grasp of all the factors dominating any problem he tackled' but perhaps more interestingly in his manner – 'in his walk and pose, and in his speech'. In November 1912, a piece in the American magazine *Town Topics* went a step further by declaring that Lever was 'more ruthless, more autocratic, more dogmatic than Napoleon'; the metaphor was employed again a couple of years later when A. G. Gardiner included Lever in his pantheon *Pillars of Society*, as a man 'who would have been the Napoleon of tea or of oil or of empires, if not in war then in peace'. Finally, after Lever's death in 1925, at the age of seventy-four, the *Liverpool Daily Post* printed a memorial address which returned again to the idea: 'There was something Napoleonic about him . . . he thought not in terms of cities or towns but of continents.'[1]

As proof of his Napoleonic determination and energy, Lever's new company was to expand at a ferocious pace. By 1897, his younger brother James had resigned his directorship on the grounds of ill health, but William pressed on alone; by 1909 the Port Sunlight factory was employing 3,600 workers to produce a variety of brands which were shipped across the world – there were subsidiaries in the United States and Canada, Switzerland, Germany, West Africa and Australia – and in 1925 the different enterprises came together to form the modern conglomerate Unilever which, within five years, was the largest company in Britain, employing a quarter of a million people.

Having outgrown the challenges of his family's grocery business, Lever turned his attention to soap. Soap manufacture was profitable and cut-throat; it was the ideal business for a determined entrepreneur with an aggressive streak. In 1885, Lever rented a factory in Warrington and began manufacturing the brand that would ensure the company's early success – Sunlight. But the Warrington site was cramped, hemmed in on all sides by the Mersey, the railway and unsavoury pumping stations. Lever needed something bigger and better. He enlisted the help of a local architect, William Owen, and together the two men took the train up and down the Mersey in search of the perfect manufacturing base. After many months of frustration they finally discovered fifty-six acres of cheap land with good rail facilities, easy access to the river and a potential workforce at Birkenhead: a marshy collection of fields which Lever was to christen Port Sunlight.

At the turn of the century, Lever Brothers would add new brands to its range of soap – Lifebuoy (1894) followed by Lux Flakes in 1900 and Vim in 1904. But it was Sunlight that made the early market breakthrough, in part thanks to technical innovation. Lever teamed up with William Hough Watson, a chemist from his home town, who invented a process for making soap from glycerin and vegetable oils, rather than animal fats. The new product was an immediate improvement on anything previously available on the market: free-lathering and effective, most importantly it was pleasant to use, without the lingering greasy smell of tallow.

But technical advance alone was not enough to explain Sunlight's

rapid progress in the marketplace. The second factor in Lever's favour
was his apparently natural talent for promotion. He appreciated the
theatricality and playfulness of branding and marketing; he had an
astute understanding of the potentially intimate relationship between
consumers and the merchandise they liked to buy. The new product
was not presented simply as 'carbolic soap', but instead was given a
distinct identity and a name that conjured bright days, ease, happiness
and clean living. This was Sunlight Soap. Buying a bar was more than
a transaction in spotless laundry: it was an investment in a pleasurable
and beautiful lifestyle. The new company aimed, Lever explained, 'to
make cleanliness commonplace; to lessen work for women; to foster
health and contribute to personal attractiveness, that life may be more
enjoyable and rewarding for the people who use our products'. Sunlight
Soap, then, could change your life. It's a mission statement – rather
alarmingly perhaps – still used proudly by Unilever today.[2]

It was just two years after the launch of this apparently revolutionary
soap that Lever began work on a village for the people who would be
employed to make it. Naming the settlement Port Sunlight, he branded
this new community with the same values as were implied in the marketing of his bar of soap: this place would be fresh, healthy and satisfying.
It would offer a radical departure from the dark yards and narrow streets
of existing working towns. Port Sunlight: a place of clean air and clean
living, of beginnings and arrival and promise. It's a name that encourages a smile, a frolic even. It's a name that advertises Lever's intentions
to reinvent and rearrange the entire notion of community.

From the middle of the nineteenth century, businesses began steadily
to invest more time and energy into the evolving discipline of advertising. This was a period when most ordinary people could aspire to
own something other than the necessities of clothing and food; when
objects could be desired not for their usefulness but for their glamour
or their luxury. Skilled workers and the middle classes on a steady
wage began to have more and more disposable income to spend on
things to improve their houses – polishes and starches – or their tea
tables – teas and jams, potted meats and pickles. Perhaps most significantly, these commodities increasingly came canned or packeted, so
giving new opportunities for branding: one of the advantages of
Sunlight Soap, for example, was that it was sold in pre-wrapped bars

instead of being cut from a single large block on the grocer's counter. This meant it could be more easily stored at home – it also, of course, offered Lever the opportunity to print his mark on every single sale and place his advertising on every pantry shelf.

The increasing move towards packaging in the middle of the nineteenth century had created more of these pristine sites for labelling and so encouraged companies to develop their brands more aggressively: John Horniman started to sell tea in packets rather than loose in 1826; pills were neatly packed in boxes by Thomas Beecham in 1848; tobacco started to be pre-packed and named by the 1840s and by 1877, John Player was registering his first brand name – Gold Leaf – and first trademark – Nottingham Castle – and giving them prominent place on his packets. By 1882, cigarette advertising had developed still further with the introduction of distinctive pictures and a catchy marketing slogan on every pack: 'Player's Please'.

In addition to packaging, there were wordy, earnest printed advertisements which appeared in the press. Holloway's Pills and Ointments, for example, urged readers in 1853 to try its 'invaluable remedy' as a cure for the widespread misery of consumption: 'The alleviative and tonic influence of Holloway's invaluable remedy operates like a charm in subduing the formidable symptoms,' it boasted. The *Illustrated London News*, the world's first fully illustrated weekly newspaper, launched in 1842, was the favourite home for advertisers; its pages were soon full of colourful claims and elaborate artwork publicising the leading brands. The 1844 special Christmas supplement featured advertisements for Schweppes Table Waters, Brown & Polson, Allen & Hanburys, Eno's Fruit Salt and two rival soap products, Wright's Coal Tar Soap and Pears, which placed a large sepia illustration on the back cover. By 1891, demand for advertising space had expanded still further and that winter the paper's Christmas special featured full pages for Edwards' Harlene products for the hair, Titan Soap, Sunlight Soap, Brooke's Soap – Monkey Brand, Phillips's Crystal Glass by Webb, Vinolia Soap, John Brinsmead & Sons – Pianos, Beecham's Pills, and Carter's Little Liver Pills.

The advertisements were aimed largely at the burgeoning middle classes, with money to spend and fashionable status to maintain. Most advertising space was taken in middle-class journals, with a focus on those products which were seen to contribute to an aspirational lifestyle. An examination of the profile of advertisers in the *Illustrated London News* reveals that soap – along with other cleaning and domestic products – provided one of the liveliest battlegrounds. The promise of cleanliness effectively offered the chance to rise magnificently above the grime of the working-class slum, and the grubby habits associated with it. The home which invested in efficient new products was portrayed as a respectable place for family, where the female members of the household were freed from the drudgery of endless cleaning, and where moral, religious and social conventions could be comfortably upheld: 'Less Labour; Greater Comfort' ran the Sunlight Soap slogan of 1890.

Promoting powerful messages of personal and domestic improvement, the advertising campaigns undoubtedly began to have an effect on the way people viewed themselves and their families. The female consumer, for example, was no longer just the secluded housewife guided by her husband's tastes and buying power, but could be reached in her own home on a daily basis: her important role in the advertisers' machinations began to liberate women, empowering the female consumer (albeit on a modest scale) by giving her choices about what to buy and by making her the focus of expensive campaigns. In addition, the invasion of brand names, images and slogans into the kitchen, pantry and parlour mitigated against the idea of the home as a secluded place of purity and abstinence – as portrayed in Patmore's poem 'The Angel of the House' – making clear instead its links to a bustling commercial world beyond. The middle-class family was increasingly defined not by its ability to remain apart in a cocoon of innocence but in material terms, by which brands it bought and used.

Today we are completely accustomed – and hence rather blind – to the onslaught of the advertiser. But for the Victorians this was a new and radical departure. For the first time, manufacturers were publicly clamouring for attention, wooing the customer with remarkable promises. While the soap battle was largely played out in the colourful, full-page spreads aimed at the wife at home, advertising had become such a widespread phenomenon that it was by no means restricted to the pages of the press. There was also, for example, the occasional outbreak of a more direct, guerrilla approach with tantalisingly obscure adverts graffitied in urban centres. *The Ladies' Cabinet of Fashion, Music and Romance* – a forerunner of the contemporary woman's magazine – ran a story of 'A Summer Ramble from Oxford to London' in 1866 which described one such campaign:

> We found that the chief object of interest was the following inscription upon every wall and untenanted house: "Who's Griffiths?" Wherever we went, this legend, like the monster of Frankenstein, haunted us— now deftly executed, now rudely serrated, like the Runic rhymes of our forefathers. We had to wait long for a solution; but at length it came, and at an especially pretty part of the river. With Denman's lyrically-praised "Cooper's Hill" to our right, and a gem of an ivy-towered church in front, in the most gigantic characters, there met our eye the following: "Try Griffith's Patent Lucifers." Wondrous power of advertisement!

Griffith's campaign, with its melodrama and lengthy narrative, its mystery and visually striking denouement, could easily have taken its place among the bright, bold pages of the Victorian Penny Dreadful; it shrewdly tapped into the Victorian fondness for drama and spectacle. Nor was it a one-off phenomenon: the writer of the article goes on to explain that while, in the middle of the century, 'advertising vans' were 'thought a marvellous thing', just a decade later advertising had become much more colourful, ambitious and immediate: 'One is not surprised to see an army of boys or embattled hosts of seedy men, with placards before and behind,' she explains, as well as 'gigantic vans of the colours of the rainbow'.[3]

In the scramble to ensure the best exposure for new and memorable slogans, distinctive artwork, posters and billboards – to create colour and sparkle and excitement – any vacant space was regarded as a potential advertising site, from terrace walls to trams. Not everyone greeted the new fashion with delight: disgruntled traditionalists wrote to *The Times* in 1892 to express their horror at the 'sordid and disorderly spectacle' that was blighting England 'from sea to sea'.[4] But the process seemed unstoppable. Railway stations and alongside railway tracks were a particular favourite for advertising hoardings, targeting the movers and shakers who were making use of the expanding rail network to further their businesses and transform their lives, while Thomas Beecham recognised that those taking the air at seaside resorts

– often on doctors' orders – might be a fruitful market for his medicines: he supplied boatmen with free sails on which flapped the slogan, 'What are the wild waves saying? Try Beecham's Pills.'

The amounts invested in these campaigns were a clear indication of the manufacturers' confidence in the efficacy of the direct approach: Thomas Holloway, maker of pills and potions, was spending £40,000 a year on advertisements as early as the 1860s; by the end of the century the Beecham brand of cures was investing over £100,000 a year. Lever spent £2 million – a colossal sum – during his first twenty years of making soap, often turning a product's weakness into its strength with a nifty sleight of hand. Lever Brothers' Lifebuoy, for example, used remnants from the manufacture of Sunlight Soap and so had a strong carbolic acid content which gave it a distinctive sweet tarry smell; the associated marketing campaign positioned it, successfully, as a disinfectant soap, reminding consumers that the whiff of hospital wards was a guarantee of health and cleanliness.

During the course of the nineteenth century, the consumption of soap increased significantly from about 3.5 pounds per person per year to around 17 pounds per person per year. In addition, the population almost tripled. The market for soap had never been larger. William Lever was quick to recognise the power of advertising and its capacity to transform his business. He admitted quite openly that 'people already in the soap business could have put rings round me on manufacturing', but he was also astutely aware of their weakness and his particular talent: 'None of them knew how to sell soap, and therefore I concentrated on the selling side of soap, advertising, agencies, etc., and left others to look after the works.'[5]

He introduced free paper dolls with soap purchases, each coming with the promise of interchangeable outfits to encourage children to collect the range – and their mothers to remain loyal to the brand. He also devised schemes offering series of encyclopedias, and designed wrappers that could be exchanged for gifts: a rolled-gold watch was the reward for a collection of 4,000 wrappers. Most famously, perhaps, soap manufacturers also turned their attention to using works of art as a novel means of selling their products. The best-known example is the first: *Bubbles* by Sir John Everett Millais, which was bought from the artist – along with the copyright – by Sir William Ingram, proprietor of the *Illustrated London News*, and destined for the Christmas edition in 1887.

While previous festive numbers had published Millais's paintings of children to great acclaim, this was the year when advertising took a hold: before its appearance in the magazine, the painting and its copyright were sold to A. & F. Pears who turned it into an advertisement by adding a bar of soap in the foreground. Millais was horrified. But despite his protestations, the manoeuvre was a great success, creating a buzz of public excitement and boosting sales. Lever – momentarily on the back foot – responded by purchasing a similarly sentimental painting two years later, advertising Sunlight Soap with *The New Frock* by William Powell Frith, in which a winsome young girl shows off a spotless peach-and-white dress – with the caption 'So Clean'.

Other paintings followed, including John Bacon's *The Wedding Morning* and Albert Tayler's *A Dress Rehearsal*, in which bars of Sunlight Soap were substituted for details in the originals such as mantel clocks and crockery, and which drew on the image of the pretty, wholesome bride in her pristine gown to emphasise values of romance, family and purity. Lever's entire art collection – which finally numbered over 20,000 works of painting, sculpture, furniture, ceramics and textiles – developed from these advertising experiments, which continued to be printed in illustrated journals until the early years of the twentieth century. At the end of my visit to Port Sunlight, I spend an hour or so in the quiet rooms of the Lady Lever Art Gallery where I see some of the works that were part of these original advertising campaigns. Here they are, as the artists meant them to be, without their bars of soap, but the lingering influence of the magazine spreads is so strong – and their reproductions so numerous – that I find it's impossible to dissociate these paintings from the products they came to represent. It's testament to the cleverness of the original advertising campaigns, I suppose, and to the tenacious grip of innovative promotional material, even more than a century after its first appearance.

William Lever was born in 1851, the year of the Great Exhibition at the Crystal Palace; he grew up when events, displays, exhibitions, entertainments – and advertisements – were becoming more and more elaborate, impressive and dramatic. In later life, he enjoyed the glitz and glamour of ballroom dancing; as a young man he was familiar with all kinds of travelling shows and fairs. By the mid-nineteenth century Britain was home to hundreds of circuses alone. Trick riding was the main attraction, but jugglers and aerial acts, trapeze and high-wire artists, exotic animals and freak shows also drew the crowds. Such events were so popular with the general public that George Sanger, the most successful circus entrepreneur, quickly became a millionaire. Barnum & Bailey's in London's Olympia employed 1,200 people and 380 horses, and laid on aquatic acts, military band recitals, ballet, trapeze stunts and a spectacular re-enactment of a sea battle at Santiago. Outside London, circuses toured to even the smallest towns and by the 1870s, with the expansion and improvement of the railway network, huge touring juggernauts were rolling up with two or three trains loaded with acts, animals and equipment. Central to these tours was the circus parade which drew enormous and energetic crowds. These were impressive choreographed spectacles in their own right – when Sanger's Circus arrived at a new venue it paraded Mrs Sanger dressed as Britannia, with Nero, the circus lion, at her feet, a string of camels, a herd of elephants, costumed characters leading exotic animals, and a series of bands – and they were perhaps the most impressive example of the fluid boundaries between performance and advertising.

Some advertisers adopted the pattern of the circus parade directly, bringing animals and caravans on to the streets to attract attention. In 1881 Hudson's Soap organised a stagecoach drive using 100 horses to cover the distance from London to York in twelve hours – a journey which could take more than three days in inclement weather. Thomas Lipton, the Scottish grocer and tea merchant, stencilled the sides of pigs, tied ribbons to their tails and paraded them through the streets bearing the (rather unnerving) announcement that they were shortly to be slaughtered, sliced and jointed for purchase in a Lipton's store; taking a different route every day he made sure of reaching as many potential customers as possible. In other stunts, he choreographed processions of Indians and Ceylonese to market his teas and in the 1880s he made himself a name for selling enormous cheeses – each more than four feet thick, twenty feet in circumference and weighing around two tons – which were paraded through the streets to great popular acclaim and split open in full view to reveal sovereigns and half-sovereigns, like giant Christmas puddings. To complete the spectacle, it was not unknown for Lipton and his store managers to hire an elephant from the local circus to be decorated in Lipton banners and haul the cheese through the streets. With such manoeuvres, the link between circus and advertising was made obvious, each using the other for mutual benefit.

While Lever's village at Port Sunlight is, of course, more than just an elaborate and costly advertisement, his lifelong fascination with branding, marketing and publicity is seen in its eclectic mix of visual stimuli, and in its attempt to 'sell' a particular philosophy of home life. The architecture combines drama, illusion and sleight of hand to create a distinct and calculated impression on the visitor. It is a place where gentility is imposed through a series of visual messages: a sense of softness is evoked, for example, by the roundness of so much of the building, the towers and circles and curves, the looping garden pathways; similarly an impression of ease and comfort is suggested both by the profusion of seating and benches – often built into the houses – which offer social warmth, and by the abundance of chimneys, from massive Lutyens-style edifices to delicate twisting brick examples, promising practical warmth and cosy firesides. Some of the styles capture the relaxed, holiday spirit of the sports pavilion or seaside villa, with sky-blue woodwork, verandahs and decks. Elsewhere, I notice a row of cottages called 'Poet's Corner', where romantic rooms nestle in low eaves. In a village planned for factory workers, there is an emphasis on pleasure and relaxation; the houses propose a different life – a different world – from the one their tenants are inhabiting.

Port Sunlight disorientates me. I spend too long wandering aimlessly, passing from street to street and from style to style as though I'm browsing some kind of architectural catalogue; it's pleasant enough but disengaging. My attempts at reflection are foiled by the superficial. This is a place designed to prevent you from knowing where you are, either in time or place, from grounding your thoughts. It's a village where impact is everything: the ordinary mechanisms of ordinary life – washing lines and wheelie bins – are diligently concealed and the internal elevations, often stark and utilitarian, are out of sight, cowering behind the decorative and the beautiful. Quality construction and detailing are all focused on the forward view; the functional equipment which allows the illusions of the village to operate is kept hidden. In this respect, too, Port Sunlight draws on the optimistic, cosmetic priorities of advertising, but also on theatrical precedents – particularly nineteenth-century innovations in scenery and lighting – and the irrepressible fashion for magic and mystery.

In the age of serial Gothic fiction, the magic trick, and the seance, there was an explosion of publications claiming to reveal magicians' secrets, for example. In 1876, a London barrister Angelo John Lewis wrote *Modern Magic: a practical treatise on the art of conjuring*, under the name of Professor Louis Hoffman. It was such a publishing sensation that similar books soon packed the shelves, culminating in the authoritative and popular 1903 work, *Hermann's Book of Magic: black art fully exposed: a complete and practical guide to drawing-room and stage magic for professionals and amateurs*. Magic was big business, and the attraction cut across class boundaries. For a magic performance at Drury Lane Theatre in 1887, seats were sold in the upper gallery at 6d; the level below cost 1 shilling, and was marketed at servants, private soldiers and apprentices. Boxes at 4 shillings were occupied by dignitaries and the elite.

By the later decades of the century – when Port Sunlight was under construction – these magic performances had been supplemented by the lecture-hall phenomenon of mediums and mesmerists and, at home, the popularity of spiritualist seances. These seances were the particular favourite of the educated middle classes; they formed a new kind of social pastime, a reinvention of the staid traditions of the tea party offering thrill and spectacle in a sexually charged atmosphere. The fashion consumed men and women from bankers and journalists to royalty: 'The higher the class, the more fiercely did it rage through it,' claimed the *Westminster Review* in 1858. There were some attempts to create an academic framework to lend authority to the process and to offer thoughtful and philosophical approaches aimed at integrating spiritualism with debates about religion, science and morality, but most participants were there for the sheer sensual pleasure of the occasion, to experience the relaxation of the strict social mores of the period. They were more than happy to enter into the illusion, which often centred on easily fabricated phenomena such as rappings and table tilting. Indeed, the writer George Eliot pointed out that the more bizarre and dramatic the 'palpable trickeries' the more delighted people seemed to be, while the *Westminster Review* concluded its examination of the craze by explaining that it was the sense of artifice and mystery that most appealed to believers, 'anything that puts science to rout and confounds the philosophers'.[6]

The entire village at Port Sunlight can be seen as part of this taste for legerdemain and performance; a weaving of reality and illusion, an attempt to make public a personal, unreliable world view. But it required more than a few noisy tables and recalcitrant ghosts. The project demanded enormous energy and planning, determination, imagination – and constant intervention. The village's overall effect, as Pevsner points out, is only made possible – and sustained – by 'high maintenance [and] tight control'. The vision was an intimate one, and even in the face of exhausting business commitments, William Lever wasn't prepared to relinquish a single element of its development.

As a young man, Lever had aspirations to be an architect himself; throughout his life he took a close personal interest in buildings and their environment. As trade flourished, he travelled extensively, visiting a variety of towns and examining them in detail at first hand. He kept accounts of his discoveries, often publishing them in the Lever Brothers' house journal, *Progress*. In 1892, for example, he wrote a long piece following a visit to Chicago, noting approvingly of one particular district: 'Each building from a purely architectural point of view is well-conceived, duly proportioned and most admirably executed.' In contrast, a visit closer to home, to Horwich near Bolton, drew criticism of new housing which was, according to Lever, arranged 'on the same crowded plan' as the Manchester slums.

Observation of other people's efforts gave Lever a confident and unshakeable philosophy of the best way to build; he articulated these principles during an address to the International Housing Conference, on site at Port Sunlight in 1907:

> The building of ten to twelve houses to the acre is the maximum that ought to be allowed . . . Houses should be built a minimum of 15 feet from the road . . . every house should have space available in the rear for a vegetable garden . . . open spaces for recreation should be laid

out at frequent and convenient centres . . . A home requires a green-
sward and garden in front of it, just as much as a cup requires a
saucer.[7]

These were the principles he was determined to make real at Port
Sunlight: in fact, with the large gardens, broad tree-lined roads and
open communal spaces, building density is well below Lever's maximum
of ten houses to the acre. To achieve his vision, he employed thirty
different architects, supervising their work closely: 'The architects . . .
all looked upon him as unique,' his son said, probably without irony.
'He did not employ them – he collaborated with them.'[8] Lever selected
a combination of local men, often already well known to him, and
the best and brightest architectural stars of his generation: he
employed, for example, obscure Bolton architect John Joseph Talbot
who lived in the village himself and designed many of the cottages,
as well as Sir Edwin Landseer Lutyens who designed 17–23 Corniche
Road at Port Sunlight before moving on to larger projects at Hampstead
Garden Suburb and, ultimately, the city of New Delhi in India. By
using so many architects on the project, from such a variety of backgrounds and with such different styles, Lever not only ensured a unique
visual diversity, he also made it difficult for any professional to establish an overview or to move into a position of influence. The system
enabled him to maintain firm control so that even as building
progressed under other hands, it was he who expressed the principles
under which it developed and who shaped its distinctive identity.

By the time Port Sunlight was finally complete, there were over
800 houses and a population of 3,500, as well as allotments, a cottage
hospital, schools, a concert hall, an open-air swimming pool, a church
and a temperance hotel. The emphasis on cleanliness, outdoor recreation and regular employment created, as usual, the conditions for
better living: it was noted by those living outside the village that Port
Sunlight children were 'fat, rosy and irrepressibly cheerful' and such
anecdotal evidence was supported by the figures: the average annual
death rate and the infant mortality rates in the village were half those
in the rest of Liverpool.

Under Lever's control, each house, or block of housing, was designed
by a different architect and each is unique. It offers a marked contrast

from the terraces of the mid-century planned villages: as I walk up from the factory towards the station and bowling green, I'm struck by the insistence of different roof lines and materials, black-and-white timbered frontages side by side with pebbledash and red brick, white-faced villas across from Flemish cottages with bulging hipped gables. The wide stone window frames and sculpted friezes of the rather squat cottages on Central Road seem so very different from the dramatic sloping red-tiled roofs and high chimneys of Greendale Road, just a few steps further on, that I'm disorientated. My personal geography shifts; my understanding of the place is challenged. This kind of resolute variety has for several decades been much copied by builder-developers and much approved by town planners, and so the originality of the effect here at Port Sunlight threatens to become diluted to modern eyes. But Lever's commitment to diversity marked a radical departure from anything that had preceded it: it was an entirely new look, owing nothing to the regular symmetry of the Georgian street or the Victorian terrace. When I allow it to hit me with full force, when I enter completely into the skittering series of illusions, it feels playful and experimental and ultimately unknowable, like a complicated game of some kind.

At the heart of this effect is a complex paradox. Architectural individuality is, as I can clearly see, strictly imposed. Yet while any visual sense of community is purposely avoided, the social and political structures of the village depended upon conformity. Port Sunlight was a place where common values were explicit, and where residents were expected to act for the general good. Participation in shared cultural and sporting activities was expected; Lever vetted everyone who came to live and work here and was clear that some people just did not make the grade: 'A good workman may have a wife of objectionable habits,' he explained, 'or may have objectionable habits himself, which make it undesirable for us to have him in the village.' Just as his own character was complex and often contradictory, so his village sets up a dichotomy between what you see, which celebrates individualism, innovation and difference, and the values inherent in the concept: orthodoxy, agreement and control. It is this uncertainty and intrinsic opposition that makes Port Sunlight so fascinating, and which also ensures that the village remains outside easy categorisations and appraisal. On my walk along the mercurial streets, I find it increasingly difficult to define the identity of the place, or even to understand it.

The bridge over the Dell can be partly explained by the fact that Port Sunlight was originally designed around a twenty-six-acre sea inlet, with tidal fingers which stretched along the streets and into open land. The gabled row of cottages built by Grayson and Ould in 1896, for example, was called 1–8 Riverside; they fronted flat marshy scrub which was cut through by the main tidal channel. When Lever began the village, he developed plans for an informal, Picturesque response to the unique demands of the terrain, a small cluster of houses that sat within the dips of the landscape, making a feature of scattered trees and the natural rivers and crossings. The vision was something like a watery Wirral version of Blaise Hamlet, looking back to the principles of eighteenth-century landscape design. By the mid-1890s, however, a period of intense building activity corresponded with Lever's acquisition of yet more land: he allowed his ambition free rein. He funded a competition to encourage architects to consider how the village could be expanded and completed. The winner, Ernest Prestwich, a third-year student at Liverpool School of Architecture and the Department of Civic Design, proposed a complete remodelling of the original plan and, most significantly, a change to the very nature of the village, moving away from a loose Arcadian spirit towards a much more structured and formal approach.

The channels were filled in to above high-water mark and cut off from the sea by a series of dams; most were subsequently levelled. At the heart of the site, in place of the sweeping roads and branching waterways, was a symmetrical layout of streets and gardens called the Diamond, as well as a formal square; the introduction of straight avenues created a strong axis from one end of the village to the other. The terrain which had informed the original, partly constructed village was obliterated, and Port Sunlight was redesigned along neoclassical lines, strongly influenced by the fashionable Beaux Arts style that took inspiration from conservative European examples and turn-of-the-century architecture in the USA, such as the terminal at New York's Grand Central Station which opened in 1903.

Just as the idiosyncrasies of the land were tamed and its contours sculpted, so the lives of the factory workers were similarly reinvented and reimagined when they were brought from the surrounding districts to populate the new village. 'I shall provide for you everything that makes life pleasant – nice houses, comfortable homes and healthy recreation,' Lever explained.[9] His rhetoric was translated into two types of residence – a three-bedroom kitchen cottage and a slightly larger parlour cottage which had an extra living room and bedroom – with allotments behind, now mostly converted into garages, which offered space for growing food. The factory was modern, clean and well-ventilated, and staff were provided with regular medical inspections. There were activities and team sports, gardens and outings. But despite Lever's apparently unequivocal view of the 'pleasant life', a move to Port Sunlight was not a simple undertaking, nor was it to be entered into lightly. Workers coming to live here were participating in a subtle process of exchange both with Lever Brothers and with Lever himself, by which they were provided with comfortable conditions in return for playing their appointed role without hesitation or deviation. Just as landlords in search of the Picturesque took to employing handsome urchins to animate their village greens, so Lever was on a quest to people his village with inhabitants who would contribute to his exhaustive vision. Rents were subsidised but good-quality housing and extensive communal facilities were given an overtly moral purpose: the village was created 'to socialise and Christianise business relations and get back to that close family brotherhood that existed in the good old days of hand labour,' he explained.[10]

Such statements bring us again to what we've seen so often before: a nostalgia for an undefined past – the 'good old days' – and a romanticised view of home and family. Lever expected his workers to commit to a fantasy of Port Sunlight as an idyll rooted in the rural past by obeying his rules and living up to the considerable burden of moral and social expectation he placed upon them. As if this was not enough, Lever, like Robert Owen a century earlier, intended domestic improvements to yield increased productivity in the workplace. His focus was the factory, and better business. So workers were expected to regulate their lives not only for the sake of the perfect village but in the profitable interests of the company. He demanded that they simultaneously fulfil the role of contented and devout peasant, part of an embracing 'family brotherhood' that peopled the neat cottages, and that of the committed, efficient factory hand operating modern machinery in the most productive way.

Not surprisingly, perhaps, these demands often proved too difficult and contradictory to create a harmonious lifestyle. From the 1830s onwards, workers had been moving away from the ideals of beneficent paternalism tried out at Cromford and Lanark Mills towards a more independent, self-regulating authority. By the time Port Sunlight was being developed, the relationship between entrepreneurial manufacturers and their workers had shifted substantially from the mid-nineteenth-century conditions which had given rise to earlier philanthropic settlements such as Saltaire. Rather than looking back to Victorian hierarchical models, the inhabitants of Lever's new town were more concerned with a twentieth-century focus on cooperative action and new class structures. The balance of power had changed, so that while Lever positioned himself as the archetypal Victorian factory owner, assuming authority and knowledge and arranging the lives of his employees in all respects, the workers themselves were resisting their assigned role in this scenario. Instead they were asserting their own right to drive change and looking beyond the company to wider structures of support and community.

Lever was apparently unconcerned by the rise of the working class in political circles; he believed in trades unions and always paid above agreed union rates. A lifelong supporter of William Gladstone, he was invited to contest elections for the Liberal Party, finally becoming MP for the Wirral between 1906 and 1909; he used his maiden speech in the House of Commons to urge the government, then led by Henry Campbell-Bannerman, to introduce an old-age pension scheme like the one he already provided for employees. But this magnanimity was counterbalanced by the practical arrangements at Port Sunlight which, in echoes of the situation at New Lanark, was operated on a system of surveillance and self-policing. The company had a right to send an official into any of the houses at any time 'for the purpose of seeing that due regard is being paid to order and cleanliness' while any workman whose behaviour was considered doubtful could find his tenancy refused and his employment terminated.

Such a culture of conformity had its advantages for employers and those who liked to see civic propriety maintained: the system in the village created what one contemporary commentator called 'a revolution . . . in the habits of the people' founded on 'wonderfully rigid' standards.[11] But unsurprisingly others found the atmosphere too oppressive. The Secretary of the Bolton branch of the Engineers' Union voiced many of his members' concerns in a letter to Lever in which he highlighted the drawbacks of the restrictive relationship between the villagers and their employer:

> No man of an independent turn of mind can breathe for long in the atmosphere of Port Sunlight . . . The profit-sharing system not only enslaves and degrades the workers, it tends to make them servile and sycophant, it lowers them to the level of machines tending machines.[12]

So widespread was this objection to the feeling of old-fashioned servility that many of the inhabitants of the village were embarrassed to admit that they lived there. The clean conditions and subsidised housing were viewed not as a benefit but as an oddity which set the workers apart from those who should be their equals and companions; the conditions at Port Sunlight were seen to create a second-class workman who lived under patronage in a tied and subsidised house. What had been regarded in the mid-nineteenth century as a largely beneficent gesture on the part of the employer was now viewed simply as demeaning: some of the village residents apparently felt their wretched status so strongly that they refused to own up to living in Port Sunlight at all, giving their postal address as Bebington and accepting the inevitable delay in letter delivery as a small price to pay for independence and respectability.

The restrictive covenants which bound tenants are still in place today and include directions such as those governing the style, colour and state of front doors, or forbidding flower borders in the front gardens. In a village whose main street names – King George's Drive and Queen Mary's Drive – are resonant of hierarchy and power, and whose design consciously glances towards the ideal aristocratic estate, many residents rebelled against Lever's apparently outdated personal doctrine, one which provided the sole coherence upon which the village was built. Not everyone moved out by any means but there was only half-hearted demand for the carefully constructed homes at Port Sunlight, and in time there was a real threat of depopulation. Although the entire village remained occupied by company employees until the mid-1980s, there was enough of a resistance to suggest that individuals were increasingly locating their identity beyond the employer and the houses he provided.

Social reform from the middle of the nineteenth century had often been focused on the question of good-quality, affordable housing which meant for many workers that there was now a more independent alternative to the restrictive atmosphere of the model village. Henry Mayhew, co-founder of *Punch* magazine, had brought the plight of the shabbiest districts to public attention during the 1840s and '50s through newspaper series such as 'London Labour and the London Poor':

> In one house that I visited there was a family of five persons, living on the ground floor and occupying two rooms. The boards were strewn with red sand, and the front apartment had three beds in it, with the printed curtains drawn closely round. In a dark room, at the back, lived the family itself. It was fitted up as a parlour, and crowded to excess with chairs and tables, the very staircase having pictures fastened against the wooden partition. The fire, although it was midday, and a warm autumn morning, served as much for light as for heat, and round it crouched the mother, children, and visitors, bending over the flame as if in the severest winter time.[13]

Similarly, Octavia Hill had pioneered the provision of sanitary, refurbished accommodation for unskilled labourers in London's Marylebone as early as the 1860s. In addition to individual efforts, local councils were being encouraged to provide economical, practical housing for working families – the Housing of the Working Classes Act of 1890 pressed for improved conditions and wider availability – and the idiosyncratic buildings and layout of the Port Sunlight village were soon surpassed, in many residents' estimation, by the functional advantages of the council house. From the outset, it was not uncommon for Lever's staff to refuse to live in the cottages, preferring the more modern settlements being developed elsewhere.

Despite some residents' reservations, however, the basic principles on which Port Sunlight was constructed were widely admired and copied, particularly by other companies developing similar schemes for employees. Almost exactly contemporaneous with much of Lever's model village is Bournville in Birmingham, which was then a rural site – with noted bluebell woods – developed by the Cadbury brothers as a healthier alternative to urban living: by 1900 there were over 300 cottages for workers at the chocolate factories, mostly designed in a coherent Arts and Crafts style by the resident architect William Alexander Harvey. The buildings were well built and carefully planned: the three-storey block of firemen's houses on Sycamore Road was close to the factory in case of an emergency, for example, while a quadrangle of plain brick almshouses was provided for retired employees. But in addition to practical considerations there was also an emphasis on pleasing the eye. Walking around Bournville village today – if you can resist the sugary lure of the 'Cadbury's Experience' close by – is very like walking around Port Sunlight: there's a lot of black-and-white timber framing, some extremely neat gardens, well-kept open spaces. The green at the village's heart, surrounded by shops and community buildings, has a charming octagonal 'Rest House' at its centre, with bench seats within and without, built by the workers and presented to Sir George and Lady Elizabeth Cadbury on their silver wedding in 1914. This, like Port Sunlight, is a place of apparent community and ease.

Further north, another confectioner and Quaker, Joseph Rowntree, built his model village, New Earswick, near York in the early years of the twentieth century. Open to any workers, not just those employed at the Rowntree's factory, the village architecture is, on the whole, plainer than at Port Sunlight but the overall effect is not very different: again, the Arts and Crafts style is much in evidence, while the layout of streets, greens and planting is strongly reminiscent of Lever's village across the Pennines. It was designed by the town planner Raymond Unwin and the architect Barry Parker, who collaborated in the writing of *The Art of Building a Home* in 1901, which applied the Arts and Crafts dictums to working-class housing. The following year they were invited to create the village at New Earswick, and in 1904, their design for a much larger development at Letchworth was adopted by the Garden City Pioneer Company.

The garden-city movement owed much to the principles of the model village: garden cities were planned as self-contained communities, with areas for living, working and agriculture. The idea came largely from Ebenezer Howard who, after emigrating to America to try his hand unsuccessfully at farming, came back to London to a modest administrative job; in his spare time he read widely, socialised with anarchists and reformers and published *To-Morrow: A Peaceful Path to Real Reform*. This Utopian view of communities living in harmony with nature was revised by 1902 to *Garden Cities of To-morrow* which was illustrated with a number of diagrams and designs for the perfect city. Proposing the creation of completely new towns of limited size, surrounded by agricultural land, Howard envisaged a network of garden cities which were largely independent of old economic structures and social hierarchies, managed by their own citizens and financed by ground rents.

In 1899, Howard founded the Garden Cities Association to turn his ideas into reality. He promoted his vision to a growing number of followers as the perfect conjunction of urban benefits – entertainments, high employment, good wages – with the natural delights and low rental costs of the countryside. His intention was to inspire a long-term migration of the population away from the overcrowded cities towards rural areas and simultaneously to change the political land-scape of the nation by creating opportunities for cooperation in a socialist model of equality and community.

Like the garden suburbs at Bedford Park or Wavertree, of course, these were not villages: they were conceived, as the word 'city' suggests, on a more expansive scale. But by the beginning of the twentieth century, the distinctions between the model village, the garden suburb and the garden city were becoming increasingly blurred, both in the intentions of their founders and in how they appeared on the ground. Having worked on the philanthropic village at New Earswick and the garden city at Letchworth, for example, Unwin and Parker went on to design Hampstead Garden Suburb with Edwin Lutyens. The central boulevards of the Broadway at Letchworth, the Parkway at Welwyn Garden City and the Causeway at Port Sunlight share a similar sense of symmetry and classical grandeur as well as a taste for fountains and memorials. A commitment to green open spaces, healthy living and attractive housing was no longer the preserve of the one-off philanthropist building his model village, but had become the cornerstone for urban development, driving a widespread move to recast the failing city and, in time, inspiring the

influential development of the New Towns following the Second
World War.

Port Sunlight, like many of the villages I've visited, sits at this point
of change; it inhabits the moment when the model village of the
nineteenth century was evolving into a new form to meet the urban
demands of the twentieth. Ten years before Ebenezer Howard outlined
his plans for garden cities, Lever was drawing on traditions of the past
to create his vision for a more efficient and pleasant future. The bridge
over the Dell yokes together a series of contradictions: beneficence
and authority; ancient and modern; rural and urban; home and work;
industrial housing and picturesque cottages. It both conceals and
reveals the illusion of the homogeneous, harmonious village. It simultaneously seduces you with its fantasy and artifice, and asks you to
interrogate it. It draws you into a vague pastoral idyll of the past, and
then delivers you across the road into a car park.

Lever went some way towards recognising these tensions but in
the face of criticism from political rivals and his own employees, he
nonetheless persisted with his crusade to create an alternative family
structure centred on the company, because for him it was about
broader issues than simply private living conditions; it was a question
of hierarchy and public power. In an address of 1898, explaining why
it was important to provide settlements like Port Sunlight, he indulges
in the language of poetry to draw direct links between decent housing,
moral responsibility and acceptable social behaviour:

> A child that knows nothing of God's earth, of green fields, or sparkling
> brooks, of breezy hill and springy heather, and whose mind is stored
> with none of the beauties of nature, but knows only the drunkenness
> prevalent in the hideous slum it is forced to live in, and whose walks
> abroad have never extended beyond the corner public-house and the
> pawnshop, cannot be benefited by education. Such children grow up
> depraved and become a terror and a danger to the State; wealth-
> destroyers instead of wealth-producers.[14]

He deploys the spectre of 'depraved' young adults not to illustrate
a waste of individual potential or a matter of social justice, but
because they present 'a terror and a danger to the State'. He binds

the experiment at Port Sunlight to matters of national importance, with implications for Britain's public order and economy. In statements such as this, it is clear that Lever was not, in his own mind, playing with architectural illusion, advertising follies and theatrical effect, but engaging with some of the most weighty and difficult issues of the time. In the streets he has so carefully created we are encouraged to see beyond his own personality and vision, to the construction of a respectable, productive and profitable nation. The imperatives of Lever's project are, he suggests, the same imperatives that faced Britain in a new and uncertain century.

A few years after Lever's death, looking back on his father's success in marketing soap, Lever's son wrote that 'the advertiser of our times . . . is laying his foundations deep. He is building for those who will follow him. It should be the same with nations.'[15] His comment – Lever's epitaph – neatly encapsulates the feeling at Port Sunlight where the fundamental frivolity, even pointlessness, of advertising is united with the idea of 'deep foundations', the sense that what was happening here had international implications to do with the building of nations. Walking through Lever's particular vision of a particular kind of Englishness, with a cold, grey drizzle clamping low over the village, I'm walking through a blueprint of nationhood which was to become significant far beyond these few Merseyside acres.

As the nineteenth century gave way to the twentieth, William Lever invested some of his enormous wealth in a world trip – a voyage that was to be about business expansion as much as pleasure. He quickly recognised the potential for using coconut and palm oils – high-quality vegetable oils – as the basis for soap manufacture and in 1902 he established Lever Pacific Plantations Ltd in the British Solomon Islands with the intention of mass-planting coconuts over 300,000 acres of prime land.

For a man accustomed to reshaping landscapes, the move to distant soil seemed to make little difference. The plantation sites were quickly cleared of their original inhabitants, while labour was imported from other islands to clear the bush, plant new saplings and manage the estate. Conditions were far removed from the model village at Port Sunlight: labourers were housed in basic sheds and employed on binding two-year contracts at the rate of £8 a year. Beatings were commonplace while lack of sanitation and medical care meant that outbreaks of dysentery could be deadly: an epidemic in 1913–14 killed almost one in ten workers on the Lever Brothers' plantations, leading to an investigation by the Colonial Office.

The Pacific venture failed to make much of a mark. It suffered from chronic labour shortages which slowed progress to something of a standstill; by the 1920s Lever Brothers had planted only 20,000 of the proposed 300,000 acres. But the company's colonial interests were not confined to the Solomon Islands: there were 300 square miles of palm oil plantations and a processing factory in Sierra Leone, mills for crushing palm oil kernels in Nigeria and, most significantly by far, five huge areas of palm exploitation – and a new town – in the Congo.

The history of Lever Brothers' interests in, and impact on, West Africa is enough to fill another book entirely. There have been several studies devoted to unearthing Lever's activities abroad, and as historians begin to piece together the stories of late-nineteenth- and early-twentieth-century colonialism, the scramble for profitable raw resources and industrial wealth is constantly being updated and reconsidered. But I can't make a convincing attempt here on this jungle of information: within the context of my rambles around cottage and terrace, what I'm interested in is the relationship – if there is one – between the village at Port Sunlight and the African enterprises; both an integral part of Lever's vision.

Lever Brothers' interests in the Congo were based on the search for affordable supplies of palm oil. On his first trip to the area in 1913, Lever noted enthusiastically that strong and healthy palm trees covered almost half a million hectares of the Belgian Congo – with a plentiful supply of native labour it was simply a matter of negotiating with the Belgian government for the rights to manage and harvest the crop. On 14 April 1911, a deal was agreed which granted concessions to a new Lever Brothers subsidiary – Huileries du Congo Belge – over a vast area of 750,000 hectares. Lever was delighted: the agreement, he claimed, would improve the area and its people 'on sound practical sensible lines' while benefiting the British consumer by providing cheap raw materials which, in turn, would keep retail prices low.

Lever was entering into business with one of the most feared and brutal regimes in a history of terrifying and brutal colonial regimes. Having lobbied across Europe for over ten years to win 'a slice of this magnificent African cake', King Leopold II of Belgium had managed to gain official recognition for his private state, the Congo Free State, in the 1880s. This amounted to over 2 million square kilometres of land – mostly unmapped jungle – and around 30 million people. Leopold claimed that his intervention in the area had philanthropic motives: he insisted that improvements in transport and infrastructure would benefit the entire populace and he became a champion of the anti-slavery campaign in a bid to drive out the Arab slave trade based in the area. But his real interests were in the region's unparalleled natural resources; together with some hand-picked European entrepreneurs, the new regime set about ravaging the land and people in the pursuit of ivory and minerals as well as exploiting a lucrative new trade in rubber fed by the nascent motor industry.

Leopold's reign in the Congo was a humanitarian disaster. His enforcement agency, La Force Publique, was armed with guns and the chicotte, a bull whip made from hippopotamus hide. Workers' failure to meet their rubber collection quotas was punishable by death; the wives and children of those who failed to meet their quota commonly had a hand cut off. When the conditions and methods gradually became known outside the region there was an outcry. The campaigning Congo Reform Association was established with a high-profile membership which included Mark Twain, Joseph Conrad and Bertrand Russell, while missionaries, journalists, government consuls and photographers joined forces in an attempt to reveal the extent of the atrocities: 'A perusal of all of these sources of information will show that there is not a grotesque, obscene or ferocious torture which human ingenuity could invent which had not been used against these harmless and helpless people,' railed Arthur Conan Doyle in his booklet *The Crime of the Congo*. In an impassioned preface he went further: 'Never before has there been such a mixture of wholesale expropriation and wholesale massacre all done under the odious guise of philanthropy.' Eventually, world opinion forced Leopold to relinquish power to the Belgium Parliament in 1908 but the damage had been done: it's estimated that a combination of starvation, exhaustion, disease, torture and murder reduced the population of the Congo by as much as half in the forty years after 1880.[16]

Lever's deal necessarily implicated him in Leopold's activities. The first consignment of palm oil extracted by the new Huileries du Congo

Belge was delivered to the Belgium business hub of Antwerp in March 1912 and a month later a special bar of soap was presented to King Leopold. Some of those watching, including the vocal members of the Congo Reform Association, believed Lever might be strong enough to become a power for good; they hoped that he would not risk losing his – and his company's – excellent reputation for the sake of profit. But such optimism was probably misplaced. There can be no doubt that Lever Brothers played an active role in the damaging scramble for Africa while Lever's own position remains murky. He certainly expressed some sympathy for those who lived on the land and, like the Belgian king, he seems to have believed wholeheartedly in the power of his own philanthropy, but his interests in the Congo were entirely commercial: his commitment was to managing the land and its communities to produce the largest yield. Just as his village at Port Sunlight was inescapably linked to the factory alongside, so his presence in Africa was intrinsically connected to the market for soap.

Lever's plans for developing Congo estates faced direct opposition from the British government which had resisted all his previous requests for concessions. In general, official policy was aimed at protecting African land rights and native production. Government administrators were shipped abroad to uphold a system of indirect rule which was cheap to manage and which suited a sense of the nation as enlightened and humanitarian, watching over the world from a position of superior knowledge and power. But Lever was convinced that twentieth-century enterprise required a more active approach: like many of his contemporaries, he believed that the African people were immature and naive, 'children' on the long scale of evolution. We are now all too clearly aware of the racism inherent in such a position, but Lever was convinced that business intervention on African land could help speed up the process of education and development: 'If you really wish to give to native races the blessings of our civilisation and religion,' he suggested in his 1893 journal, 'let us first teach them to make for themselves and their families the best use of their lands.' A few years later he went further: 'The land of the world, in any part of the world,' he claimed, 'ought to be in the possession of those people who can develop it and its resources.'[17]

This rather uncomfortable conjunction of paternalistic impulse and uncontainable business ambition is what we've seen at work, of course, in many of the model villages. Lever himself recognised the connection: he drew parallels between his African enterprises and the community he was continuing to construct at Port Sunlight. In both cases, he had a fairly contemptuous view of the workforce as industrious but ultimately limited: in both the Congo and the Wirral, he claimed that only a system of close supervision and assiduous management could keep workers on track, so allowing them to play their proper role in business and creating the best conditions for profit. With this need for constant monitoring and guidance in mind, he was as fully involved in his Congo operations as he was in the detailed development of Port Sunlight. He made the taxing journey across continents several times and according to his son 'not a palm area was selected not a site chosen, except on his authority; not a building was erected unless the plans had been passed by him'.[18]

Perhaps most central to this increasing sense of interchange between Merseyside and the Congo was the development of Lever Brothers' African town: Leverville. Amongst the 'darkest forests' and 'steaming swamps' which both intrigued and terrified Europeans, Lever constructed the main coordinating base for the palm oil concession of Huileries du Congo Belge. The new settlement had all the hallmarks of any model Victorian village – schools and hospitals, workers, housing (in brick and thatch), wide thoroughfares and public spaces – but it shared particular features with Port Sunlight. Some of the company buildings in Leverville were designed by James Lomax Simpson, who also designed rows of cottages at Port Sunlight, and even the street layouts were similar, with the main streets converging on to five wide European-style avenues. The fabric of the new town seemed purposely designed to recall its counterpart overseas: 'Leverville in the Belgian Congo and other villages in Africa . . . were, in their way, akin to Port Sunlight,' noted one Lever Brothers' manager.[19]

But it was not just the architecture at Leverville which recalled the model settlements back in Britain. Given Lever's views on the childish and unformed nature of his African workers, it's perhaps not surprising that he followed the pattern we've seen in many of the other model villages, by placing formal education at the heart of his new town. A century after the London Lead Company aimed to make schooling the key to personal development and commercial efficiency among the untamed mining families of the isolated North Pennines, Lever was adopting the same approach with the apparently uncivilised plantation workers in the jungle wilderness. 'The education of the native in the Congo is of supreme importance,' he wrote to one of the company agents. A decent system of schools, he claimed, would not only win over the hearts of the local population but, more fundamentally, would be of benefit by 'advancing them in civilization, increasing their wants, and raising them in the social scale of humanity'. Lever's schools were intended to shape a society, inculcating European ways of doing things and advancing a process of evolution that would in time promote a nation 'in the social scale of humanity'. With so much at stake, teaching was entrusted to a small group of Catholic priests in a religious monopoly that would not risk confusing local families or 'upsetting . . . their mentality to know that the white man had many religions'; the most promising students were kept at school until the age of sixteen to be trained in the skills the company needed.[20]

For all the familiar patterns, however, the difference at Leverville compared to Port Sunlight, or indeed any of the other model villages, was one of sheer scale. The concessions for Huileries du Congo Belge covered five discrete areas, each of a 60-kilometre radius, with a requirement to provide hospital and education facilities for all the people they contained. This was a massive undertaking, recklessly ambitious and perhaps indicative of an attitude which regarded African life as somehow small and insignificant. Providing for the practical needs of the few thousand employees on the Wirral and providing for tens of thousands of local workers in the Congo is not, we can see now, the same thing at all – but Lever did not seem to be at all daunted by the prospect.

Lever made his final visit to the Congo in autumn 1924 at the age of seventy-three. He had not been to the region for twelve years, and he was delighted with what he observed: he noted with enthusiasm that 'sick and underfed people' had been transformed into 'men, women, and children happy, contented and well fed'. He admired the new roads and railways, a river fleet of steamers and barges, the network of processing plants, the maternity and midwifery facilities and the detached family houses provided for employees. Floating down the Congo on his luxury barge, what sprang to his mind was a comparison with Port Sunlight, and what had been achieved there: 'It is a business like none other we have. Perhaps Port Sunlight comes nearest to it in social work,' he boasted.[21]

When I first came to Port Sunlight I didn't know very much about Lever's activity in Africa. I had some idea that the company history was not all Sunlight Soap pristine, but this amounted to little more than a vague impression of a squalid past. We're all fully aware now, even if only in general terms, of how much Victorian wealth was built on vicious injustice and abuse, although the details of many of these interactions are often difficult to unearth and we're generally left with little more than a ubiquitous impression of unsavoury colonial enterprise. The history of model villages is inevitably constructed upon half-concealed narratives of misery and exploitation, as well as heart-warming tales of resistance and reparation: the cotton mills of New Lanark and Cromford were implicated in the horrors of the transatlantic slave trade, for example, while the Cadbury brothers were prominent members of the British and Foreign Anti-Slavery Society, challenging the conditions of African labourers working in the chocolate plantations in Portuguese colonies.

In time, however, I found out more specific details about the working of Huileries du Congo Belge – and other, more short-lived, Lever Brothers' enterprises – and my subsequent visits are necessarily coloured by what I discover. I sit for a while on a bench. The rose beds behind me are bare: the gardeners have already been here and finished the trimming; the soil is turned. To one side of me is the copse of trees which surrounds the church. Ahead, there's one of the village's many patches of open ground, a wide but shapeless area of grass with a couple of slight trees at the far end and, beyond, a block of large white cottages, their eaves picked out in black and white timber, the doors (eleven of them) a shade of pale yellow. It's an exposed bench, and I feel quickly cold. But it's easier to sit still for a moment, because I have a picture to consult, a photograph from the Lever Brothers' archives. It shows a building in Leverville, long and white, with a verandah across its length. When I hold it up in front of me I can play about with perspective so that the Leverville building and the Port Sunlight cottages ahead of me sit alongside each other. The sky in both views is the same, greyish and flat. The long, low roofs, too, are very similar. At Port Sunlight the building's vertical interest comes from the strong lines of the mock-Elizabethan detailing and black drainpipes; in Leverville it's provided by the verandah supports. The rows of small windows could be interchangeable. It's a disconcerting game.

With a century or more of post-colonial guilt behind us, it's easy to judge Leverville with modern eyes. But I'm trying to avoid this. What's interesting for me about the juxtaposition of the two Lever settlements is not so much what it might reveal about the nature of activity in the Congo but the way my impressions of Port Sunlight might be clarified by considering its relationship to the African town. In both interventions, it seems clear, Lever was indulging a personal enthusiasm for ordering and managing people's lives, alongside fulfilling the business imperatives of a multinational conglomerate. In both he clearly positioned himself as generous, caring and enlightened, the forward thinker expressing his most treasured values in the ideal of community he was creating. These values were important, not just on account of personal pride, but because the village developments were so closely linked to a sense of national identity: acts of generosity and enlightened humanity at home and abroad, it suggested, was how a British man knew himself and, by extension, how Britain saw itself and wished to be seen. The Lever Brothers magazine described its founder as 'the kind of man who made the British Empire possible'. Lever titled his travel journal *Following the Flag* – his 'jottings of a jaunt round the world' were not just personal anecdotes for the delight of friends but were also marking British interests on the map, shaping the world through his impressions and defining the places he visited by their ability to hoist the Union flag.

Despite such nationalist idealism, however, it's evident that at Leverville the villagers were often exploited, mistreated and thoroughly miserable. Since Lever's time, many of the weaknesses, prejudices and false assumptions which underpinned the colonial adventure have been revealed, and it's easier now to view the experiment as problematic. But if we can see the ways in which Leverville was flawed, where does this leave its counterpart at Port Sunlight? Here, too, residents were often discontented or resistant. Here, too, the village was seen by some as an imposition, an autocratic step too far, and an anachronism. Here there is a bridge, a pretty English country bridge, that crosses nothing and leads only to the factory floor. Sitting on my bench, examining the views of Lever's buildings, I wonder whether mistakes and stupidities are better concealed by Port Sunlight's closeness to home and charming indigenous architecture than by the starker oddity of European dreamstreets in the African jungle.

7

Portmeirion, Gwynedd

This is something of an indulgence on my part, perhaps. Portmeirion is not an industrial village built for workers, nor perhaps even a model village in the true sense: it's a holiday village, a place of hotels and self-catering cottages; it's a personal fable, a whim, an architectural indiscretion. But it's also, in many ways, the logical place to end my ramble because it brings to conclusion – to their ultimate end – many of the ideas and principles that underlie the places I've already visited. It seems more interesting to come here than simply to produce more examples of the same; it seems as though this odd, extravagant, twentieth-century folly on the edge of Wales might give away some secrets. Portmeirion is a village out of time and out of place, which seems a fitting way to end.

The site, tucked away on the Dwyryd Estuary in Gwynedd, was acquired in 1925 by the architect Clough Williams-Ellis. It was a private peninsula on the coast of Snowdonia, 'a neglected wilderness' with the mountains towering behind. Hidden and almost mystical, it was something of a Garden of Eden, breathlessly described by Williams-Ellis as a place of excess:

> A tumbling cascade falls to a sandy bay between two rocky headlands
> . . . twenty miles of cliff and woodland rides and paths that crisscross
> the whole headland between high crags, great forest trees and the
> exuberant jungle of exotic and subtropical flowering shrubs with which
> a succession of devoted owners had prodigally adorned it.[1]

But this was not a place to remain secret: Williams-Ellis bought the land in order to transform it. Born in 1883, he was at architectural school briefly in 1902–3 and began private practice in 1905: he repeatedly and proudly referred to himself as a town planner, and was at his most creatively impressionable during the same years which saw the completion of the model villages at Port Sunlight, Bournville and New Earswick and the laying-out of the first garden city at Letchworth. He had seen that it was possible to build new settlements from nothing, to reinvent the idea of the village on the basis of a personal vision, to create a place with a distinct and distinctive identity embodied in its design and architecture. And this is what he set out to achieve for himself. This little retreat in Wales, which he called Portmeirion, was to be for and about Williams-Ellis, clearly and visibly articulating the deeply intimate nature of the model village and its relationship to those who created it:

> Its long pre-natal history, its period of imaginative gestation, actually began when I was a small boy of five or six. Some day, somewhere, I would even assuredly erect a whole group of buildings on my own chosen site for my own satisfaction; an ensemble that would body forth my chafing ideas of fitness and gaiety and indeed *be* me.[2]

With his heart initially set on an island site – and he was determined to choose somewhere he could have complete freedom and control – Williams-Ellis took many months to find a suitable spot for his new enterprise: 'Clearly, I must be free from all outside interference what-soever and sole master of all I surveyed.'[3] But having found the place he wanted, he moved quickly and by January 1926 he was already 'engaged upon plans and models for the laying of an entire small township'.[4] His concept was precise and ambitious, a practical expression of a belief in the close relationship between architecture and environment, and a declaration of the importance of lavishness and display. Over the following fifteen years the first stage of the village was laid out, including the cottages known as Neptune and Angel, the Arts and Crafts Town Hall, and the distinctive bell tower which was to set the tone for the rest of the development: 'The need for a Campanile was obvious enough,' Williams-Ellis explained. 'It was imperative that I should open my performance with a dramatic gesture of some sort.'[5] After building restrictions were lifted following the end of the Second World War, a further period of development from 1954 to 1976 added a number of classical and Palladian-style buildings as well as an observatory tower with a camera obscura and a painted Coadestone figure of Napoleon, a folly lighthouse, a rococo triumphal arch, a bandstand flanked by a statue of Hercules, a Gothic pavilion, a piazza with a fountain pool, and a grotto whose walls are plastered with shells.

I arrive in this place of multiple histories and deceptive whimsies on a quiet afternoon when the car park is almost empty and the man taking entrance fees is dozing in the pink-painted tollbooth. It's a very calm, mild day, the air still and the woodland hushed. It evokes a certain composure, almost a lethargy, and I don't feel any excitement or expectation on arrival; I wonder if I'm even looking properly at anything. Once I've bought my ticket, I follow the pedestrian route into the village, an unprepossessing stretch of bland tarmacked road with a tin-roofed toilet block on the right and on the left a china outlet selling cut-price seconds. The estuary is hidden, the trees unremark-able. There are one or two of Williams-Ellis's later buildings here, bolstering the outskirts of the village, but they don't make much of an impression. I walk on in the dreaminess of the tranquil afternoon, and it's not until I reach Bridge House that – with a jolt – I'm thrown into the strangeness and the commotion of Portmeirion.

Bridge House is painted in blocks of ochre and pale blue and yellow; there's a large Venetian window with diamond panes; the entire building seems to sprout from the rough rock to one side, like layers of exotic fungi, while through a gap in the wall to the other I catch glimpses of water, calm shallow rills swirling between vast flats of low-tide sand. There's a wide, tempting arch, the simple building piled above as it would be in a medieval village, but then, as I pass beneath, everything changes: I'm suddenly in a townscape, with buildings and tended gardens all around me, and when I turn back to look behind, the ad-hoc lines of Bridge House have become, from this side, precise and symmetrical, a pale classical facade with sash windows and bays, Doric pilasters and plaster cornices which recall the most conventional of eighteenth-century villas. What had seemed one thing has become another; I've been tricked, or at least surprised.

I'm quickly thrust into a place of excess: more picturesque and eccentric than Edensor; the eclectic mix of architectures more striking than at Port Sunlight; the Arts and Crafts, the villa, the terrace, the country cottage all mishmashed together in the narrow strip of land between the wooded hills and the sea. 'Where I judged I had perhaps a trifle overplayed the picturesque, I would pop up a blank façade of serene classical formality,' Williams-Ellis explained matter-of-factly.[6] The only obvious connection between the buildings – the overriding impression of the village – is an undefined Italianate character. Taking the architectural influences of Arkwright's and Titus Salt's mills to extremes, this is a place that attempts to capture and recreate the essence of Italian village life, even down to the naming of the village 'in affectionate memory of Portofino', a celebrity resort near Gerona.

With its architectural playfulness, its colourful facades, towers and turrets and changing vistas, the taste for theatricality and display which is inherent in varying degrees in many of the model villages is given free rein here at Portmeirion. Many of the buildings play quite open games with illusion and sleight of hand. I sweep around towards the main square to find a row of pastel-painted cottages sitting in pretty gardens on a rise of land to my left. I follow a narrow path up through the flower beds to take a closer look – this is Chantry Row, a single building made to look like a terrace, our eyes easily deceived by the false divisions painted on the facade in baby pink and primrose yellow.

But this is not the extent of the trickery – such *trompe l'oeil* is little more than a cheeky inversion of what can be seen in the Georgian terraces of a fine Bath square – and it takes me a little while to realise that the row of smaller windows set below the eaves is entirely false, each one painted, complete with reflections and worn window frames and curtains peeping behind. Furthermore, in a final brazen flourish, the octagonal tower with its bright blue onion dome which marks the end of the row and rises as a landmark for the village, is revealed from here to be only half of what it seems: the tower and its dome have been sliced cleanly in two and behind the mock copper and sandstone turret there's a very ordinary, practical chimney with a grubby chimney pot. Chantry Row is in no way what it appears; its workings have been concealed, its structure obscured, its presence exaggerated.

The delight in illusion is uncontainable: two walls of the classical-style Cliff House are covered in *trompe l'oeil* windows; the grand Palladian mansion named Unicorn, resplendent with Doric pilasters and a pediment, turns out to be a flat-roofed bungalow with an over-sized facade; dummy attic windows occur again and again; seagulls perched on roofs and towers are revealed to be fashioned from copper;

from the top of Government House, a painted devil peeps from a window, looking out over the lawns and the estuary beyond. Here, the hierarchies of order and scrutiny which we explored in some of the mill villages are unsettled and interrogated: who is watching whom at Portmeirion? Can we believe anything of what we see, or are the structures all telling tales of dissembling and affectation?

Williams-Ellis's enthusiasm for salvage, for creating what he called 'a home for fallen buildings', further adds to the turbulence here, the sense of place and history being disrupted and manipulated. All kinds of bits and pieces have been installed on site, trailing with them whispers of other lives: there are two small cannon from Belan Fort on the Menai Strait, a stronghold built to repel the Napoleonic threat; there's a chiming turret clock from a demolished nineteenth-century London brewery; ionic columns rescued from the colonnade constructed at Hooton Hall in Cheshire by Samuel Wyatt now form the basis of 'the Gloriette', a Palladian concoction named after the huge eighteenth-century example which acts as a focal point to the Schönbrunn Palace Garden in Vienna; the mermaid panels on the bandstand, gazebo and Pantheon were acquired from the Liverpool Sailors' Home. Nothing quite belongs here, or perhaps everything does, given a new lease of life by Williams-Ellis's eclecticism and resuscitated by the bracing coastal breezes.

I spend a few minutes sitting on the low wall surrounding one of the ponds in the central piazza. In the distance, gulls wheel, their cry an unmistakably seaside sound; closer to, a blackbird sings. Above the still water at my side, midges swarm in the mild air. The surface is thick with lily leaves, and beyond it a cluster of palm trees rises inappropriately from beds of English roses. There are salvaged pieces on view around the cottages here too: a cast-iron coat of arms bought by Williams-Ellis from an island lighthouse keeper and a National Benzole petrol pump, embellished with an early nineteenth-century pine figurehead, the head of an androgynous bystander with a feathered hat and a rather vacant stare, of the sort that might once have stood outside a shop or at the prow of a smallish ship. But I've been garnering my energies for the Town Hall, poised just behind, at the far end of the village, and this is where I head to see the most extensive evidence of Williams-Ellis's magpie habits.

This is one of the most successful buildings of the collection at
Portmeirion. Its location, on the edge of things, with tall pines and
mature broad-leaf trees massed behind, lends it a certain gravitas while
the Arts and Crafts-style frontage is elegant and mature. The light-blue
wrought-iron gates, dated 1908, are graceful and airy. But the gates
once belonged elsewhere and the Town Hall is a conglomeration, a
yoking of new and old, of lost and found. This is a building purposely
designed as a place to store and display some of the best features of
another, older building with a much longer history: Emral Hall in
Maelor, Flintshire.

Emral Hall was a huge, solid, three-sided house, protected by a moat
168 feet long and 37 feet wide and owned by the Puleston family. It had
a romantic place in Welsh history. The first master, Roger de Puleston,
described himself as 'de Embers-hall' in 1283, and ten years later was
appointed first Sheriff of Anglesey by Edward I, collecting taxes on
behalf of the English king and precipitating the revolt led by Madog
ap Llywelyn in the autumn of 1294; at the height of the rising, the hated
Sheriff was seized and hanged. A century later, Robert Puleston married
the sister of Owain Glyndŵr, temporarily losing his estates for joining
forces with his brother-in-law. The house and family were steeped in
local and national folklore, but in 1936 Emral Hall was demolished – the
direct Puleston line had died out and nobody wanted such a vast,
unwieldy old place whatever its past claims to fame.

The chief treasure of Emral was a barrel-vaulted plaster ceiling
depicting the labour of Hercules. It was installed in the central part of
the house around 1600 and used in later years as the major feature
of an extravagant ballroom. A notice in *Country Life* magazine, giving
details of the demolition at Emral, attracted Williams-Ellis's attention;
he was immediately determined to save the ceiling: 'Aghast at the
news . . . I rang up the National Trust . . . Too late and no money.
Then the V&A Museum . . . no room,' he explained, his prose still
breathless at the memory. With official rescue routes closed, 'I felt I
must instantly do something about it myself'; he threw himself into
a project that was to become larger and more unwieldy than he had
imagined:

> . . . packed a bag, caught a train, and reached Emral just as the sale
> was starting . . . So far as the ballroom was concerned, the ceiling

came up first, and there being next to no bidding for so awkward and
speculative a lot, it was knocked down to me for a derisory thirteen
pounds. But then of course I had to buy all the rest of the room at
any cost; the old leaded glass in its mullioned windows, its fire grate,
its oak cornices and architraves – the lot. And committed that far, it
was but prudent to buy a great deal more of the old house wherewith
to contrive an apt new building in which to embed my reconstructed
ballroom. Whence the somewhat hybrid aspect of what is now
Portmeirion's Town Hall, an unabashed pastiche of venerable Jacobean
bits and pieces adding interest and dignity, as I think, to an otherwise
straightforward modern structure.[7]

Something about Williams-Ellis's obvious excitement and delight
– even recounting the tale years later – reminds me of Titus Salt's
plan to bring the Crystal Palace to a village on the Bradford moors:
Portmeirion shares much of the same sense of adventure and drama
as Tremadog or Saltaire; it reveals the same strength of purpose and
ebullience of character as Edensor or Port Sunlight. Is the result so
very different, or does this secluded concoction of holiday homes
stand in direct relation to the model villages of the eighteenth and
nineteenth centuries?

In one crucial respect, it's true, Portmeirion differs from the other
villages we've explored: it's a place built without people. There are
vestiges of industry here – a short-lived lead mine which now acts as
the hotel wine cellar and an unsuccessful gold mine concealed in the
woodland – but unlike the model villages which had a working
community at their heart, Portmeirion is primarily about landscape
and architecture, rather than about those who might live here. For
Williams-Ellis, there was no imperative to construct schools or leisure
facilities; the housing need not be cost-effective or practical to manage.
He was concerned with appearance and display, with attracting attention, rather than with how the place might function for the families
who lived here.

On the day I visit there are few visitors. I can peer through the
windows of the unlet holiday cottages; the cafés are deserted. A young
woman quickly negotiates the narrow flight of stone steps alongside
a red baroque building and disappears behind. An American in one

of the souvenir shops explains to the assistant – at great length – how he and his wife are here as part of their honeymoon; it's the perfect romantic hideaway, he says. A man with a bulky camera helps push an old lady in a wheelchair up the steep incline from the harbour to the piazza, her grateful daughter puffing alongside, the three of them laughing at the idiosyncrasies of such a crazy village, a place that perhaps inspires such random acts of kindness.

In the absence of families and coach parties, I become aware of the strange way in which the village is, in fact, peopled: with statues and busts and painted figures, faces everywhere at all angles and in all views, a rather unnerving host of false bodies in this place of fake buildings. There's an eroded sandstone statue of a huntsman with a staff and an eighteenth-century Portland stone figure of the Saxon goddess Friga, acquired by Williams-Ellis when the Duke of Buckingham's house at Stowe was being converted into a school. There's St Peter preaching from a balcony, looking over newcomers as they arrive through the entrance archway; a bust of Shakespeare bent over the quayside; a gilt Buddha; Hercules heaving his great stone globe outside the Town Hall; eighteenth-century marble busts of the Duke and Duchess of Argyll tucked away into dark niches; a marble statue of a Roman woman with flowing robes; a child clutching a puppy or a lamb; another child, a kind of fish-child, with scales and fins; golden Balinese dancing figures atop stone columns; angels, mermaids, cherubs and goddesses . . . This is a village inhabited by a strange, ad-hoc, disconnected public, set adrift here from other contexts. It's also the village where the cult 1960s television programme, *The Prisoner*, was filmed – filling the streets with another surreal community, odd characters without names or purpose. Portmeirion, it seems to me, takes to extremes the Picturesque taste for peopling a village with pretty peasants: the residents here are set props, easily manageable and interchangeable, attractive but undemanding.

I've wandered the little pathways and climbed the twisting flights of steps; I've taken photographs and bought a souvenir in one of the shops. Now I make my way to the grotto of shells. I dip down from the village towards the estuary, the buildings sinking out of view behind me, and I follow a well-trodden track around a bend until I reach what looks like a circular concrete bunker, not unlike a Second World War pillbox, an apparently solid piece of no-nonsense defence.

There's a small arched entrance to one side. Inside, the grotto looks dark and uninviting; it feels like stepping into an underpass or one of those public lavatories below ground – you're intimidated by the change of light, not quite sure of the smells, anxious to spot an exit. But of course I go in anyway, and it's not, in the end, as close and gloomy as it had appeared; not quite. But it's shabby and worn, none-theless, the hard grey surface of the concrete not really decorated so much as scarred by a mass of white scallops with, here and there, a larger conch shell slightly pinkish and some green roundels of glass. It has the air of an unloved, outdated piece of public art in a forgotten urban corner; it feels, oddly, like bus stations did when I was young. It has nothing like the natural excitement and charm of the Cavern Cascade on the Hafod Estate.

At the heart of the grotto there's a fountain pressed into the wall, blue and ornate, a pair of twined fishes designed to spout into the pool. But there's no water today and the thing seems desolate. The ceiling is low; the indentations of more shells create dry shallow wounds which catch the light from the estuary, slanting in from the openings which ring the cobbled walkway. It's a bizarre kind of wonderland. I pass through the painted arch at the far end with relief and make my way instead on to the roof, where there's a viewing platform with a circular metal bench. From here I can look across the sands of the estuary to the far bank, less wooded than this one, dotted with farms – in the distance I can just make out the town of Harlech with the castle perched above. Seabirds swirl in small flocks across the pools and channels of shallow water left by the tide; a flag flutters half-heartedly outside the hotel at the harbour below me and further along the sea wall two people in bright coats approach the lighthouse-cum-lookout-tower on the promontory. It's a tranquil moment; with my back to the artifice of Portmeirion I am quickly beguiled again by the undramatic authenticity of this corner of Wales.

Unlike many of the model villages I've visited, which seem designed to allow those within to be watched, Portmeirion is a place made for views outwards: balconies, platforms, benches, follies all direct the gaze away from the village to the estuary or the hills. The rise and fall of the land is used to advantage so that vistas are as open as possible; the planting of gardens and trees frames rather than conceals the landscape. This somehow reinforces the idea of Portmeirion as a place to distract and amuse rather than fully engage; it's a place that continually offers escape. If the model villages of the nineteenth century were made to forge and contain communities over genera-tions, this seems a twentieth-century amusement intended briefly to seduce the individual before letting her loose again into the real world. I sit on the bench and admire the view, looking outwards as was intended.

Returning later to the main part of the village, I'm attracted by a board from the 1950s hung now in the Pantheon. It gives the original admission price for visitors – by means of a turning disc, the board displays a fee on a gradated sequence up to as much as 10 shillings (the maximum was charged only once, when King Edward VIII was staying in the village). The inscription reads: 'That visitors to Portmeirion may be sufficiently discouraged and so kept to acceptable numbers a toll per head has had to be imposed. To avoid it – please turn back here.'

The principle of 'sufficiently discouraging' visitors to the peninsula was not without precedent: in 1869, Sir William Fothergill Cooke – inventor of the electric telegraph and then owner of the land – not only demolished the twelfth-century castle on the site but went to great lengths to obliterate it completely 'lest the ruins should become known and attract visitors to this place'. The entrance board a century later seems to express a similar rebuff but in more ambivalent terms: in this place built for sightseers, for hotel guests and weekend lodgers, how many visitors was too many? Was this a private village or a public one? Could the correct type of visitor be admitted while a raised entrance fee deterred the less welcome?

When Williams-Ellis discussed visitors to his village, this ambiva-lence was certainly evident. Although he recognised Portmeirion's reliance on the tourist trade, in his writing he expresses a lurking snobbery about what this might actually mean. The 'perfectly pleasant bread-and-butter' visitor, he notes with relief, is 'sweetened' with the 'jam' of the artistic and the elite: he goes to great lengths to note the names of prestigious guests, in particular listing over half a page of authors such as H. G. Wells and Noël Coward. There's an air of the country-house party to his description of events at the hotel; he revels in the idea of a discreet hideaway for those who could afford it, noting at one point – with disturbing echoes of Coleridge's 'Rime of the Ancient Mariner' – that 'before my time, a flamingo had been seen and ungratefully shot from the lower lawn'.

Just as we've seen at Port Sunlight, Williams-Ellis was concerned to control not only how his village looked, but how it was used and by whom. His graded scale of entrance fees gave him, in effect, a veto over unwelcome visitors; it demonstrates a subtle distrust of ordinary people and their antics. This was a place where public access sat uncomfortably with private invitation and where a residency in the village – however short term – was seen as some kind of potential reward for a sanctioned moral or intellectual contribution to national life: 'I wish it could somehow be contrived that, without too invidious distinctions, credit points could be awarded to the deserving poor,' Williams-Ellis wrote, before further defining what he meant as: 'approved academics and intelligentsia, especially if with families – so that such could afford what was originally and primarily designed for their particular enjoyment.'[8]

Since Williams-Ellis's death in 1978, at the age of ninety-four, some of these tensions have been resolved: Portmeirion is now unequivo-cally a tourist attraction; it hosts 240,000 visitors a year and the holiday cottages are energetically marketed. But it feels as though there's a lingering regret that the village never amounted to anything more than a day tripper's destination; the entire place seems to rue its light-heartedness at the same time as celebrating it – like the stereotype of the tearful clown, Portmeirion is brash and preposterous while simul-taneously giving the impression that it wants to impress us with its substance. With its architectural experimentation and ambitious plan-ning, its gardens and green spaces, its clusters of cottages and imposing public buildings, Portmeirion is a direct descendant of the nineteenth-century model village but, divorced from the workers' needs and philanthropic ideals of the earlier model villages, it has become a plaything.

Williams-Ellis seemed fully aware that his life's work could be criticised for its lack of substance. 'I'm frequently asked what it was "in aid of",' he says defensively. His answer is interesting: Portmeirion, he suggests, is a place 'wherein the irrational, para-poetic needs of those seeking relaxation and relief, on holiday from a work-a-day world, are given as much attention as their need for physical well-being.'[9] This shift of emphasis from practical needs to emotional ones, from the basic supply of food and shelter to the provision of facilities for relaxation and retreat, seems to demonstrate perfectly the evolution from the earliest model villages to this twentieth-century example. It shows how the 'work-a-day world' has changed, and the demands of the worker with it. Portmeirion's flimsiness – if that's what it is – is not so much a reflection on the village itself, perhaps, as a vindication of the earlier settlements, proof that for all their inconsistencies, their troubles and tensions and confusions, they succeeded in revolutionising the way people lived; they did not offer a diversion from the 'work-a-day world' but an intrinsically new way of constructing and managing it, in so doing transforming the ways in which we think about work and home, about the past, and about ourselves.

And so I end at Portmeirion's Gothic Pavilion, another piece of salvage, once the portico at Nerquis Hall in Flintshire. It is pink and flouncy, set in the lawns and shrubberies at the end of the formal piazza gardens, the campanile rising to one side of it and a view of the estuary visible at the other. It's flanked by the gilt Balinese dancers on their podiums. Even in the context of Portmeirion it is something of a trinket, a frippery with no purpose beyond ornament. But as I walk around the back, I look above the trefoil arch and notice a plaque erected by Williams-Ellis in 1973. It's an elaborate four-leafed clover shape, in keeping with the rest of the building, with a twisted-rope edging; it's also very worn and the inscription is difficult to make out but I persevere and read: 'This re-erected Gothick Porch from Nerquis Hall aptly commemorates William Madocks 1773–1828 who loved this region and strove mightily to increase its fame and its prosperity. Portmeirion hereby acknowledges her debt to this man of vigorous virtue.'

I wonder how many visitors to Portmeirion know who Madocks was, or of his commitment to a model village at Tremadog 150 years before Williams-Ellis embarked on his enterprise here. I doubt there are many. But I like ending my exploration with the connection between the two places made manifest, written in stone. I take the path that cuts down the hill towards the harbour and the hotel. The tide is starting to come in; I find a sheltered spot and watch the waters begin to fill the estuary. I wonder a little about the relationship between fame and prosperity and building villages, and then I'm distracted by a flock of birds dipping in from the distance, skimming the sea.

Endnotes

1: Cromford, Derbyshire

• **1** The exact date of Byng's visit is disputed but seems to have taken place in 1789 when he was invited to view Arkwright's work to build his home at Willersley Castle. 'Prospect View of Sir Richard Arkwright's House at Cromford', 1792, British Library Topographical Collection, K., Top. Vol. 11, p. 13. • **2** R. Owen, 'A New View of Society, 1813' in A. L. Morton, *The Life and Ideas of Robert Owen* (New York: International Publishers, 1962), pp. 73–6. • **3** Robert Owen, *Report to the County of Lanark of a Plan for Relieving Public Distress* (London, 1832), pp. 27–8. • **4** Robert Owen, *Life of Owen, written by himself* (London: Effingham Wilson, 1857), p. 103. • **5** William Hazlitt, 'A New View of Society; or, Essays on the Principle of the Formation of Human Character, and the Application of the Principles to Practice', in *Political Essays: With Sketches of Public Characters* (London: William Hone, 1819), pp. 97–8. • **6** William Allen, *Life of William Allen* (3 vols, 1846–7), Vol. I, p. 245. • **7** William Urwick, *Biographical Sketches of James Diggs La Touche* (Dublin, 1868), pp. 60–1. • **8** Robert Owen, diary entry, 24 March 1825, quoted in Edward Royle, *Robert Owen and the Commencement of the Millennium: A Study of the Harmony Community* (Manchester: Manchester University Press, 1998), p. 33. • **9** For a fuller description of the Institute, see Ian Donnachie, *Robert Owen: Owen of New Lanark and New Harmony* (East Linton: Tuckwell Press, 2000), pp. 156–171. • **10** Letters between Madocks and Williams are in the archives of Gwynedd Council, XD8/2. • **11** 'Bray's Tour into Derbyshire &c' in John Pinkerton, *A General Collection of the Best and Most Interesting Voyages and Travels in All Parts of the World* (London: Longman, 1808), p. 375.

2: Nenthead, Cumbria

• **1** 'Alston. By the Rev. W. Nall, M. A. Read at that place, July 10th, 1884' in *Transactions of the Cumberland and Westmorland Antiquarian & Archaeological Society*, Vol. VIII, pt 1, 1885. • **2** Manuscript book of surveyors' and mine notes, quoted in Raistrick, Arthur, *Two Centuries of Industrial Welfare: the London (Quaker) Lead Company 1692–1905* (Buxton: Moorland, 1938), pp. 35–6, which offers a detailed history of the mines. • **3** Part of the inquiry preceding the Mines and Collieries Act, 1842; the Royal Commission known as the Kinnaird Commission, 1862–4. • **4** Quoted in Raistrick, p. 36. • **5** W. M. Patterson, *Northern Primitive Methodism* (London: E. Dalton, 1909), p. 171. • **6** C. J. Hunt, *The Lead Miners of the Northern Pennines in the Eighteenth and Nineteenth Centuries* (Manchester: Manchester University Press, 1970), p. 224. • **7** Records of the Society for Bettering the Conditions of the Poor (Vol. III, pp. 300–12); the Hadow Report, 'The Education of the Adolescent' (1926), pp. 3–4. • **8** The Hadow Report, p. 9. • **9** The Hadow Report, 'The Primary School' (1931), p. 3. • **10** R. Williams, *The Long Revolution* (London: Chatto and Windus, 1961), p. 135. • **11** These details from the Stagg reports are quoted in Raistrick, p. 63. • **12** Quoted in Hunt, p. 234. • **13** Letter, William Penn, 4 August 1682. • **14** Middleton District Report 1834, quoted in Raistrick, p. 27. • **15** Ibid.

3: Edensor, Derbyshire

• **1** Quoted in Deborah, Duchess of Devonshire, *The Garden at Chatsworth* (London: Francis Lincoln, 1999), p. 48. • **2** Diary, 6th Duke of Devonshire. The Duke's diaries are in the archives at Chatsworth. • **3** William Gilpin, *Three Essays: On Picturesque Beauty; On Picturesque Travel; and On Sketching Landscape* (London: R. Blamire, 2nd edition, 1794), pp. 49–50. • **4** R. H. Newell, *Letters on the Scenery of Wales* (London: Baldwin, Cradock and Joy, 1821), p. 30. • **5** *Gardener's Chronicle* (1842), quoted in Gillian Darley, *Villages of Vision* (London: The Architectural Press, 1975), p. 39. • **6** Uvedale Price, *Essays on the Picturesque* (London: Newman, 1810), p. 345. • **7** Daniel Defoe, *A tour thro' the whole island of Great Britain, divided into circuits or journies* (London: J. M. Dent and Co., 1927), Letter 8, Part 2. • **8** Watkins, Charles and Ben Cowell, *Uvedale Price: Decoding the Picturesque* (Woodbridge: the Boydell Press, 2012), p. 104. • **9** Letter from George Repton to John Scandrett Harford (23 August 1810), the Harford Papers, Bristol Record Office, 28048/P52/5. • **10** Perhaps in an attempt to placate critics, the title of 'Deputy' was added to the post especially for Nash. • **11** *Quarterly Review*, XXXIV (1826), p. 193. • **12** James

Boswell, *The Life of Samuel Johnson*, Vol. 2 (London and Oxford: William Pickering, 1826), p. 249.• **13** John Claudius Loudon, *Encyclopaedia of Cottage, Farm and Villa Architecture and Furniture* (London: Longman, revised edition 1842), p. 1,191. • **14** Nathaniel Kent, *Hints to Gentlemen of Landed Property* (London: Dodsley, 1775), p. 235. • **15** George Smith, *Essay on the Construction of Cottages Suited for the Dwellings of the Labouring Classes* (Glasgow: Blackie, 1834), p. 27. • **16** Price, *Essays on the Picturesque*, p. 63. • **17** Loudon, *Encyclopaedia*, p. 811. • **18** The comment was apparently made during a production staged in London by Mme Vestris. Quoted in Barranger, Milly, *Theatre Past and Present: An Introduction* (London: Wadsworth, 1984), p. 241. • **19** Helmholtz, quoted in Crary, Jonathan, 'Techniques of the Observer', in *The Nineteenth Century Visual Culture Reader* (New York: Routledge, 2004), p. 85. • **20** David Watkin, *The English Vision: the picturesque in architecture, landscape and garden design* (New York: Harper & Row, 1982), p. vii.

4: Saltaire, West Yorkshire

• **1** Corman O'Grada, *The Great Irish Famine* (Cambridge: Cambridge University Press, 1995), p. 45. • **2** Susan Zlotnick, *Women, Writing and the Industrial Revolution* (Baltimore: John Hopkins University Press: 2001), p. 233. • **3** William Rathbone Greg, *Why Are Women Redundant?* (London: Trübner, 1869), pp. 12–15. • **4** Friedrich Engels, *The Condition of the Working Class in England, with a preface written in 1892* (London: Allen & Unwin, 1943), pp. 148–9. • **5** I haven't been able to find the source of the original comment which is quoted in Alan Hall's booklet, *The Story of Bradford* (Stroud: the History Press, 2013), n.p. • **6** *Punch*, 21 (July 1851), p. 10. • **7** *Art Treasures Examiner: A Pictorial, Critical and Historical Record of the Art Treasures Exhibition at Manchester in 1857* (Manchester: A. Ireland, 1857), p. 252. • **8** Quoted in Thomas Richards, *The Commodity Culture of Victorian England: Advertising and Spectacle, 1851–1914* (Stanford: Stanford University Press, 1990), p. 29. Richards's book offers a fascinating account of the Great Exhibition and its contexts, the complexity of which I can only touch on here. • **9** Richards, *The Commodity Culture of Victorian England*, p. 31. • **10** The *Bradford Observer* (22 September 1853). • **11** *Diaries of Sir Daniel Gooch, Baronet* (London: Kegan Paul, 1892), p. xi. • **12** Muthesius, Stefan, *The English Terraced House* (New Haven and London: Yale University Press, 1982), p. 15. • **13** Virginia Woolf, 'Professions for Women', read to the Women's Service League in 1931. • **14** Charles Eastlake, *Hints on Household Taste* (London: Longmans and Green, 1878), p. 126. • **15** Joan Perkin, 'Sewing Machines: Liberation or Drudgery for Women?', *History Today*, (52: 2002), p. 12. • **16** *Hampshire Telegraph*, 1839. • **17** Samuel Smiles, *Self-Help;*

with Illustrations of Conduct and Perseverence (London: John Murray, 1859), pp. 19, 21. • **18** Ibid., p. 96. • **19** Daniel Merrick, *The Warp of Life* (Leicester: C. Merrick, 1876), pp. 14–18, 23, 24.

5: Creswell, Derbyshire

• **1** Emerson Bainbridge, quoted in Roy Church, *Strikes and Solidarity: Coalfield Conflict in Britain, 1889–1966* (Cambridge: Cambridge University Press, 1998), p. 134; *The Times* (1 December 1913), p. 12. • **2** Dr W. Ewart, quoted in Hunt, *The Lead Miners of the Northern Pennines*, p. 210. • **3** A comprehensive description of the physical and psychological impact of mining is given in Kevin White (ed.), *The Early Sociology of Health and Illness: hygiene, diseases and morality of occupations* (London and New York: Routledge, 2001). This quote is from Vol. V, p. 268. • **4** Report from the Select Committee on the South Kensington Museum (1860), National Art Library (NAL), pp. 10–11. • **5** Quoted in Fiona MacCarthy, *William Morris: A Life for Our Time* (London: Faber and Faber, 1994), p. 181. • **6** *The Times* (14 November 1887), p. 6. • **7** Krishan Kumar (ed.), *Cambridge Texts in the History of Political Thought. News from Nowhere* (Cambridge: Cambridge University Press, 1995), p. 136. • **8** Bryce Leicester, 'Life in a Garden Suburb', *Garden Suburbs, Villages and Homes*, 2 (London: Co-partnership Publishers Ltd, 1912), n.p. • **9** C. R. Ashbee, *Craftsmanship in Competitive Industry* (London: Essex House Press, 1908).

6: Port Sunlight, the Wirral

• **1** These examples are quoted in Brian Lewis, *So Clean: Lord Leverhulme, Soap and Civilization* (Manchester and New York: Manchester University Press, 2008), p. 2. The discussion in the book's opening chapter of the Napoleon comparison is illuminating. • **2** Lever's words are reproduced extensively on the Unilever website and in marketing material from the company. • **3** H. J. S., 'A Summer Ramble from Oxford to London', *The Ladies' Cabinet of Fashion, Music and Romance* (London: Vickerson, 1866), XXVIII, p. 256. • **4** *The Times* (22 November 1892), p. 11. • **5** William Hesketh Lever, letter to G. Edward Atkinson, 5 November 1923, quoted in Lewis, *So Clean*, p. 56. • **6** 'Spirits and Spirit Rapping', *Westminster Review*, 69 (January 1858), p. 16. • **7** William Hesketh Lever, *The Six Hour Day and Other Industrial Questions* (London: Allen & Unwin, 1919), p. 181. • **8** William Hulme Lever, *Viscount Leverhulme* (Boston, Mass., and New York: Houghton Mifflin, 1927), p. 86. • **9** Ibid., p. 167. • **10** This is an oft-repeated quote of Lever's. See, for example, the

Unilever website or Elizabeth Outka, *Consuming Traditions: Modernity, Modernism and the Commodified Authentic* (Oxford: Oxford University Press, 2008), p. 46. • **11** W. L. George, popular novelist and campaigner, *Labour and Housing at Port Sunlight* (London: Alston Rivers, 1909), p. 180. • **12** Quoted in Alison Ravetz, *Council Housing and Culture: The History of a Social Experiment* (London: Routledge, 2001), p. 37. • **13** Henry Mayhew, *London Labour and the London Poor: a cyclopaedia of the condition and earnings of those that will work, those that cannot work, and those that will not work* (London: Griffin, Bohn and Company, 1861), VI, p. 110. • **14** Quoted in Darley, *Villages of Vision*, p. 75. • **15** Lever, *Viscount Leverhulme*, pp. 306–7. • **16** Arthur Conan Doyle, *The Crime of the Congo* (New York: Doubleday, 1909), p. iii. For a more detailed discussion of Lever Brothers' and King Leopold's impact on the Congo see, for example, Adam Hochschild, *King Leopold's Ghost: A Story of Greed, Terror and Heroism in Colonial Africa* (London: Macmillan, 2000). • **17** William Hesketh Lever, *Following the Flag: Jottings of a Jaunt Around the World* (London: Simpkin Marshall, 1893), pp. 32–3. The second quote is from a letter to the campaigner and journalist Edmund Dene Morel, quoted in Lewis, *So Clean*, p. 168. • **18** Lever, *Viscount Leverhulme*, p. 167. • **19** Jervis Babb, head of Lever Brothers USA during the 1950s, quoted in Lewis, *So Clean*, p. 154. • **20** Letters to L. H. Mosley, 19 May 1916 and 11 April 1916. Unilever archives, Port Sunlight. • **21** Letter to Myrtle Husband, 11 November 1924. Unilever archives, Port Sunlight.

7: Portmeirion, Gwynedd

• **1** Clough Williams-Ellis, *Portmeirion: The Place and its Meaning* (London: Faber, 1963), p. 15. • **2** Ibid., p. 13. • **3** Ibid., p. 14. • **4** *The Architects Journal* (6 January 1926), quoted in Robin Llywelyn, *Portmeirion*, p. 2. • **5** Williams-Ellis, *Portmeirion: The Place and its Meaning*, p. 32. • **6** Ibid., p. 37. • **7** Ibid., pp. 32–3. • **8** Ibid., pp. 56, 63. • **9** Clough Williams-Ellis, *The Pleasures of Architecture* (London: Jonathan Cape, 1924), p. 204.

Select Bibliography

Altick, Richard, *The Shows of London* (Cambridge, Mass., and London: Harvard University Press, 1978)

Anon., 'Shelley and the Tremadoc Embankment', *Welsh Outlook*, 17, No. 6 (June 1930)

Appadurai, Arjun, *The Social Life of Things: Commodities in Cultural Perspective* (Cambridge: Cambridge University Press, 1986)

Barnatt, John, 'Chatsworth: the parkland archaeology', in *Landscape, Archaeology and Ecology*, Vol. 6, 2007, pp. 13–17

Berg, Maxine, *Technology and Toil in Nineteenth-Century Britain* (London: CSE, 1979)

Booth, Michael R., *Theatre in the Victorian Age* (Cambridge: Cambridge University Press, 1991)

Briggs, Asa, *Victorian Things* (London: Penguin, 1998)

Buder, Stanley, *Visionaries and Planners: The Garden City Movement and the Modern Community* (New York and Oxford: Oxford University Press, 1990)

Carey, John, ed., *The Faber Book of Utopias* (London: Faber and Faber, 1999)

Cherry, Gordon E., *Cities and Plans: The Shaping of Urban Britain in the Nineteenth and Twentieth Centuries* (London: Edward Arnold, 1988)

Colley, Linda, *Britons: Forging the Nation 1707–1837* (New Haven and London: Yale University Press, 1992)

Crary, Jonathan, *Techniques of the Observer: On Vision and Modernity in the Nineteenth Century* (Cambridge, Mass., and London: MIT Press, 1990)

Suspensions of Perception, Attention, Spectacle and Modern Culture (Cambridge, Mass., and London: MIT Press, 2001)

Creese, Walter L., *The Search for Environment: The Garden City Before and After* (Baltimore: John Hopkins University Press, expanded edition 1992)

Cyfeillion Cadw Tremadog, *Tremadog: Historic Planned Town* (CCT: Tremadog, 2008)

Darley, Gillian, *Villages of Vision* (London: The Architectural Press, 1975)

Davis, Terence, *The Architecture of John Nash* (London: Longacre Press, 1960)

Devonshire, Deborah, Duchess of, *The Garden at Chatsworth* (London: Francis Lincoln, 1999)

De Vries, Leonard, *Victorian Advertisements* (London: John Murray, 1968)

Dyer, Gillian, *Advertising as Communication* (London: Routledge, 1989)

Eaton, Ruth, *Ideal Cities: Utopianism and the (Un)Built Environment* (London: Thames and Hudson, 2002)

Evans, Martin, *European Atrocity, African Catastrophe: Leopold II, the Congo Free State and its Aftermath* (London and New York: Routledge, 2002)

Flint, Kate, *The Victorians and the Visual Imagination* (Cambridge: Cambridge University Press, 2000)

Gaskell, S. Martin, *Model Housing from the Great Exhibition to the Festival of Britain* (London and New York: Mansell, 1987)

Gilpin, William, *Three Essays: On Picturesque Beauty; On Picturesque Travel; and On Sketching Landscape* (London: R. Blamire, 2nd edition, 1794)

Ginswick, J., *Labour and the Poor in England and Wales 1849–1851* (London: Frank Cass, 1983)

Grant, Kevin, *A Civilised Savagery: Britain and the New Slaveries in Africa 1884–1926* (London and New York: Routledge, 2005)

Gunn, Simon, *The Public Culture of the Victorian Middle Class, Ritual and Authority and the English Industrial City, 1840–1914* (Manchester: Manchester University Press, 2000)

Harrison, J. F. C., *Robert Owen and the Owenites in Britain and America: the Quest for the New Moral World* (London: Routledge & Kegan Paul, 1969)

Hilton, Matthew, *Consumerism in Twentieth-Century Britain: The Search for a Historical Movement* (Cambridge: Cambridge University Press, 2003)

Hochschild, Adam, *King Leopold's Ghost: A Story of Greed, Terror and Heroism in Colonial Africa* (London: Macmillan, 2000)

Hunt, Christopher J., *Lead Miners of the Northern Pennines in the 18th and 19th Centuries* (Manchester: Manchester University Press, 1970)

Jeremy, David J., 'The Enlightened Paternalist in Action: William Hesketh Lever at Port Sunlight before 1914', *Business History*, 33.1 (January 1991)

Lever, William Hulme, *Viscount Leverhulme* (Boston, Mass., and New York: Houghton Mifflin, 1927)

Levine, Philippa, *The Amateur and the Professional: Antiquarians, Historians and Archaeologists in Victorian England 1838–1886* (Cambridge, Cambridge University Press, 1986)

Lewis, Brian, *So Clean: Lord Leverhulme, Soap and Civilization* (Manchester and New York: Manchester University Press, 2008)

Llywelyn, Robin, *Portmeirion* (Portmeirion: Portmeirion Ltd, n.d.)

Loeb, Lori Anne, *Consuming Angels: Advertising and Victorian Women* (New York: Oxford University Press, 1994)

MacKenzie, John M., ed., *Imperialism and Popular Culture* (Manchester: Manchester University Press, 1986)

Mangan, J. A. and James Walvin, eds, *Manliness and Morality: Middle-Class Masculinity in Britain and America 1800–1940* (Manchester, Manchester University Press, 1987)

Marchal, Jules, *Lord Leverhulme's Ghosts: Colonial Exploitation in the Congo* (London: Verso, 2008)

MacCarthy, Fiona, *William Morris: A Life for Our Time* (London: Faber and Faber, 1994)

Miller, Andrew H., *Novels Behind Glass: Commodity Culture and Victorian Narrative* (New York and Cambridge: Cambridge University Press, 1995)

Muthesius, Stefan, *The English Terraced House* (New Haven and London: Yale University Press, 1982)

Outka, Elizabeth, *Consuming Traditions: Modernity, Modernism and the Commodified Authentic* (Oxford: Oxford University Press, 2008)

Pollard, Sidney and John Salt, *Robert Owen: Prophet of the Poor. Essays in Honour of the Two Hundredth Anniversary of his Birth* (London: Macmillan, 1971)

Price, Richard, *British Society 1680–1880: Dynamism, Containment and Change* (New York: Cambridge University Press, 1999)

Price, Uvedale, *Essays on the Picturesque* (London: Newman, 1810)

Raistrick, Arthur, *Two Centuries of Industrial Welfare: the London (Quaker) Lead Company 1692–1905* (Buxton: Moorland, 1938)

Ravetz, Alison, *Council Housing and Culture: The History of a Social Experiment* (London: Routledge, 2001)

Richards, Thomas, *The Commodity Culture of Victorian England: Advertising and Spectacle, 1851–1914* (Stanford: Stanford University Press, 1990)

Royle, Edward, *Robert Owen and the Commencement of the Millennium: A Study of the Harmony Community* (Manchester: Manchester University Press, 1998)

Steegman, John, *Victorian Taste: A Study of the Arts and Architecture from 1830 to 1870* (Cambridge, Mass.: MIT Press, 1970)

Stewart, Susan, *On Longing: Narratives of the Miniature, the Gigantic, the Souvenir, the Collection* (Baltimore: the Johns Hopkins University Press, 1984)

Storry, Mike and Peter Childs, eds, *British Cultural Identities*, 2nd edition (London: Routledge, 2002)

Summerson, John, *John Nash* (London: George Allen, 1935)

Vernon, Anne, *A Quaker Business Man: The Life of Joseph Rowntree 1836–1925* (London: Allen & Unwin, 1958)

Watkin, David, *The English Vision: the picturesque in architecture, landscape and garden design* (New York: Harper & Row, 1982)

Watkins, Charles and Ben Cowell, *Uvedale Price: Decoding the Picturesque* (Woodbridge: the Boydell Press, 2012)

Weiner, Martin J., *English Culture and the Decline of the Industrial Spirit 1850–1980* (Cambridge: Cambridge University Press, 1981)

Williams-Ellis, Clough, *The Pleasures of Architecture* (London: Jonathan Cape, 1924)

Portmeirion: The Place and its Meaning (London: Faber, 1963)

Wohl, Anthony S., *Endangered Lives: Public Health in Victorian Britain* (London: Dent, 1983)

Zlotnick, Susan, *Women, Writing and the Industrial Revolution* (Baltimore: Johns Hopkins University Press: 2001)

Index